The Right and the recession

MANCHESTER
1824
Manchester University Press

New Perspectives on the Right

Series editor
Richard Hayton

The study of conservative politics, broadly defined, is of enduring scholarly interest and importance, and is also of great significance beyond the academy. In spite of this, for a variety of reasons the study of conservatism and conservative politics was traditionally regarded as something of a poor relation in comparison to the intellectual interest in 'the Left'. In the British context this changed with the emergence of Thatcherism, which prompted a greater critical focus on the Conservative Party and its ideology, and a revitalization of Conservative historiography. *New Perspectives on the Right* aims to build on this legacy by establishing a series identity for work in this field. It will publish the best and most innovative titles drawn from the fields of sociology, history, cultural studies and political science and hopes to stimulate debate and interest across disciplinary boundaries. *New Perspectives* is not limited in its historical coverage or geographical scope, but is united by its concern to critically interrogate and better understand the history, development, intellectual basis and impact of the Right. Nor is the series restricted by its methodological approach: it will encourage original research from a plurality of perspectives. Consequently, the series will act as a voice and forum for work by scholars engaging with the politics of the Right in new and imaginative ways.

Reconstructing conservatism? The Conservative party in opposition, 1997–2010
Richard Hayton

Conservative orators from Baldwin to Cameron
Edited by Richard Hayton and Andrew S. Crines

The Right and the recession

Edward Ashbee

Manchester University Press

Published by Manchester University Press
Altrincham Street, Manchester M1 7JA
www.manchesteruniversitypress.co.uk

British Library Cataloguing-in-Publication Data
A catalogue record for this book is available from the British Library

Library of Congress Cataloging-in-Publication Data applied for

ISBN 978 0 7190 90820 hardback

First published 2015

Typeset by Out of House Publishing
Printed in Great Britain by
CPI Group (UK) Ltd, Croydon, CR0 4YY

Contents

Acknowledgements *page* vii

Introduction: Charting the Right 1
1 Intercurrence and its implications 20
2 The state and processes of change 31
3 Embedded neoliberalism 54
4 The advent of crisis and the building of narratives 78
5 Rallying around the Gadsden Flag 97
6 Britain, retrenchment and the 'Big Society' 120
7 Chafing, abrasion and the contemporary Right 148
8 A permanently leaner state? 170

Bibliography 179
Index 196

Acknowledgements

I am very grateful to Richard Hayton (University of Leeds), the series editor, for both his backing and the invariably astute comments that he made as the project proceeded. I should also extend my thanks to Tony Mason, commissioning editor at Manchester University Press, and my appreciation to friends and colleagues in the Department of Business and Politics at Copenhagen Business School. Their justly acerbic observations (which usually began with the words 'this is very interesting but …') at the Department's weekly work-in-progress seminars helped my thinking enormously.

Introduction: Charting the Right

The phrase 'Great Recession' and references to crisis conditions eventually gave way to talk of recovery. In the United States (US), Gross Domestic Product (GDP) had, when adjusted for inflation, at least recovered sufficiently to surpass its 2007 total by 2011. British national output took longer to recover but finally matched its pre-recession figure in mid-2014.

Nonetheless, despite this and rising prices in some property markets, most of the references to recovery remained cautious and tentative. The financial crisis that erupted in 2008 and the recession that followed in 2009 had been the prelude to a prolonged period of fitful growth and were followed by persistent anxieties about the possibility of a 'double-dip' or even a 'triple-dip' recession. Earlier hopes of a more full-blooded recovery during the first few months of each year had to be abandoned as growth stalled just a few months later (*BBC News*, 2013a).

Although 'recovery' was redefined downwards so even the most modest signs of economic activity were hailed as evidence of such, few were reckless enough to talk in unqualified terms about future economic prospects. Even in mid-2014, despite talk of interest rate rises and the Federal Reserve's limited and experimental 'tapering' as the rate at which quantitative easing (that had, as the crisis continued, become the primary form of macroeconomic management) was taking place was gradually reduced, forecasters were asserting that there would not be a return to monetary policy normality for a very long period to come.

At the same time, although unemployment never reached the peak that some had predicted when the crisis first struck, and there were encouraging signs in both the US and the United Kingdom (UK) (where by mid-2014 the rate was – at 6.6 per cent – the lowest rate since the crisis broke out), the joblessness figures took a long time to fall. Indeed, despite large numbers abandoning the labour market altogether, the long-term unemployed numbered four million in the US at the beginning of 2014 (Thompson, 2014). And, as of July 2013, around 915,000 people in Britain had been unemployed for a year or more (Dugan, 2013). The figures for youth unemployment were even more striking. In January 2014, the *New York Times* reported that 15 per cent of workers aged 16 to 24 were unemployed (Dewan, 2014). The same figure was given in the UK for the proportion of young people who were defined as

NEETs (not in education, employment or training) during the third quarter of 2013 (Mirza-Davies, 2014: 1).

Yet, despite the painfully slow character of the economic recovery (which led some commentators to talk of a 'lost decade' or long-run stagnation), the primary focus of attention had long shifted away from growth and employment and instead towards deficits and debt. What had initially been defined and represented as a crisis created by the banking sector had become, within a relatively short period, defined and represented as a crisis of excessive government expenditure. Both the UK and the US turned to fiscal retrenchment policies. For much of the Left as well as the Right the debate quickly became structured around the intensity and pace of retrenchment rather than the principle of retrenchment itself. The call went out for budget cuts and they became the defining policy of the Conservative-led coalition government that took office after the May 2010 general election. In the US, amidst intense partisan conflict, expenditure cuts were enacted through budget agreements and the federal government budget sequester, which took effect in March 2013.

Some on the free market Right have argued that the expenditure cuts that have been imposed in both the US and UK are not that significant or far-reaching. Daniel Mitchell of the Cato Institute, a libertarian think tank in Washington, DC, has referred to the 'United Kingdom's faux austerity' (Mitchell, 2012). He compared what he saw as the very limited nature of the Cameron government's budget cuts with those enacted in Canada between 1994–95 and 1996–97, which amounted, in nominal terms, to an overall reduction of 4.95 per cent. At the time at which he was writing, Mitchell noted that the British government foresaw a nominal cut of only 1.6 per cent (Mitchell, 2012).

Nonetheless, this line of argument should be treated with a degree of caution. The cuts were differentially applied and some sectors were ring-fenced so that retrenchment was felt much more severely in other sectors. Just as importantly, if projected population growth, shifts in the demographic structure of the country, probable economic growth (however limited) and inflation are factored in, this reduces projected government expenditure as a share of GDP significantly. In October 2012, the International Monetary Fund forecast a drop from 45.5 per cent in 2012 to 39.2 per cent in 2017 (International Monetary Fund, 2012). This relative form of measurement provides much more of a guide to the size and scale of government spending than do the raw numbers.

Studies and commentaries

Inevitably, the moment of crisis and its prolonged aftermath have given rise to a substantial number of reports, commentaries and scholarly studies reflecting upon the causes, course and consequences of the crisis. Some of these have been narrative accounts informed by insider sources, often recounting personal conversations. For example, the events of autumn 2008, when, at least according to legend, President George W. Bush, while seeking Congressional backing for the financial sector bailout, proclaimed 'if money isn't loosened up, this sucker could go down', have been described in some depth (quoted in Herszenhorn *et al.*, 2008).

Other accounts shift, at times uneasily, between analysis and polemic but also consider underlying economic processes. In most, the 'sucker' to which Bush referred was represented as world capitalism or, at the least, the financial system. Such accounts reflect upon the causes of the crisis and its roots in the structural imbalances between the US and Asia and the asymmetric flows of funds that stemmed from them. They also point to the impact of increased economic inequalities in the US and the ways in which stagnating real earnings created a demand for large-scale, and often 'subprime', borrowing from a largely unregulated financial sector that was structured around a lust for quick, speculative returns and a blind faith in the spreading of risk through the securitization of loans. In striking contrast, the rather smaller number of free market studies that have been published have emphasized the part played by swollen government budget deficits during the Bush years, market-distorting interventionism in the housing market (through, for example, the government-sponsored enterprises Fannie Mae and Freddie Mac, which securitized mortgages) and in some cases what they see as the political manipulation of the interest rate that led to the misallocation of investment funds and the incessant fuelling of an asset bubble.

There is also a growing literature (much of it also lying on the divide between analysis and polemic) considering, to paraphrase the much-cited phrase from the Sherlock Holmes stories, the case of the dog that didn't bark. Why, these studies ask, did the crisis fail to generate more sustained and radical departures from the neoliberal paradigm? Why, after seeming to hold out the prospect of radical reform and 'the return of the master' (the subtitle of Robert Skidelsky's 2009 study of John Maynard Keynes, his ideas and their impact), did the pursuit of activist fiscal policies quickly give way to an emphasis upon 'austerity', the retrenchment of government spending and then, as the narrative developed, the need for a shrunken state (Skidelsky, 2009)?

Other questions have also been asked. Why, insofar as stimulus policies were still pursued after the crisis had moved beyond its opening phases, did they shift from fiscal to monetary policy and become a matter for central banks rather than government? Why, instead of reinvigorating the Left, did the unfolding crisis provide a backcloth to the emergence of the Tea Party movement in the US, contribute to the spread of Rightist populism in much of Europe and, in many countries, bolster the mainstream liberal and conservative Right?[1]

Affinities

This book builds upon these accounts and studies by surveying the ways in which the Right in both the UK and the US responded to the 2008 financial crash, the ensuing recession and the years of prolonged economic uncertainty that followed.

The two countries are often spoken of in the same breath, and they are, after all, at the forefront of the 'Anglosphere'. In recent years, they have been bound together more closely than ever in the foreign policy arena. There are also institutional affinities. Although the UK has now embraced a multiplicity of voting systems for elections other than those for the Westminster Parliament, both nations use the first-past-the-post system and face the sometimes intense forms of partisan competition that it facilitates and encourages.

Those who assess countries in terms of economic models or welfare regimes almost always place the countries together. As the crisis took hold, French president Nicolas Sarkozy scornfully referred to the 'Anglo-Saxon model' and attributed the crisis to what he saw as its structural weaknesses and failings. More scholarly accounts have sought to draw a distinction between seemingly more managed economies and economies such as those of the US and the UK that take a 'purer' liberal form. The Varieties of Capitalism school, which takes the different forms of coordination between firms as its starting point, placed the US and UK together as 'liberal market economies', while the countries in much of continental Europe are represented in very different terms as 'coordinated market economies'.

Although academic opinion is often emotionally drawn to the coordinated market economies or, to an even greater extent, its Nordic social-democratic variant, the liberal economies have a resilience that often disappoints and dismays their many critics. While President Sarkozy asserted that, as a consequence of the crash, the world 'had turned the page' on the Anglo-Saxon model, little has happened to modify its fundamental characteristics (Hall *et al.*, 2009). Indeed, they have in many ways been bolstered in recent years and the model continues to play a major role in shaping the overall character of the world economy.

The structural similarities between the US and the UK provide a basis for comparative study. Because political activity in the countries of continental Europe has been structured by the relationship between the state and economic interests, the character of the labour market, the effects of proportional voting systems, the nature of political coalitions and extended welfare regimes, it inevitably takes a very different form from that found in much of the 'Anglosphere'. Comparisons between the liberal and the coordinated economies therefore only serve limited purposes. Comparative study within the different structural types is, however, much more fruitful. It can identify the variables that played a part in bringing certain actors to the fore while sidelining others, shaped the policy thinking that emerged during the crash and its aftermath, and brought forth particular policy outcomes.

Purpose of the book

The Right and the Recession tracks all of this. It looks at the principal actors, the ideas that emerged and were pursued, and the policies that were either sought or enacted. It surveys the efforts of the Right in both countries to shrink the post-war state during the years that preceded the crisis, its initial responses once the extent of the crisis became evident, the shift to a retrenchment narrative during 2009 and 2010, and the changing character of that narrative during the years that followed.

The book is not, however, a chronology or description of events and policy processes or a listing of the similarities and differences between the US and the UK. The focus of the book instead considers the ways in which circumstances in the two countries opened up political opportunities for the Right while at the same time closing off others. Rahm Emanuel, who was to become President Obama's first White House Chief of Staff (and later Mayor of Chicago) said shortly after the November 2008 election, using phrases that the Right claimed were full of menace:

> You never want a serious crisis to go to waste ... Things that we had postponed for too long, that were long-term, are now immediate and must be dealt with. This crisis provides the opportunity for us to do things that you could not do before.
>
> (quoted in *The Wall Street Journal*, 2008)

The Right and the Recession assesses the efforts of the Right to ensure that the crisis did not go to waste and to 'do things that you could not do before'. It looks, in particular, at the ways in which the Right, during the crisis period in both the UK and the US and once the initial shock had passed, sought to shrink and reconfigure the role of the state.

In doing this, the book looks at the ways in which 'big government' came to be defined as *the* pivotal economic and political problem, and assesses the attempts to shrink the size and limit the scope of the state in its role as a service provider and curtail its role in ameliorating perceived market failures by recasting American conservatism and transforming the character of the Republican Party and its elected representatives through the Tea Party movement. And, as noted above, it also considers the impact of the Conservative-led coalition's programme of spending reductions and the shift away from a narrative that framed austerity as a pragmatic and necessary response to a structural deficit and the embrace of a restructuring process.

The Right and the Recession argues that the political responses to the crisis were shaped and moulded in large part by the relative failure of both the 'Reagan revolution' and Thatcherism, in particular the former, to bring about the lasting neoliberal transformation of the state in both the US and UK that the Right had hoped to secure. Thus, events and processes during the decades that preceded the crisis were as important as events and processes during the crisis itself.

The book has two further purposes. First, it considers the drivers of institutional and ideational change. There are, as the Introduction outlines, five principal literatures surveying the contemporary Right. Each considers its development at a different level or, put another way, within a different tier. Some accounts, for example, concentrate on actors and their judgements or actions. Either implicitly or explicitly they suggest that the Right has been driven by actors' discretion and agency. Others, in contrast, consider the logic of neoliberalism and the ways in which neoliberalism has forced an economic and political agenda upon countries. Another set of accounts points to the different constituencies and groupings from which contemporary conservatism is drawn and the role of, for example, white evangelical Protestantism in shaping the American Right. Institutional studies point to the character of the contemporary state, in particular that in the US where structures take a sprawling form and the demarcation lines between the state and civil society are often hard to identify with certainty, and the ways in which structures and policy legacies constrain neoliberal reformers as well as other actors.

The book argues that a comprehensive portrait of the Right must draw on all these levels or tiers but it seeks to go further. It employs some of the approaches associated with American Political Development (APD) that consider the relationships between political orders and emphasizes the stresses, strains and conflicts that characterize those relationships. The tiers or levels described in the contemporary literature are in some ways akin to the 'orders' around which APD accounts are structured. The relationships between them can therefore be considered in similar ways. While there are at times fits between different levels or tiers there are more often than not processes of 'chafing' and 'abrasion' between them. Each has its own set of logics and pace of development. There are inevitably stresses and tensions as levels or tiers abrade each other and interact. As APD theorists suggest in their studies of orders, it is these processes of 'intercurrence' that bring forth change.[2]

Second, *The Right and the Recession* seeks to assess the extent to which the change mechanisms enacted by the Cameron government in the UK might be expected to bring forth enduring change. Change is a subject about which much has been written in recent years, particularly within the framework of historical institutionalism. The point of departure for this literature has been the concept of path dependence. From this perspective, significant, path-departing change is largely confined to periods of acute crisis when there is intense ideational and institutional flux. During such periods, decisions are taken (often in difficult and contingent circumstances, with a rushed framework) that form the basis of paths that, over time, are established, reinforced and bolstered. The relative costs of abandoning such a path rise over time and it thus becomes increasingly difficult to depart from it. Expectations shift so as to fit around paths and they quickly become 'common sense'. In other words, path-departing alternatives are not considered or regarded as legitimate. Thus, path-departing change only again becomes credible in a further moment of crisis. If a long-run perspective is adopted, patterns of development can be understood as a process of *punctuated equilibrium*. There are short bursts of radical change followed by long periods of continuity within which the change that takes place is limited in character and path-maintaining or path-reinforcing.

Few would now subscribe to a picture as crude or structurally determined as this. It does, however, often serve, either implicitly or explicitly, as a starting point for discussions. Increasingly, however, attention has now turned to the forms of path-departing change that can, despite the claims of those who adhere to punctuated equilibrium models, take place outside, and between, periods of crisis. Recent studies, perhaps most notably work by Jacob Hacker, Wolfgang Streeck, Kathleen Thelen and James Mahoney, have been structured around processes such as policy drift (whereby the impact of particular policy structures changes because the context within which they are situated changes in character), conversion (whereby the uses to which an institution is put are changed) and layering (whereby new structures are placed 'on top' of existing structures) (Hacker, 2004; Streeck and Thelen, 2005; Mahoney and Thelen, 2010). Over time, it is said, drift, conversion or layering undermine or 'subvert' existing institutional arrangements so as to bring forth long-run transformational change.

The history of the neoliberal Right abounds with examples of gradualist strategies. In October 1995, Newt Gingrich, then a leading Republican and Speaker of the US House of Representatives, caught their spirit when he said that he and fellow conservatives should, despite their commitment to the free market, avoid frontal assaults on government social provision (because it was so ideationally and institutionally embedded) and instead seek to ensure that programmes such as Medicare, the system of health provision for senior citizens, were eroded over time through the effects of gradual change mechanisms:

> Now, we don't get rid of it in round one because we don't think that that's politically smart, and we don't think that's the right way to go through a transition. But we believe it's going to wither on the vine because we think people are voluntarily going to leave it – voluntarily.
>
> (Newt Gingrich, quoted in *The New York Times*, 1996)

Yet, so far as Medicare is concerned Gingrich's hopes have been largely dashed. Indeed, far from withering, Medicare was bolstered and extended by the backing that Congressional Republicans and President George W. Bush gave to the 2003 Medicare Modernization Act. If reform processes more broadly are considered, gradualism has brought significant, indeed transformational change in some spheres, but in other spheres it has been reined in or rolled back. *The Right and the Recession* seeks to assess the extent to which gradualist strategies have least, when the role and structure of the state is considered, had a transformational character.

All in all, despite the loud assertions made at the beginning of the crisis years that the crash would usher in the resurrection of Keynesianism (or even Marxism), it has instead brought the Right (and in some instances the radical Right) to the forefront of politics. Furthermore, in Britain, the Cameron leadership has declared its commitment not only to fiscal retrenchment as a pragmatic necessity but also to a permanently 'leaner' state. Nonetheless, the processes that shape the character of the Right, at least in the UK and the US, and the nature of change mechanisms have at the same time placed limits upon the durability and staying power of the state restructuring processes that are taking place.

Thus, after the financial crisis, the prolonged period of recession and barely visible growth and the efforts to create a permanently 'leaner' state, the extent of overall and long-run structural change may well be rather limited. Put another way, the state structures that emerged from the Depression of the 1930s or the Second World War and its aftermath, and the relationships that those structures created, have a striking resilience. As the book will argue, those who seek radical reform may secure periodic political victories but they may in the longer run remain disappointed.

Literatures

Although there have been periodic lulls in interest, the Right in both the US and UK has been subject to extended scrutiny by both scholars and media commentators, particularly from the late 1970s onwards.

In assessing the responses of the Right to the economic crisis and its political fate, the book builds upon these earlier studies. Although there are, of course, extensive and far-reaching overlaps between them, these studies can be categorized in terms of five distinct and discrete literatures. The five should of course be regarded as ideal types, and it would be easy to find accounts that only fit uneasily with this schema.

First, the British Right has largely been considered through elite-based accounts that owe much, theoretically and methodologically, to political history. Indeed, there is no readily visible dividing line between studies that place themselves within politics and those that place themselves within history. In these accounts, there is a particular focus on processes, events and mechanisms within Westminster, Whitehall and the Conservative Party apparatus. In their classic form, the emphasis upon 'high politics' led not only to the neglect of broader settings and institutional contexts but also to the treatment of backbenchers and party members as an 'off-stage' presence (Bale, 2010: 14). In recent years, however, there has been an analytical broadening out because of both party democratization (which increased the visibility of the role played by the party membership) and the increasing use of quantitative surveys that have facilitated the more rigorous study of party attitudes and public opinion.

For the most part, these studies concentrate on short-term patterns and processes as much as longer-run trends. Actors and their ideas are at the forefront and the personalities of those who have at different times led the Conservative Party are afforded extensive coverage. In particular, early studies of Margaret Thatcher's governments readily lent themselves to this type of elite-based and actor-centred approach. All too often, developments and processes during the 1980s seemed to depend upon the decisions that she herself made, her seemingly strident personality, her character as an 'outsider' and her sustained efforts to remake the Conservative Party in her own image by sidelining dissident 'wets'. Certainly, it is difficult to represent the drama and intrigue that led to Margaret Thatcher's political demise in November 1990 in terms other than the discretion of well-placed actors.

Two features of this literature deserve close attention. First, there are methodological difficulties insofar as there is often a degree of analytical wavering when the motivations of actors are considered. At times, accounts stress personalities or the ideas and ideologies to which actors adhere or seek to promote. However, they also point to the importance of electoral considerations, the drive to maximize support at the ballot box, and (although usually only asserted implicitly) the search to win over the median voter. These different variables are rarely weighted. Second, although generally treated as secondary, there is also a recognition in much of the elite-level literature on conservatism that politics is, as Chancellor Bismarck noted in his celebrated phrase, the 'art of the possible'. In other words, and in the language of contemporary political science, actors are constrained (although sometimes empowered) by their institutional circumstances. In most of these accounts the institutions that are brought under the spotlight are limited to the formal structures and rules that define the work of the executive and legislative branches of government rather than the informal institutions that are considered by other theoretical approaches.[3] The focus is therefore upon the parliamentary arithmetic at any given point in time or the ways in which particular actors are constrained by the dictates of collective cabinet responsibility.

There is a second literature of conservatism that has to be considered. In contrast to the accounts published in the UK, many of the scholarly studies of US conservatism and the Republican Party over the past half-century are structured around shifts within broad political constituencies and among particular demographic groupings.[4] Kevin Phillips's studies, most notably *The Emerging Republican Majority* (1969) which considered the impact of the Republicans' 'southern strategy', and Thomas B. Edsall's accounts of the political challenges facing the Democrats, such as *Chain Reaction: The Impact of Race, Rights, and Taxes on American Politics* (1992), which he co-authored with his wife, are broadly representative of the genre. Daniel Williams's more recent book, *God's Own Party: The Making of the Christian Right*, is another such study (Williams, 2010).

Seen in terms of constituencies, the Republican ascendancy from the late 1970s onwards can be attributed to the realignment of political allegiances as the white South abandoned the Democrats in the wake of desegregation, the party's seeming embrace of cultural liberalism and the re-entry of white evangelical Protestantism, through organizations such as the Moral Majority and, later, the Christian Coalition, into the political process as a core component of the new Republican bloc. Republican operatives exploited the openings that cultural and demographic shifts created. In short, they went (to invoke Senator Barry Goldwater's celebrated phrase) 'hunting where the ducks are' (quoted in Schreiber, 1971: 157).

In these accounts, there has sometimes been an implicit recognition of the part played by particular institutional arrangements. Certainly the use of the direct primary in selecting federal and state candidates for public office gave some constituencies a disproportionate degree of political leverage that would otherwise have been largely absent. Although, within this context, the efforts of political entrepreneurs, such as those who forged the 'new Right', have been recorded, their efforts are often treated as secondary.

Third, the emergence and growth of 'neoliberalism', and the dislodging of earlier economic thinking based upon Keynesianism and extended state social provision, have been the object of widespread study. In contrast with the literature of British Conservatism (which, as has been noted, is largely at elite level) and US conservatism (largely at constituency level), much of the neoliberalism literature is at regime level or multi-regime level.[5] Its focus on, for example, the 'Washington Consensus' has also been informed or at least tinged by class-based or at the least class-related perspectives. The neoliberalism literature's loci of study have generally been normative frameworks, public policy, broad institutional structures, long-run socioeconomic processes and the relationship between such structures and processes, as well as capitalist interests or those of particular fractions of capital. Although there is sometimes a degree of wavering in the account, there is for the most part a stress upon long-run neoliberal logics and impulses, which can be distinguished from what particular firms seek at a particular point in time and are instead a function of what actors believe can be secured within the settings in which they are located.

Within this framework, there have also been important studies of 'embedded neoliberalism' and the processes through which neoliberalism has attached itself to other ideational frameworks or has been implanted and reshaped by the contours of particular settings and contexts. If we briefly look beyond the UK and the US, Bastiaan van Apeldoorn considers neoliberalism as it is embedded within the discourses and structures that play a part in defining the European Union (EU). There were, he has argued, different and competing projects within the EU. Neoliberalism coexisted, and at the same time competed, with a 'neo-mercantilist' discourse and social democracy (van Apeldoorn, 2009: 23). Whereas neo-mercantilism sought a European economy that was protected from, and in competition with, the remainder of the globe, social democracy stressed the need to flank or 'soften' the market's harsher edges while its Third Way variant focused on investment in human social capital through both education and training as well as more rigorous disincentives directed against those who proved resistant to processes of labour market inclusion.[6] Within such a setting, embedded neoliberalism incorporated and to some degree made its peace with these other projects.

Nonetheless, although there is almost always an acknowledgement that neoliberalism takes embedded forms, the neoliberalism literature has for the most part shied away from the specificities of Thatcherism, Reaganomics (the economic policy thinking and policies pursued by the Reagan administration) or other, nationally defined and structured applications of neoliberalism, although there have been studies of the relationships between particular class fractions (such as finance capital or 'sunbelt capitalism') and processes of policy formation during the 1980s.

Fourth, there is a literature associated with historical institutionalism (HI). Its starting point is to stress the extent to which in considering the impact of Thatcherism or Reaganomics there have been continuities rather than change. Put another way, there are processes of path dependence. Although there was a recognition that neo-liberal reforms had been far-reaching in some policy areas, such as the sale of council housing enacted early in the Thatcher years, there was an emphasis on the failure of reformers to restructure some of the basic building blocks of the British welfare state, most notably the National Health Service (NHS). This has been represented as testimony to the strength of path dependency.[7] Once particular paths – or logics – establish themselves they are reinforced and bolstered by institutional complementarities and adaptive expectations that militate against path-departing changes. Within such a perspective, fundamental change is largely limited to moments of crisis and the periods of institutional and ideational flux that they bring forth.[8]

Having said this, the 'stricter' path-dependence perspectives have not gone unchallenged. At a theoretical level, there has been an increasing emphasis upon gradual change processes that, taken cumulatively, have had a transformative and path-departing character (Mahoney and Thelen, 2010). At a more empirical level, and although not explicitly written within an historical institutionalist framework, there have been important appraisals of Thatcherite radicalism (in other words, the extent to which it was 'path-departing') and the points in historical time at which that radicalism began to take hold, and the differences between the extent of reform in different policy areas (Hay and Farrall, 2014: 10–19).

Last, there have been studies of Thatcherism and, to a much lesser extent, Reaganism and their political specificities. As Richard Hayton argues, these studies marked an important shift away from the elite-based studies that had, as noted above, rested either implicitly or explicitly upon the claim that political outcomes are largely shaped by the discretion of actors. The Thatcherism literature thus marked a 'movement towards more structurally inclined modes of explanation, in contrast to the agency-focused historical narratives that preceded them' (Hayton, 2012: 10). Having said this, accounts of Thatcherism have taken very different forms and indeed there is no single entity to be explained. The phenomenon has instead been represented and understood through its co-option or absorption into different political narratives: 'there is no essentialist account of "Thatcherism"' (Bevir and Rhodes, 1998: 111). As David Marsh notes in a parallel survey essay, Thatcherism has been understood in political, economic and ideological terms (Marsh, 1995: 598). Thus, whereas some (primarily Marxian) accounts represent Thatcherism as a response to the long-run crisis of international capitalism and efforts to restore profitability, others emphasize the ways in which uncertainties of the 1970s and the 1978–79 'winter of discontent' enabled the Conservatives to secure political advantage.[9] Seen in this way, Thatcherism was a form of 'statecraft' driven by raw political calculus (Bevir and Rhodes, 1998: 101–102). Broken down into its component parts, 'statecraft' rests upon successes or failures in party management, the construction and deployment of a winning electoral strategy, the securing of political argument hegemony around the most salient issues, demonstrations of governing competence and the winning of a further election (Bulpitt, 1986: 21–23).

Nonetheless, although 'Thatcherism' has been understood and discussed in these different ways, it is most usually depicted as an ideational order. Such representations have their origins in the debates that took place in the journal *Marxism Today* at the end of the 1970s and during the early 1980s about the changing character of hegemony. The debate was tied to the growth of 'Eurocommunism' and the move away from economistic and more militant versions of Marxism that had stressed labour militancy and sometimes seemed to attribute the relative weakness of socialist politics to the 'false consciousness' and the repressiveness of the state apparatus. 'Hegemony' was rooted in the ideas of the Italian Marxist theorist Antonio Gramsci and placed an emphasis on the pivotal role of ideas, their contested character and the ways in which they were tied to 'real' material experience. There was likely, from a Gramscian perspective, to be a prolonged 'war of position', during which conflict would often take a hidden form or be fought in the nooks and crannies of the cultural terrain.

Approached in this way, Thatcherism was, as Stuart Hall noted even before Margaret Thatcher secured the premiership, a 'rich mix'. It combined 'organic Toryism' structured around the enforcement of 'standards', representations of the nation, the centrality of family, the imperative of duty, as well as notions of authority and tradition with 'the aggressive themes of a revived neo-liberalism – self-interest, competitive individualism, anti-statism' (Hall, 1983: 29). It tied the repertoire of anti-collectivism to the promises of reversing Britain's long-run economic decline and making Britain 'Great' again (Hall, 1988: 49). In a phrase that was widely quoted, Thatcherite hegemony was structured around 'authoritarian populism'.

These reconfigurations of hegemony built upon the declining hold of social democracy and the changes that took place in the 1970s when, amidst successive crises and moral panics around issues such as race, law and order and social 'permissiveness', 'the popular mood shifted decisively against the Left' (Hall, 1988: 40). Seen in this way, Thatcherism should not be regarded as 'false consciousness' in the ways that the more simplified versions of Marxism suggested. Instead, its guiding assumptions and claims corresponded with the lived experience of those on the lower rungs of the class ladder. Insofar as Thatcherism was a critique of the post-war welfare state, that state was seen and experienced by many as a cumbersome, unresponsive and bureaucratic apparatus. Thus, the anti-statist sentiments that Thatcherism conveyed had a 'material' basis:

> Thatcherite ideology tapped discontents arising from popular experience in a range of fields extending far beyond what the Left, in general, normally thinks of as 'political', and linked them both to Thatcher's central policy themes and to 'deep', traditional feelings and identities.
>
> (Leys, 1990: 125)

Despite the Labour Party's later general election victories, 'New Labour' only won back some of those drawn to Thatcherism for a limited period and to a limited extent. Indeed, the growth of the United Kingdom Independence Party (UKIP) shows the ways in which 'authoritarian populism' continues to shape the British political landscape.

Although far less has been written about Reaganism and Republicanism as cultural processes, much the same could be said of those white, male manual workers who recoiled against the Democrats' seeming associations with 'acid, amnesty and abortion' at the time of the Vietnam War, backed President Nixon in his 1972 re-election victory over the hapless Senator George McGovern, acquired the mantle of 'Reagan Democrats' and were progressively drawn into the ranks of the Republican Party's core voting base over the years that followed. Thomas Frank's 2004 book, *What's the Matter with Kansas? How Conservatives Won the Heart of America,* looked at this by studying processes in just one state. It considered the ways in which moral issues drew workers and farmers away from economic issues and opposition to economic elites and instead pulled them into the Republican fold. Moral concerns were thereby used to obscure economic realities and lure workers away from class-based politics.

Levels and tiers

Each of these five literatures (considering party, constituency, regime, institutional settings and ideas and culture, respectively) has its own terms of reference, guiding assumptions and parameters. All contribute to a broad and comprehensive understanding of the contemporary Right and the contextual circumstances within which it has taken shape and exerted political leverage during recent decades. Each captures political processes and their dynamics at a particular level or tier.

Nonetheless, each level or tier tells only part of the story. Taken on its own, each of the literatures necessarily presents only a limited and partial account. Party- or elite-level studies often fail to consider the broader contexts and settings within which the processes that they describe are driven. Either explicitly or implicitly, they generally accord very considerable, arguably excessive, weight to agency and all its indeterminacies. Constituency-based studies often neglect the often layered character of socioeconomic shifts and transformations that shape the political horizons of those constituencies. As has been noted, regime-level accounts pay relatively little attention to the mechanisms through which changes in public policy are enacted, modified or in many instances blocked. Path-dependence arguments can underestimate the degree to which, although formal structures have remained largely unchanged, there have been important shifts in the character of the settings within which those structures operate since the 1970s (a process of 'policy drift'), thereby exposing individuals and households to much greater levels of social risk than formerly (Hacker, 2004). And, discursive studies structured around questions of hegemony may over-estimate the extent to which neoliberal ideas have secured popular assent and can therefore neglect processes of sometimes fierce ideational contestation or underestimate 'material' considerations. In other words, such accounts may be guilty of 'ideologism' (Bonnett *et al.*, 1985: 73).

Interaction and intercurrence

Put another way, while all five literatures, levels or tiers are part of the story, none should be considered alone or in isolation from the others. A rounded and comprehensive portrait of the Right has to incorporate all of the tiers and consider the patterns of interaction and exchange between them. It is a premise of the book that the contemporary Right is shaped and driven by processes of interaction and exchange between party, constituencies, regime, broader institutional structures and ideational orders.

Nonetheless, that having been said, the character of that interaction between levels or tiers demands consideration. It is of course commonplace to plead for different literatures or foci of study to 'talk to each other' or become in some way reconciled. Yet, like the celebrated slogan of the late 1960s, 'give peace a chance', it fails to consider the terms on and the processes through which reconciliation should or could take place.

In place of such an approach, the book instead draws, albeit loosely, upon the concept of *intercurrence*. 'Intercurrence' is found in some studies of American Political Development (APD) and refers to the processes of contact and interaction between different institutional and ideational orders.[10] Whereas many institutionalist accounts point to the 'fits' or complementarities between institutions that develop over time as paths (which often owe their origins to decisions taken at a moment of crisis) take shape and are subsequently bolstered, thereby raising the costs and reducing the likelihood of path-departing change, accounts employing intercurrence tend to suggest that any such 'fits' or complementarities are largely circumstantial or contingent. Indeed, in many instances, their existence depends upon the creativity and political entrepreneurship of actors or coalitions of actors. For the most part, however, there will be friction, 'chafing' and 'abrasion' between those orders because they came into being at different periods, in different settings, for different purposes and with different logics. Amidst this, the efforts of actors may well be frustrated. In other words, intercurrence suggests that although party, constituencies and regime may not be equal players, they each have their own separate logics and 'laws of motion'.

Thus, to take the concept away from its place in the study of US political development, Britain's health policy order or regime, largely structured around the NHS, was shaped and formed by the politics of the Second World War and the immediate post-war period. Despite incremental changes and efforts at reform by successive governments, the NHS's structural character still bears the imprint of the political dynamics in play at the time of Clement Attlee's premiership and Aneurin Bevan's stewardship at the Ministry of Health. Given this, there has inevitably been sustained 'chafing' and 'abrasion' between the health policy regime and the structures of the labour market, as ideational orders structured around a commitment to markets and quasi-markets, new public management systems, shifting perceptions of health needs, changed demography and the contemporary fiscal policy regime clash and abrade with the structures, capacity and commitments around which the NHS is based.

Applying intercurrence

All of this has significant theoretical and methodological implications that, as Britain's NHS suggests, stretch way beyond the immediate concerns of APD. As intercurrence implies, accounts of political processes should move away from a search for 'fits' and compatibilities and instead concentrate more on the tensions and stresses between orders and the ways in which these, as well as the efforts of actors, can drive forward processes of political and social change.

The study of intercurrence has to date largely been confined to the study of relationships between political (or racial) 'orders' in the US. The book will argue that intercurrence or processes akin to it can be found in other settings. In many other settings, political outcomes are shaped by the relationships between differently structured logics. If the contemporary Right is considered, there are the different and separate logics associated with party, constituencies, regime, institutions and political cultures. Each of these has its own origins and dynamics. While there are at times fits and compatibilities, the book will argue that there are in many instances significant stresses and tensions between them.

If, for example, the dilemmas confronting the contemporary British Right and its relationship with the EU are considered along the lines suggested by intercurrence, an account would stress the profound tensions between a broadly neoliberal regime that, although segmented, rests in significant part upon securing gains from the transnational mobility of capital, labour, goods and services, a party elite and apparatus that have become far more resolutely 'Eurosceptic' over the past thirty years, and different constituencies and potential constituencies across the country that are, at least in generalized terms, fearful of immigration, regulations imposed in an alien Brussels apparatus, a distant political class and the seemingly relentless loss of British sovereignty to the EU. Furthermore, the institutional structures within which much of the European debate has been conducted and broader political processes have taken place have at times limited and constrained the Eurosceptic challenge while intensifying it in other settings. Elections to the European Parliament, held every five years, direct attention towards European issues and, through the use of the party list electoral system, allow minor or 'infant' parties to secure seats whereas other systems would stifle them. Parliamentary elections, held on a different cycle and still using the single-member constituency first-past-the-post plurality system, continue to present almost insuperable barriers to such parties unless their support is geographically concentrated.

Understood through the spirit of intercurrence, the making of policy and policy outcomes are largely shaped by the friction, 'chafing' and 'abrasion' between party, constituencies, regime institutions and ideational orders. Put another way, outcomes are shaped and moulded by processes at the edges of each of these levels or tiers. These outcomes may be stasis and 'gridlock' or, if there is political change, it may well be in a form that is unanticipated and perhaps undesired by actors. Or, it may be that processes based upon mutual stresses and tensions open the way for the creativity of actors as they wrestle with different and conflicting demands. If the Conservative Party's policy towards the EU is considered, the tensions and clashes between tiers has led the Cameron leadership to pledge itself to a referendum on continued British membership and join together in the European Parliament with Rightist populist parties coming from markedly different traditions, but at the same time insist that negotiations with other member countries could produce fundamental reforms or allow the development of a 'two-speed' Europe that many British business interests would like to secure. The efforts of actors to navigate their way around these issues, and the friction points between the different tiers, will demand considerable judgement and luck.

Structure and outline

Aside from this Introduction, the book has eight chapters. Chapter 1 outlines the concept of intercurrence, around which the later arguments are structured, in greater depth. It addresses some of the questions that have been posed in commentaries critical of the concept. The chapter argues that the concept has a value and relevance to accounts of political development in both the US and beyond.

Chapter 2 returns to consider the structural development of the British and American states over recent decades. It suggests that despite the efforts of neoliberal reformers, and notwithstanding the processes of 'hollowing out' in the UK as many established state responsibilities and functions have been transferred to agencies, sub-contractors or the EU, the post-war state in both the UK and the US has proved remarkably resilient. Indeed, if the size of the state and its character as a social provider is considered through the simple proxy of measuring government expenditure as a proportion of GDP, the state has repeatedly 'bounced back'.

These increases in state spending took place in part because of the 'automatic' processes by which government expenditure grows during economic downturns (because there are many more demands upon government social provision) and discretionary spending decisions that took place because political actors sought to secure particular domestic policy objectives or national security goals. Thus, to the chagrin of neoliberal reformers, both the British and American states have proved obstinately 'sticky' in terms of size over recent decades.

Chapter 3 considers the ways in which the Right and its different factions responded to this 'stickiness'. It outlines the competing and contending strategies that emerged. These included, for example, 'civic conservatism'. The term refers to efforts to strengthen and bolster civil society, in particular the provision of social services and civic projects, in the hope that civil society and 'third sector' or 'not-for-profit' organizations and networks of volunteers would pick up the slack and assume far greater responsibility for social provision.

Chapter 4 considers the initial responses of the British and American Right as the extent and scale of the economic crisis began to become evident during the closing months of 2008. It looks at the financial bailout packages and, as the consequences of the financial crash for the 'real economy' became increasingly visible, the very limited 'return of the master' as policymakers in both the UK and the US seemed, albeit hesitantly and without recapturing the economic convictions of the mid-century decades when demand management had been ascendant, to rediscover Keynesian fiscal strategies.

In Chapter 5, the book surveys developments in the US that followed in the wake of the initial crisis and Barack Obama's inauguration as president, in particular the emergence and development of the Tea Party movement. Within days of the passage of the American Recovery and Reinvestment Act, the recession was being redefined as a crisis of excess government rather than a banking crisis or a consequence of market failure. The shifting agenda allowed the shrinkage and redefinition of the post-war state to come into the open and secure legitimacy as a political project. The porous character of the party system, the largely empty character of the Republican Party at precinct level and the intensity of ideological and partisan polarization all laid a basis for the growth of the Tea Party movement and its efforts to mobilize independently, confront the Republican Party 'establishment' and at the same time pull the party towards a more abrasive and confrontational form of conservatism.

Chapter 6 turns to consider the UK. While Labour had foreseen a switch from stimulus measures to fiscal retrenchment at an early stage, the Conservatives had by early 2009 embraced the concept of a 'structural deficit'. Through Labour's persistent over-spending from 2001 onwards, it was said, the UK would be in deficit even when the economy recovered. Such a deficit threatened the country's overall stability and threatened to choke off economic recovery. The sovereign debt crises in the Mediterranean countries, and the spillover effects for the eurozone as a whole, stood out as an object lesson. Nonetheless, once in government, the Conservatives moved, almost by stealth, from framing 'austerity' in pragmatic terms towards a proclaimed faith in the long-run shrinkage of the state and a fundamental redefinition of its role and relationships. There were suggestions of this as some talked about the promise of the 'Big Society' at the time of the May 2010 general election, but, as noted above, it became explicit by 2013–14. At the same time, just as the American Right turned towards the Tea Party movement and 'constitutional government', significant sections of the British Right (in particular UKIP and its associated constituencies) embraced populist themes while fusing them with particular representations of the British nation.

Chapter 7 brings the preceding chapters together and returns to the concept of intercurrence that was introduced in Chapter 1. It surveys the ways in which the tensions, stresses and clashes between party, constituencies, regime, institutions and ideas and cultures shaped many of the outcomes described earlier. It also seeks to explain the differences in the character of political responses by the Right in the UK and the US.

The final chapter (Chapter 8) looks ahead. On the face of it, particularly if the UK is considered, a process of transformational change is taking place. The strategies pursued by neoliberal reformers appear to have secured far-reaching changes. Nonetheless, the book concludes, those changes are relatively fragile and the shrinking of the British state may prove relatively short-lived. The pressures and forces that have in recent decades repeatedly 'brought the state back in' remain in place.

Notes

1 The term 'liberal' is used here in its European sense to refer to what is sometimes termed classical liberalism or economic liberalism.

2 See pp. 22–23.

3 Such an approach is sometimes now termed 'old institutionalism'.

4 There is also, as noted above, a rich US literature lying on the boundaries between journalism and political studies describing actors and their decisions. Ron Suskind's book, *Confidence Men*, which charts the Obama administration responses to the economic crisis, is one of many examples (Suskind, 2011). Such literature is often informed by unattributed briefings given to the authors.

5 A 'regime' is, in this context, a set of structures, relationships, ideas and rules that holds sway for a particular period. Within each, particular interests are hegemonic.

6 Akin to physical capital, social capital is defined by the World Bank with reference to groups and networks, trust and solidarity, collective action and cooperation, social cohesion and inclusion, as well as information and communication (The World Bank, 2011). It is at its simplest 'getting things done' (Foley and Edwards, 1997: 551). It rests upon reciprocity, mutuality, participation and connectedness and is a driver of economic growth. As Robert Putnam asserted, social capital at least partially explains the differential in terms of growth rates between the Italian north and south. It encompasses civic engagement, institutional structures and associated value systems (dubbed the 'habits of the heart' in another context). Put another way, social capital consists of 'values that people hold and the resources that they can access, which both result in, and are the result of, collective and socially negotiated ties and relationships. The focus is on networks, norms and trust, and resources, and the relationship between them' (Edwards, 2004: 2).

7 Seen in this way, institutional arrangements do not only restrict and inhibit actors. They can also facilitate political action. Arguably, the institutional obstacles that the Thatcher governments encountered in their efforts to reduce public expenditure paved the way for privatization programmes that offered another means of reducing the Public Sector Borrowing Requirement (Marsh, 1995: 601–602).

8 Some studies of conservatism are also informed, albeit implicitly, by other forms of path dependence. In some accounts, one event or process leads to, and shapes, a further event or process. There is, in other words, a sequential chain. During the 1980s, the popularity of council house sales may well have encouraged the Thatcher government in its pursuit of privatization and a more widely based property-owning democracy. There may at times also be processes based upon reactive sequences. See p. 113.

9 As David Marsh notes, many of these accounts overplay the coherence of the policy initiatives pursued during the Thatcher years. Policy disaggregation and the more detailed study of, for example, industrial relations policy, suggests that there was rather less coherence and consistency than accounts often suggest (Marsh, 1995: 603).

10 'Orders' are, however, defined in different ways within the APD literature. See Chapter 2.

1

Intercurrence and its implications

This chapter sets the scene for later chapters by considering the relationship between the tiers established in the Introduction. As was noted, each of these tiers is described in one of the different literatures that survey the contemporary Right. The chapter introduces the concept of intercurrence within this context.

The Introduction to the book surveyed the five literatures, structured around party, constituencies, regime, institutions, ideas and cultures, through which the Right in the UK and the US has been studied and understood. It argued that each of these literatures describes and captures political and social processes within a particular level or tier. Each has played an important part in structuring the overall character and trajectory of the contemporary Right.

A rounded account of the British and American Right will therefore draw on each of these levels or tiers. In doing so, it is tempting simply to appropriate one or 'pick and mix' between them as seems appropriate at any point during the narrative or discussion. At times, after all, certain constituencies have hit the headlines and seemed pivotal. It would be difficult, after all, to describe and discuss the Republican Party's fortunes in recent years without making reference to the different networks of economic and social conservatives (who, as the terms suggest, stress market and cultural issues, respectively) as well the 'neoconservatives', all of whom have sought to remake the party in their own image. Other accounts draw freely on, and quickly move backwards and forwards (sometimes rather erratically and unpredictably) between, ideas and cultures, constituencies and deliberations within party organizations.

Alternatively, studies may make efforts to identify 'fits' or complementarities between the different levels and tiers. There are good reasons for doing this. It can easily be argued that there were 'fits' or complementarities between the Conservative Party's electoral interests and the broader logic or neoliberalism in pursuing privatization policies and reining in trade union militancy through legislation and the defeat of the National Union of Mineworkers during the 1980s. There are other 'fits'. The 'right to buy' council houses established by the 1980 Housing Act extended the market through processes of commodification while at the same time creating, or at least bolstering, Conservative-leaning electoral groupings within broad demographic constituencies (particularly the 'C2s' or skilled manual workers) that had traditionally backed the Labour Party.

American Political Development (APD) and historical institutionalism

Nonetheless, although there are complementarities between the different levels or tiers, they should not be assumed or be the sole object of study. Indeed, alongside complementarities there are often *dis*complementarities.

At this point the concept of 'intercurrence' becomes relevant. It is rooted in accounts of American Political Development (APD), most notably the work of Karen Orren and Stephen Skowronek.[1] APD is the study of US historical processes within political science, in particular political change and institutional development. For the most part, the efforts of APD scholars have been concentrated on the historical development of the American state, in particular its formation and construction, architecture and long-run character, and the character of its relationship with civil society (Gerring, 2003: 82n). In more recent years APD has, at least to some degree, moved outwards, taking in themes such as the boundaries between the public and private, labour relations, the construction of markets, race and gender.

In some respects, however, APD is defined in terms of style as much as content. It is informed by a sense that, first, political processes are always taking shape and developing (or put another way they are in motion) and, second, the past matters because it structures and organizes the present.

Nonetheless, although it is sometimes difficult to pin down what does, or does not, fall within APD's auspices, it is fair to say that as a sub-field APD owes much to the theoretical propositions and methodologies underpinning historical institutionalism (HI). Indeed, there would be great difficulty finding a discernible or consistent dividing line between APD and HI. Significantly, APD's practitioners often describe themselves as historical institutionalists.

APD and HI accounts have much in common. They both suggest, at times implicitly but often explicitly, that institutions (which are understood in broad terms as policy regimes, rules and standard operating procedures) and the legacies of past policies mediate or in some accounts alter or create interests and notions of self-interest: 'institutions construct politics ... they shape action, conflict, order, change and meaning' (Orren and Skowronek, 2002: 737). Put another way, 'Institutions participate actively in politics: they shape interests and motives, configure social and economic relationships, promote as well as inhibit political change' (Orren and Skowronek, 2004: 78). Recent accounts within APD have perhaps placed rather more emphasis upon the processes of interaction between institutions and politics. Indeed, by privileging some constituencies while weakening others, policy and policy regimes not only create politics but through feedback effects forge a politics that in turn remakes those institutions. Thus, as Andrea Campbell has recorded, Social Security and the provision of Medicare improved the material circumstances of senior citizens but also drew significant numbers through interest organizations such as the AARP into lobbying and other assertive forms of political activism (Sheingate, 2014: 466).

Nonetheless, by definition, institutions remain as the core of institutionalism. From an institutionalist perspective, therefore, politics is, to use Bismarck's celebrated phrase, structured around 'the art of the possible' insofar as institutional arrangements constrain the options open to actors while at the same time (although, despite the work noted above, they receive less attention from scholars) offering opportunities and indeed resources for empowerment.

Intercurrence

The term 'intercurrence' is used in APD to describe the points of contact and the processes of interaction between different institutional and, in some accounts, ideational 'orders'. More often than not, processes of intercurrence between such orders are marked not by the presence of complementarities but instead by friction, 'chafing' and 'abrasion'.

This is because orders invariably emerge at different points in time, in different settings, for different purposes and amidst different configurations of political forces. They therefore follow different, at times very different, logics. They have profoundly different tempos: 'we can consider that any political moment or episode or outcome is situated within a *variety* of ordered institutional and ideological patterns, each with its own origins and history and each with its own logic and pace' (Lieberman, 2002: 701). Put another way, 'institutions congeal time ... within their sphere' (Orren and Skowronek, 1994: 319).

Although there will be periodic compatibilities or 'fits' between orders, intercurrence presumes that there will just as probably be disorder and incongruity: 'any realistic depiction of politics in time will include multiple orders, as well as the conflict and irresolution built into their reciprocal interactions' (Orren and Skowronek, 2004: 17). In other words, and this often places those who explore intercurrence apart from those employing other scholarly approaches, there are no 'a priori presumptions of order' (Orren, 1995: 97). Indeed, taken together, events and processes constitute 'a kind of patterned anarchy' (Orren and Skowronek, 1994: 324). Within this context, friction and abrasion between orders are among the most significant drivers of change: 'change proceeds through the push and pull of differently constituted elements simultaneously engaged' (Orren and Skowronek, 2002: 736).

Nonetheless, having said this, intercurrence suggests that despite the tensions and stresses between orders there may be periodic 'fits' and complementarities and processes of ordering. Such 'fits' may be circumstantial or contingent. For the most part, however, when they emerge they are dependent upon the imagination, creativity, innovations and skill of well-placed actors or coalitions of actors and their ability to construct ordering mechanisms: 'political order is circumstantial, something that officials within government institutions will create or not, sustain or not, depending on their own interests, on the available resources, and on the obstacles to change' (Orren and Skowronek, 2004: 92). This argument constitutes a challenge to many other representations of institutional and ideational change. First, many institutionalist accounts, at least until relatively recently, argued or implied that path-departing change had exogenous rather than endogenous sources. In these accounts, major exogenous shocks such as the dramatic oil price rises in the early 1970s have served as a trigger for a political crisis, a critical juncture and the pursuit of a different institutional path. As Stephen Skowronek has noted in a critique of these accounts and the forms of path dependence to which they are tied: 'Change comes from elsewhere and is likely to be a transition between relatively stable institutional orderings. The dynamics of the polity are taken to be essentially homeostatic, resolving exogenous disruptions in new institutional settlements' (Skowronek, 1995: 92). In sharp contrast to claims such as this, intercurrence represents change as largely endogenous, arising, as noted above, from the existence of multiple orders that necessarily conflict with each other: 'different temporalities operate simultaneously in the political construction of governance' (Orren and Skowronek, 2002: 735). Put another way, institutional arrangements themselves generate change and development: 'Rather than providing stability and coherence, as the metaphor of institutions as equilibria suggests, institutions embody contradictory purposes, which provide for an ongoing, churning process of development' (Orren and Skowronek, 2004: 113).

Second, many other institutional accounts are based upon claims that there are complementarities or coordination effects. From their perspective: 'Institutional arrangements induce complementary organizational forms, which in turn may generate new complementary institutions' (Pierson, 2000: 255). Such complementarities bolster and reinforce an institutional path and thereby change the opportunity-cost ratios if a new or different path is to be followed. Given this, path-departing change becomes much more difficult and, outside of crisis periods, there is, at least relatively, long-run stability. In contrast, intercurrence denies that orders or paths are stable over the long run in the way that these accounts suggest.

Third, although all theoretical approaches suggest that political outcomes are unpredictable and may not be optimal for any of the actors involved, the importance that APD and intercurrence attach to stresses, tensions and friction as the principal sources of change implies that outcomes invariably have a character that cannot be anticipated and was not sought.

'Adventures in intercurrence'[2]

Although the term 'intercurrence' is not always employed, important studies of the American state have been structured around it. They include not only accounts of the construction of an 'administrative state' in the US but also Robert Lieberman's survey of the public policy shift from the 'color-blindness' that underpinned the 1964 Civil Rights Act (and sought to prohibit discriminatory actions by employers or providers) to the affirmative action programmes promulgated just a few years later. By the early 1970s, the Equal Employment Opportunity Commission (EEOC), the federal government agency charged with addressing cases of discrimination against minorities, was playing a significant role in bringing forth US Supreme Court rulings that required employers to adopt race-conscious recruitment policies (Lieberman, 2002: 708). The shift took place because the EEOC did not have the capacity to monitor and 'police' individual instances of alleged discrimination and therefore had to seek broader and more generalized policy solutions based upon 'classes' of individuals: 'Expected to enforce the law but left essentially powerless to do so, the EEOC had to find other outlets to fulfill its enforcement mission' (Lieberman, 2002: 708).

Intercurrence has been applied in other ways. In a study of race and the US labour movement, Paul Frymer has considered the ways in which labour and race policy regimes developed separately from each other, thereby creating and maintaining profound differences of perceived interests. Many labour unions resented the shift towards racial rights and affirmative action through a succession of court rulings that they saw as a threat to the interests of their white memberships. There were 'two vectors of power involving labor and civil rights, created in different historical moments, each with each other, leading to unintended consequences' (Frymer, 2008: 9).

In another exploration of multiple orders and intercurrence, Desmond King and Rogers Smith consider the interaction between different and conflicting 'white supremacist' and 'transformative egalitarian' racial institutional orders (Smith, 2006: 92). Although these orders have shifted in character over the years, they have defined and divided the American experience since the colonial period and the early days of the republic. During the period when independence was declared, there was at one and the same time a commitment that all men were created equal but there were concurrently institutions and ideational structures structured around an enduring faith in a hierarchy based upon white supremacy (King and Smith, 2005: 77). These orders conflicted with each other 'with far-ranging consequences for many aspects of American life that may seem distant from race' (King and Smith, 2005: 84).

Questions

Intercurrence does, however, come with baggage. There are theoretical and methodological hazards associated with it and questions should be asked. APD accounts define and discuss intercurrence in terms of the relationships and interactions between different 'orders'. The character and composition of the 'orders' on which intercurrence rests can be uncertain. At the least, it requires some further consideration. As Rogers Smith asks: 'but just what elements in it count as political "orders" operating intercurrently, with considerable friction?' (Smith, 2006: 101).

In their account of orders, Karen Orren and Stephen Skowronek represent them as 'a constellation of rules, institutions, practices and ideas that hold together over time' (Orren and Skowronek, 2004: 16). They equate them with policy regimes, citing the 'American health-care policy regime' and the 'American pension policy regime' (Orren and Skowronek, 2004: 16). This account appears to tie institutional and ideational variables together, although it seems to give primacy to institutions insofar as ideas appear to express themselves through governing and other political institutions.

In contrast, some adopt a broader and at the same time looser perspective and refer to ideational as well as institutional orders. In these accounts, they are separate and coexist alongside each other. There are thus processes of intercurrence between different institutional orders, different ideational orders and between institutional and ideational orders (Lieberman, 2002: 703).

Others are nonetheless reluctant to represent ideas as 'free-floating' in the way that the concept of separate ideational orders suggests. Rogers Smith, for instance, insists upon the primacy of institutions. From this perspective, ideas only have political significance once they gain traction through institutional connections and bearers within an order:

> Traditions of ideas and ideologies are always carried by particular organizations or sets of organizations within the coalition that constitutes a political order ... Ideas can produce political change only when particular, identifiable political institutions, groups, and actors advance them.
>
> (Smith, 2006: 109)

Another strand within the literature offers a different perspective. It asserts that 'orders' cannot be separated from notions of power. In other words, 'orders' incorporate power relationships, assertions of power by particular interests and efforts by interests to secure power. They are 'a durable mode of organizing and exercising political power at the national level, with distinct institutions, policies, and discourses' (Plotke, 1996: 1). It is thus possible, from the early 1930s onwards, to speak of a Democratic political order structured around Democratic Party networks, national state and interest groupings and social movements (Plotke, 1996: 1). It was at the same time tied to discourses that rested upon democratization, modernization and government action. David Plotke, whose representations of ' political orders' seem broadly synonymous with 'regimes' (although his approach appears to go far beyond the policy regimes considered above), also refers in his discussions of the UK during different historical periods to both a Conservative and a Labour political order (Plotke, 1996: 59). The second half of the 1970s, for example, can be represented in terms of a Labour political order.

Desmond King and Rogers Smith similarly put forward a definition whereby an 'order' incorporates elements from within the state as well as movement actors and others and, just as importantly, ties 'orders' to the articulation and promulgation of particular interests. Orders are:

> coalitions of state institutions and other political actors and organizations that seek to secure and exercise governing power in demographically, economically, and ideologically structured contexts that define the range of opportunities open to political actors.
>
> (King and Smith, 2005: 75)

Smith himself later reiterated the part played by governing authority. Within an 'order', 'Anything worthy of that name must have among its components at least some 'governing institutions' that can assert legal authority to enforce their goals, rules, and policies against at least some outsiders' (Smith, 2006: 108). There are, then, significant differences between all these representations of 'orders'. Nonetheless, all share a presumption of internal coherence. In other words, whereas the relations *between* orders are characterized by friction and 'chafing', there are complementarities *within* an order:

> the effects of the component parts are cumulative and mutually reinforcing, that they generally point most actors in the same (or at least complementary) directions most of the time. (This is not to say there is no conflict, only that conflicts are fundamentally stable and predictable and tend to be contained and resolved within the normal political processes that constitute the order in question according to generally agreed upon or conventionally understood rules and expectations.)
>
> (Lieberman, 2002: 702)

Questions should also be asked about the place of agency and the creativity of political entrepreneurs and other actors within APD scholarship and its relationship to processes of intercurrence. Like many institutionalist accounts, those associated with APD can often seem to have a structuralist bias.[3] Indeed, while *The Search for American Political Development* asserted that 'APD highlights agency – citizens' actions, legislators' votes, politicians' designs', creative agency seemed to get fairly short shrift in practice. Indeed, as one reviewer noted: '"agency" is not among this primer's keywords' (Orren and Skowronek, 2004: 21; Rodgers, 2005).[4] Although this was perhaps rather too sweeping a judgement, *The Search for American Political Development* did appear to circumscribe the role of agency.[5]

Nonetheless, at times agency and creativity seem to have rather more of a place. Indeed, it might be argued that the processes of 'abrading' and 'chafing' might open up countless opportunities for creative discretion by actors. Within historical institutionalism more broadly, the focus in recent studies on the multiple meanings of institutions, the extent to which there is invariably institutional 'play' and gradual forms of change such as layering and conversion seems, if only implicitly, to give considerable weight to the designs of actors. The examples that are most commonly cited consider the ways in which the conservative Right in the US has sought to undermine and restrict government social provision through indirect, covert and subterranean strategies that often stretch the most creative of political imaginations.

Yet, although there have been some discussions of the ways in which, for example, political entrepreneurs use strategic techniques such as *bricolage,* whereby existing elements are recombined or the new is fused with the old, much of this remains implicit rather than explicit (Campbell, 2004: 28). Indeed, in *The Search for American Political Development,* Orren and Skowronek seemed to argue that while actors could open up opportunities their capacities were limited beyond this: 'political actors ... do not by themselves determine the course of political development, but they reverberate with greater or lesser effect throughout the whole ... agency is first of all a matter of breaking things apart' (Orren and Skowronek, 2004: 199–200). APD accounts and studies of intercurrence pose some other potential difficulties. There are (as in other accounts drawing upon historical institutionalism) tensions surrounding the relationships between actors and institutions. These go beyond questions of structure and agency.

There is a guiding assumption in many APD accounts and in much of the literature within historical institutionalism that actors are rational (or largely rational) and their behaviour is thereby shaped by the architecture of institutional incentives and disincentives in any particular setting and at any particular point in time (Orren and Skowronek, 2004: 21). Other studies suggest, however, that institutional configurations do not guide behaviour in this way but instead accord primacy to some sets of ideas by bringing them to the fore while weakening others or shifting them towards the ideational background. Alternatively, as noted above in the discussion of 'ideational orders', ideas may have much more autonomy than these approaches suggest. Studies should therefore pay more attention to the ways in which actors develop and set goals and the ways in which that process of goal-setting shapes the character of policy change. The study of

> institutional factors may help to explain why a policy alternative is defeated or enacted but it can seldom account for the reasons why actors conceived and made sense of this alternative in the first place. Failing to analyze the changing assumptions of actors as they affect the formulation and diffusion of new policy proposals makes it harder for scholars to understand the potential content and direction of policy change.
>
> (Béland, 2009: 703)

Significance

Nonetheless, despite the questions that can be asked about intercurrence, the concept has a validity and capacity for application that deserves wider acknowledgement and recognition. Studies of intercurrence and APD scholarship more broadly pose a direct challenge to what has been termed an 'iconography of order'.

As has been seen, much of the literature written within an institutionalist framework stresses the extent to which there are 'fits' or complementarities. The Varieties of Capitalism school emphasizes the ways in which the two ideal types of capitalism, both liberal market economies (LMEs) and coordinated market economies (CMEs) are held together as formations by institutional complementarities so that, for example, systems of employment training take different forms in each. Theories of path dependence, particularly the stricter versions, rest in part upon the emergence of institutional complementarities that in turn bolster the path and raise the relative costs of path-departing change.

Even within APD, at least if the sub-field is understood at its broadest, there are those who have emphasized 'fits' and the ways in which such 'fits', rather than abrasion and friction, have driven processes of change. In her 1992 book, *Protecting Soldiers and Mothers*, Theda Skocpol considered the ways in which the 'fit' between institutional structures, patterns of party competition, interests and particular ideas about the deserving and undeserving gave rise to early forms of social spending, while Richard Bensel surveyed the way in which the 'fit' between laissez-faire, the gold standard and protectionism for industries (each of which was backed by one of the three branches of the federal government) laid the basis for American industrialization (Sheingate, 2014: 468–469).

Nonetheless, as has been seen, although many accounts in the social sciences search for 'fits' and complementarities, intercurrence rightly considers the many tensions, stresses and incongruities that characterize the political, social and economic world. Intercurrence also directs us towards the ways in which political outcomes are shaped by the nature and character of relationships rather than simply being a reflection of the preferences of influential actors.

Furthermore, intercurrence and APD more broadly call attention to the many limits and constraints that even the most creative and innovative political actors face. As noted above, because of the ways in which orders clash and abrade, decisions and actions seemingly affecting just one order may well have spillover effects in other, related orders that are far removed from the original intentions of policymakers. Thus, political efforts to build ordering mechanisms may be profoundly disruptive and create *dis*complementarities:

> At any given historical juncture, however, measures aimed at alleviating strain will as likely exacerbate it … the intricacies of control were hidden from actors who did not anticipate the systematically disruptive consequences of their ordering pursuits.
>
> (Orren and Skowronek, 1994: 324)

Indeed, as Orren and Skowronek record, the War on Poverty and the Great Society programmes pursued during Lyndon Johnson's presidency were in part an effort to bolster the Democrats' electoral ties with African-Americans, who had by then become a pivotal political constituency, by addressing poverty and disadvantage. Nonetheless, once implemented, some of the Great Society programmes created a basis for a semi-autonomous mobilization by African-Americans against the established party machines in the bigger cities (Orren and Skowronek, 1994: 324). Some conservative commentators have argued that the 2010 Patient Protection and Affordable Care Act ('Obamacare') has also had consequences that were not anticipated or foreseen by its designers. Stresses and tensions between the policy regime that the Act established and the health insurance industry, in particular concerning requirements that coverage conform to particular standards and the insistence that coverage be extended to all those with pre-existing health conditions, led those insurance companies to change their commercial strategies and withdraw coverage for significant numbers of individuals.

Conclusion

The tiers or levels outlined in the Introduction all constitute important and legitimate ways of representing and understanding the politics of the contemporary Right. A comprehensive account should draw upon them. Nonetheless, the relationships between them are not straightforward or unproblematic. Because these levels or tiers are akin to the 'political orders' considered by scholars of APD, their relationship can be considered in terms of intercurrence. In other words, there are often stresses, tensions and discomplementarities. These bring forth change and shape its character. Such changes may differ profoundly from the original intentions of policymakers. The later chapters in the book will be informed by this approach.

The next chapter considers the British and American states and the extent to which they were restructured by Thatcherism and the 'Reagan revolution'.

Notes

1 The emergence of contemporary APD can, in part, be dated to efforts during the mid-1980s to 'bring the state back in' and provide a corrective to the implicit pluralism that underpinned many political science projects in the US. There were, however, earlier generations of scholars who considered the historical development of the American state from what might be termed a 'formal institutionalist' perspective. Woodrow Wilson, who served as US president between 1913 and 1921, was perhaps foremost among them. Later mid-century scholars who considered issues such as continuity and change, party development and American 'exceptionalism' include V.O. Key, Walter Dean Burnham and E.E. Schattschneider.

2 This term is taken from Richardson Dilworth's review of Stephen Skowronek and Matthew Glassman's edited collection, *Formative Acts: American Politics in the Making* (Dilworth, 2009).

3 The studies of 'political creativity' edited by Gerald Berk, Dennis Galvan and Victoria Hattam pose a direct challenge to the alleged structuralism of institutionalist accounts. In place of institutional constraints they stress that 'action is not rote playing from sheet music, nor are improvisational riffs predictable from gaps in the score. Instead, we find

actors who constantly mess with the score in unexpected and unauthorized ways, rearranging it with each performance. The creativity of situated action is a kind of recomposition' (Berk *et al.*, 2013: 3).

4 It should, however, be noted that the word 'agency' appears on ten pages of the book (Orren and Skowronek, 2004: 229).

5 *Formative Acts*, edited by Stephen Skowronek and Matthew Glassman, places much more emphasis on agency, although critical commentaries suggest that it retains an implied distinction between structure and agency. Although it is, they say, 'a necessary corrective to structuralist accounts of political development, its editors do not challenge the dualist foundations of the subfield' (Berk *et al.*, 2013: 13).

2

The state and processes of change

This chapter considers the impact of 'Thatcherism' and 'Reaganomics' and the extent to which the British and American states were restructured during the 1980s. It argues that, despite the neoliberal project, the state proved largely resistant to long-run shrinkage. It suggests, furthermore, that some of the gradual change mechanisms that were employed by policymakers in this period did not always create lasting or sustained institutional shifts.

Much has been made of 'Thatcherism' and the extent to which Margaret Thatcher's eleven years in office changed the UK. At the time of her death, almost all the obituaries hailed, for good or ill, the 'revolution' that had taken place during her premiership.

A commentary in *The New American* was representative. In the account that it gave, Britain was at the end of the 1970s 'the sick man of Europe' and there was a sense of crisis and decay as James Callaghan's Labour government staggered through its final months. The instability of a minority government, militant trade unionism culminating in the 'winter of discontent' as public sector workers took industrial action, and declining international competitiveness all came together in a composite picture. Nicholas Henderson, Britain's ambassador to Paris, said at the time:

> Today we are not only no longer a world power but we are not in the first rank even as a European one ... Our decline is shown not simply by the statistics but by the look of our towns, airports, hospitals, local amenities.
>
> (quoted in Reiland, 2013)

Seen from a Thatcherite perspective and even from the vantage point of her many critics on the Left, the UK had changed beyond recognition eleven years later when Margaret Thatcher left office. In particular, the role of government and the character of macroeconomic policy had been transformed.

The word 'revolution' was no understatement. Whereas post-war macroeconomic policy had long juggled competing policy goals between reducing unemployment, curbing inflation and reducing the balance of payments deficit, inflation had by the time the Conservatives took office in 1979 become 'public enemy number one', as it had been dubbed by President Gerald Ford five years earlier. Indeed, while the Phillips curve, which underpinned thinking by both policymakers and the economics profession during the post-war decades, had depicted unemployment and inflation as opposites (so that reductions in unemployment necessarily created upward pressure on inflation rates), it was now argued with growing intellectual self-confidence that price stability was an essential prerequisite for securing growth and employment insofar as such stability brought forth investment. In other words, for the new Right, inflation and unemployment were not opposites but were instead bound together.

In contrast with the preceding Conservative government led by Edward Heath (1970–74), Thatcherism eschewed policy U-turns ('the Lady's not for turning') and the Chancellor of the Exchequer, Geoffrey Howe, sought to reduce inflation to manageable levels through, at least initially, prescribed targets for the growth of the money supply. Thus, while inflation rates surged at the beginning of the Thatcher government's first term of office and rose again at the end of the decade as the Lawson boom ran its course, they were for the most part held under 5 per cent (falling to 3.4 per cent in 1986), which, although high by later standards, appeared to constitute a significant economic victory when set against the inflation figures for the 1970s. Although formal monetarism and the direct efforts to control the growth of the money supply that had been embraced at the start of her premiership and were enshrined in the Medium Term Financial Strategy were abandoned, the setting of interest rates and, to some degree, the fiscal policy stance adopted by her successive governments continued to be guided by the principle of inflation-targeting for much of the decade.

Even more visibly, the British trade unions, held up through representations of the 1970s as strike-prone, politically driven, excessively powerful and a threat to both price stability and Britain's international competitiveness, lost much of their former influence. The events of 1978–79 held a particular place in these representations. Indeed, as Colin Hay argues, the discursive construction of the 'winter of discontent' laid a basis for Thatcherism's ability to impose 'a new trajectory upon the institutions of the state' (Hay, 1996: 256). The National Economic Development Council, within which the unions had an important place and which was a vestige of Britain's distinctly anaemic efforts to emulate the corporatist arrangements governing economic life in much of Western Europe, was sidelined ahead of its eventual abolition in 1992. The coal miners, widely seen as the strongest and most militant vanguard of the organized labour movement, were crushed in the 1984–85 strike. The number of working days lost because of strike action was (at 3,939,000), as an annual average, during 1985–89 about a third of the corresponding figure a decade earlier (Hyman, 1999). The legislative reforms pursued by the Thatcher government and the relentless decline of traditional industries that had once been union strongholds combined to weaken the unions, or at least those in the private sector, fatally.

The 'sell-off' or privatization of public utilities by the Thatcher government should also of course be chalked up as a further victory. The wave of privatizations, which gained pace with successive general election victories, not only widened and thereby tightened the grip of the market and weakened the trade unions that had formerly been entrenched within the utilities, but also seemed to spread asset ownership more broadly. Direct share ownership (a figure that excludes *in*direct share ownership through pension and mutual funds) rose dramatically between 1984 and 1989 (reaching over a quarter of the population). The flotations included both British Telecom (1984) and British Gas (1986), although the increase in share ownership can also be tied to changes in the character of the tax regime (Banks *et al.*, 2004: 217).

The shift towards a 'property-owning democracy' was also boosted by growing rates of home ownership. From early on, council housing was made available for sale at a discounted price to sitting tenants. Indeed, 1.7 million social housing units were sold at less than their market value between 1981 and 1995 (Hills, 1998: 8). There were also changes to the pensions system. There were cuts in the State Earnings-Related Pension Scheme (SERPS), reducing the pension as a proportion of average earnings, while at the same time private pension schemes were introduced and encouraged. Opposition to the changes was, however, muted:

> These changes, though criticized, failed to generate the kind of outcry that often led the government to back off from other reforms. Offering the carrot of personal pensions diminished the pain of the cuts in public pensions (although the required tax incentives also diminished the government's budgetary savings). More important, the government's use of incremental and seemingly technical reforms limited the emergence of opposition.
>
> (Pierson, 1996: 162)

There were, alongside all of this, deregulation processes. The 1986 'Big Bang' liberalized the financial markets and ended restrictions that had prevented foreign companies buying out City firms, while at the same time introducing electronic trading. For its supporters, the move re-established the City of London as one of the world's major financial centres.

Nonetheless, Thatcherism was multifaceted. By the late 1980s, and despite passage of the 1986 Single European Act, it had an increasingly more pronounced Eurosceptic edge to it, symbolized by Margaret Thatcher's 1988 Bruges speech calling for a Europe of independent sovereign states and issuing a rallying cry against regulation: 'We have not successfully rolled back the frontiers of the state in Britain, only to see them re-imposed at a European level with a European super-state exercising a new dominance from Brussels' (Thatcher, 2008, orig. 1988).

Even more significantly, there were reforms (as noted in the Introduction) that did not decentralize but instead had a profoundly centralizing character. Local government was subject to increasing controls triggered by efforts to restrain public spending and a bid to break the hold of the Labour Left over councils in some of the bigger cities. In efforts to increase educational standards schools were made subject to a national curriculum and standardized testing. Both the Left's pleas to retain traditional local education authority control over schools and the Right's calls for school vouchers so as to create a simulated market were sidelined. Job-related training provision and the universities were placed, albeit to different degrees, under the control of local business interests.[1]

In a similar vein, other studies have pointed to new regulatory institutions and the introduction of re-regulatory processes at state level. Indeed, the neoliberal state has been portrayed as one variant of the emerging 'competition state'. The competition state (which in these accounts has displaced the welfare state) was evident in different ways. Policy has shifted from macroeconomic to microeconomic interventionism. The competition state controls inflation and promotes enterprise, innovation and profitability. In overall terms, political actors are 'attempting to reinvent the state as a quasi-"enterprise association" in a wider world context'. Thus, despite the talk of curbing and restraining the state, the neoliberal project may 'necessitate the actual expansion of *de facto* state intervention and regulation in the name of competitiveness and marketization' (Cerny, 1997: 251).

The more critical commentaries have also questioned the Conservatives' economic record and claims that the Thatcher government rejuvenated the British economy. As they note, real Gross Domestic Product (GDP) only surpassed its 1979 figure in 1983 (given the depth of the recession at the beginning of the 1980s), there were significant increases in income inequality and although labour productivity rose it still lagged substantially behind that in France and West Germany (Crafts, 2013: 3). They also argued that much of the increase in labour productivity was attributable to the growing openness of the British economy as trade barriers fell rather than to the impact of Thatcherite reforms. And as a corollary there were also those on the Right who claimed that the Thatcher governments should have gone far further in terms of cutting marginal tax rates. Thatcherism, they asserted, was insufficiently radical and the economic recovery was thereby limited in character.

Although it has been said that Thatcherism reconfigured and secured popular hegemony, others argue that it signally failed to win hearts and minds. Instead, there were repeated challenges and processes of contestation. Despite Margaret Thatcher's three general election victories and John Major's subsequent success in 1992, aggregate popular opinion remained ambivalent, particularly in the outer nations and regions of the UK. Indeed, Ivor Crewe suggested that even after almost ten years of the Thatcher government, 'the public remain wedded to the collectivist, welfare ethos of social democracy' (quoted in Heffernan, 2000: 110). Furthermore, the unpopularity of the poll tax, which displaced the rates, a property tax, and in their place levied a uniform 'price' (with some concessions for those on low incomes) for the provision of local government services, contributed much to Margaret Thatcher's abrupt and unceremonious removal from the premiership in November 1990.[2]

Nonetheless, all this having been said, Thatcherism not only presided over significant policy reforms but also stamped its imprint on Margaret Thatcher's successors as prime minister, not least those drawn from the Left. Although there have been debates about the extent to which 'New Labour' consolidated Thatcherism, rolled it forward or alternatively developed 'flanking mechanisms' so as to soften and ameliorate Thatcherism's 'two nations' (or 'them and us') narrative, Margaret Thatcher's claim, when asked to identify her greatest success, that it was 'Tony Blair' was not only widely reported but also left unchallenged.

Furthermore, the impact of Thatcherism on the ideas and narratives associated with the Left went beyond the revival of Gramscian approaches and considerations of hegemony. Influential figures on the Left, particularly those within the Communist Party's orbit, subscribed with growing vigour to the idea that Thatcherism had, when taken together with structural changes in the economy, halted the 'forward march of labour', in other words the progress of the working class and its allied organizations and the advance of collectivism. The turn away from working-class politics, and then the collapse of the Soviet bloc at the end of the 1980s, seemed to constitute a major turning point as even those who had never felt sympathetic to the USSR and the other communist states abandoned the idea of a socialist alternative to the capitalist order. A significant proportion of those who had once invoked visions of the Paris Commune of 1871 and the Petrograd Soviet turned instead to incremental reform and the adoption of measures associated with Rhineland capitalism.

The 'Reagan revolution'

Thatcherism and Reaganomics are often mentioned in the same breath. The similarities are self-evident. Stephen Skowronek's comment on US politics during the second half of the twentieth century could equally be applied to the UK: 'A conservative insurgency pushed its way to power, transformed national discourse, realigned political conflict, and brought new priorities to the fore' (Skowronek, 2009: 348).

Nonetheless, despite the similarities there were also differences. Just as the Labour government that preceded Margaret Thatcher's election as prime minister had, through its efforts to reduce inflation, begun the neoliberal turn, so the 'Reagan revolution' arguably began with President Jimmy Carter's appointment in 1979 of Paul Volcker to head the Federal Reserve and the decision to embrace monetarist strategies. However, whereas Thatcherism, fearful of increased budget deficits, shrank from radical tax-cutting measures, 'Reaganomics' was not so inhibited.

In the UK, the marginal income tax reductions in the Thatcher government's first budget were matched by a significant increase in indirect taxation. Value added tax rates were raised from 8 and 12 per cent to 15 per cent. In the US, despite the presence of figures such as Volcker at the Federal Reserve and Martin Feldstein in the Council of Economic Advisors, supply-side economics trumped monetarist fears that tax-cutting could be inflationary (Ashford, 1990). Marginal tax reductions would, supply-siders argued, bring forth a significant increase in factor supply. Entrepreneurship would flourish and investment would rise, thereby leading to an increase in economic activity and growth. Indeed, as the Laffer curve suggested, the increase in economic growth rates would be sufficient to compensate for the loss of tax revenue resulting from the marginal tax reductions.

Supply-side economics and, in particular, faith in the Laffer curve informed the new administration's pursuit of the Economic Recovery Tax Act of 1981 (ERTA). ERTA reduced marginal income tax rates by 23 per cent over a three-year period. The top rate was cut from 70 per cent to 50 per cent and the lowest rate was reduced from 14 per cent to 11 per cent. Estate, corporate and capital gains taxes were also reduced. Though the effects of these measures were partially muted by later tax rises, they nonetheless shifted the burden of taxation away from higher-income earners and capital gains.

The deregulation policies initiated during the Carter years, including the abolition of the Civil Aeronautics Board and deregulation of oil prices, continued and were extended. The defeat of the August 1981 strike by the Professional Air Traffic Controllers Organization (PATCO) had a similar symbolic value comparable with the Thatcher government's vanquishing of the coal miners in 1984–85. US trade unions, always weaker than their European counterparts, continued to shed their membership outside of the public sector, which remained as their last redoubt.

There was very little ambiguity about the overall political character of those who followed Reagan into the White House, at least during the years that preceded the 'Great Recession'. There have been few commentaries that mirror the debates about the character of the relationship between New Labour and Thatcherism. After its initial efforts to promote healthcare reform, the Clinton administration embraced the cause of the balanced budget and then in 1996 the president signed the Personal Responsibility and Work Opportunity Act that dramatically restricted and restructured welfare provision. The Act was based around time limits on assistance whereby benefits were withdrawn after two years and a lifetime limit of five years was imposed on benefits funded by the federal government. Many states introduced workfare provisions so that those receiving assistance had either to work or to undertake prescribed training programmes. Absent fathers were pursued far more vigorously for child support. While opponents argued that the Act demonized single mothers and at the same time swelled the ranks of the low-paid, thereby putting further downward pressure on wage levels, its supporters claimed that by compelling individuals to enter the labour market the reform began the process of lifting them and their dependants out of poverty.

Gradual change mechanisms

There is much to suggest, therefore, that the 1980s and 1990s were a revolutionary era. Nonetheless, all this having been said, the extent to which Thatcherism and the 'Reagan revolution' brought forth substantive change cannot simply be assessed by looking at shifts in the character and structure of formal policy regimes. The impact of Thatcherism and Reaganomics goes beyond a catalogue of legislation or a list of regulatory reforms. As Jacob Hacker as well as James Mahoney and Kathleen Thelen have argued, gradual change mechanisms can, over time, have large-scale cumulative effects even when the existing institutional arrangements remain either unchanged or very largely unchanged. They call for:

> enlarging and shifting the focus of analysis – from formal rules to their social consequences, from the welfare state narrowly defined to the broader public–private economy of welfare, and from the highly visible politics of large-scale reform to the subterranean political processes that shape ground-level policy effects.
>
> (Hacker, 2004: 243)

Seen in this way, there is much more of a focus on the consequences of seemingly marginal or hidden forms of change, covert and quasi-covert manoeuvres by political actors and the effects of (often deliberate) inactivity and inaction. Taken together, these largely subterranean forms of change have had significant consequences over recent decades as individuals and households have become much more exposed to social risk. Put another way, as the social state has retreated and the scope of its provision has lessened there have been processes of 'risk privatization' (Hacker, 2004: 243). Seen in this way, although some forms of change were not immediately visible, both the Thatcher and Reagan eras had a very substantial impact.

These processes, whereby institutional arrangements fail to keep pace with contextual shifts, have been dubbed policy *drift* (Mahoney and Thelen, 2010: 15–18). Drift occurs because of either neglect or deliberate political design. Thus, the federal minimum wage in the US was not adjusted between 1997 and 2007 so as to keep place with inflation, and it thereby lost real value. In the UK, the updating of welfare benefits was decoupled from economic growth rates and instead tied to inflation. Although this maintained their real value, their worth fell through a process of policy drift in relationship to average earnings (Hills, 1998: 4).

There are other gradual change mechanisms. Although perhaps less subterranean than policy drift, they may still be partially hidden. 'Layering' refers to the introduction of new institutional arrangements 'on top' of existing structures. The effect, over time, is to subvert and transform those earlier structures. Thus, in both the UK (as noted above) and the US, private pension schemes (through, for example, individual retirement accounts) have increasingly supplanted state pension schemes.

Government spending as a share of GDP

There are further ways in which the impact of the Thatcher and Reagan years and the actions of their successors can be considered. The process of 'rolling back' the state that both Thatcher and Reagan claimed to seek is generally understood as the reduction of 'welfare' expenditure commitments through retrenchment processes (King, 1987: 120–121).

Retrenchment is, as Paul Pierson notes, both programmatic and systemic. The former refers to reductions or cutbacks in particular programmes, while the latter refers to changes in the overall structures or environment within which social programmes are provided. Taken together, retrenchment refers to residualization so that government social provision is increasingly limited to short-run 'emergency' provision for those facing the most dire forms of proven need. As Pierson puts it, retrenchment describes 'policy changes that either cut social expenditure, restructure welfare state programs to conform more closely to the residual welfare state model, or alter the political environment in ways that enhance the probability of such outcomes in the future' (Pierson, 1994: 17).

Yet, despite the rhetoric of both Thatcherism and Reaganomics, as well as the claims made by both devotees of the two leaders and many of their detractors on the Left, and more than three decades of neoliberal reform, much of the post-war social state remains intact. Indeed, as Pierson concludes in a study of retrenchment in both the UK and the US:

> Economic, political, and social pressures have fostered an image of welfare states under siege. Yet if one turns from abstract discussions of social transformation to an examination of actual policy, it becomes difficult to sustain the proposition that these strains have generated fundamental shifts.
>
> (Pierson, 1996, 173)

This is an important argument and it has rightly commanded widespread attention. It does, however, pose a methodological question. How can the 'fundamental shifts' to which Pierson refers be measured and assessed? One answer lies in detailed case studies of particular policy regimes and the social settings within which they are placed.[3] Alternatively, the structural character of provision and the degree to which it is, for example, universal or means-tested could be assessed. Another approach to retrenchment is to consider real spending on particular programmes relative to their target populations, total social spending or overall government expenditure as a proportion of GDP.

Any proxy is of course by definition crude and open to methodological challenge. In the US (and perhaps also in those countries influenced by German *ordoliberalism*), where the relationship between the state and civil society is often blurred and imprecisely defined, the percentages understate the scale of government involvement in the lived experience of individuals. The overall figure also says nothing about the composition of the spending totals (Crawford and Johnson, 2011: 2). Unless final consumption expenditure figures are employed, the numbers include transfer payments.[4] Such social spending is inevitably vulnerable to long-run demographic shifts (and provision for pensions and health have therefore grown in recent decades) as well as the state of the economy.

Nonetheless, despite these shortcomings, the figures for government spending levels provide a rough and ready guide to the extent and scale to which there has been fiscal retrenchment or, conversely, government expansion over a given period. If the figures for the 1980s are considered, they indicate that the Thatcher governments had a measure of success in squeezing the overall size of the state. Overall public spending in the UK fell from 44.6 per cent of GDP in 1979–80 to 39.2 per cent in 1989–90. The figure then rose during the recession at the beginning of the 1990s only to fall again as the economy became more buoyant and both John Major's government and its New Labour successors sought to hold overall spending levels in check. By the beginning of the new millennium expenditure had fallen to a figure close to the proportion that had been achieved at the end of the Thatcher years. Then, in Labour's second and third terms of office, spending again began to rise, and inevitably increased again very sharply as the financial crisis and the 'Great Recession' took hold (*The Guardian*, 2013).[5]

As Table 2.1 suggests, the pattern was broadly similar in the US. If federal government spending is considered (thereby excluding the very substantial amount spent by state and local government and distributed through transfer payments), expenditure remained at just over a fifth of GDP during the Reagan years, rose as a consequence of the 1991 recession, then fell as the Clinton administration and Congress prioritized fiscal restraint as the economy surged during the second half of the 1990s, but then rose once more at a slow but perceptible rate in the aftermath of the downturn that came at the end of the dot.com boom. During Bush's years in office the figure edged upwards, reaching 18.8 per cent of GDP in 2007, the final year before the recession began to take its toll. Overall government spending, including expenditure by state and local governments as well as transfer payments, was much higher, constituting almost a third of GDP in 1980 and rather more than a third (34.2 per cent) in 2007 (US Government Spending, 2014).

The history of the neoliberal 'revolution' from the late 1980s onwards is therefore a history of the state, at least if measured in terms of the overall size of public spending in relation to GDP, returning more than once from the fate to which the free market Right had sought to consign it. Reductions in the size of the state have invariably proved time-limited and fragile. In short, the size of the state has always been vulnerable to economic downturn (in particular severe and prolonged recession) and the fiscal designs of those who have sought, for different discretionary reasons, to increase government expenditure.

Table 2.1 US federal government spending as a proportion of GDP, 1980–2007

Year	Federal government spending as a % of GDP
1980	20.64
1981	21.12
1982	22.29
1983	22.22
1984	21.08
1985	21.77
1986	21.58
1987	20.62
1988	20.26
1989	20.22
1990	20.95
1991	21.45
1992	21.13
1993	20.49
1994	20.00
1995	19.78
1996	19.26
1997	18.60
1998	18.18
1999	17.61
2000	17.39
2001	17.53
2002	18.31
2003	18.76
2004	18.68
2005	18.88
2006	19.16
2007	18.84

Source: adapted from US Government Spending (2014) *Government Spending Chart*, www.usgovernmentspending.com/spending_chart_1980_2007USp_15c2li011mcn_F0f

Reasons

Why has the post-war state proved so resilient and, indeed, 'sticky'? Why have neoliberal efforts, at least in terms of the size and scale of overall government expenditure, proved largely unsuccessful? For some on the Right, in an echo of the agency-based perspectives that have defined many studies of the Conservative Party, the answer lies in a failure of political will. In short, policymakers, including Reagan himself, buckled:

> the clamor for more government intervention in the economy was so formidable that Reagan abandoned the free-market position and acquiesced in further crippling of the economy and our liberties ... Even Ford and Carter did a better job at cutting government. Their combined presidential terms account for an increase of 1.4% – compared with Reagan's 3% – in the government's take of 'national income.' And in nominal terms, there has been a 60% increase in government spending, thanks mainly to Reagan's requested budgets, which were only marginally smaller than the spending Congress voted.
>
> (Richman, 1988)

President George W. Bush went further and, whereas Reagan became a conservative icon, Bush created disappointment and provoked anger within the conservative movement. For some this was again an issue of personal and political weakness. Bush, it was said, capitulated to the Democrats and the logic of pork-barrel politics. He not only failed to veto spending bills but expanded government by promoting the No Child Left Behind Act of 2001 (which provided federal funding for states setting standards for educational attainment) and the Medicare Modernization Act (2003), which established prescription drugs as a federal entitlement for senior citizens. In other accounts, Bush did not so much capitulate to demands upon the federal government purse but revealed himself to be a 'big government conservative'. From this perspective he was committed to the expansion of government, albeit in the service of conservative goals. According to Fred Barnes of the *Weekly Standard* and a *Fox News* contributor, who was a sympathetic commentator, conservatism has in Bush's hands moved away from faith in the small state and been 'redefined ... to fit the times and to come to grips with political reality' (quoted in Béland and Waddan, 2008: 114).

Whatever the exact motives and circumstances (and presidents have of course only limited leverage over the size and composition of the federal government budget), the expenditure increases in both countries were largely driven by rises in public social expenditure, in particular, education and health expenditures (Table 2.2). In the UK, health spending almost doubled in real terms between 1999 and 2010 and rose from 5 per cent of GDP in 1999 to over 8 per cent of GDP by 2009.

For conservative commentators such as Jesse Norman, who became a Conservative MP in 2010, the increase in British government expenditure was tied to a restructuring process and efforts to enlarge the scope and scale of the state. The Labour government was, he charged, eliminating the institutions that traditionally mediated between the citizen and the central state so as to direct and manage individual lives.

Table 2.2 Public social expenditure as a share of GDP, 1990–2012 (%)

Year	UK	US
1980	16.5	13.2
1985	19.4	13.2
1990	16.7	13.6
1995	19.9	15.5
2000	18.6	14.5
2005	20.5	16.0
2010	23.7	19.8
2012	23.9	19.7

Source: OECD StatExtracts (2013) *Social expenditure – Aggregated data*. Online: http://stats.oecd.org/Index.aspx?DataSetCode=SOCX_AGG.

> In the name of efficiency, there will be a minimum of hierarchy or other intervening institutions between the Treasury and the home. The ethos of government will be one of continuous intervention and micro-management, in which specific groups will be targeted and economic incentives tweaked in order to redistribute resources or change behavior ... Standing in the centre, mediating these transfers, and assessing merit or worth, will be central government; and in particular not merely the office, but the person, of the Chancellor.
>
> (Norman and Ganesh, 2006: 10)

Another answer, and one that attaches far less importance to agency-based variables and the discretion of actors, lies in 'automatic' rather than discretionary fiscal processes. The recessions in the early 1980s and at the beginning of the 1990s (and in both cases the relative length of the subsequent recovery period) as well as the downturn in 2000–2001 in the US inevitably put heavy demands upon the public purse and took their toll on efforts to contain and reduce spending levels.

Other reasons might be cited. Both the new arms race during the early 1980s, pursued as relations with the Soviet Union deteriorated, and some of the centralizing measures pursued by the Thatcher government required substantial additions to expenditure. Furthermore, whereas Margaret Thatcher commanded parliamentary majorities, President Reagan confronted all the perils of divided government. And, from January 1987, he had to bargain and barter with Democrats in the US Senate as well as the House of Representatives. While the Reagan administration was able to construct a conservative coalition in Congress that stretched across partisan divisions, at least around some issues, it still required strategic calculation by the White House and a willingness to give ground when necessary. Thus, Reagan's admirers assert that his efforts to contain government were thwarted.

There were at the same time demographic shifts that had implications for governments and their budgets. The inability of the Thatcher governments to cut spending levels dramatically can in part be attributed to the growth in the numbers dependent upon state social provision. As society 'greyed', there were increased numbers of pensioners. At the same time there were many more single parents as household structures changed and, by 1993, 23 per cent of families were headed by a lone parent (Hills, 1998: 5).

Alongside all of this, the cognitive perceptions and normative preferences of policymakers and the subsequent policy choices that they made are also important. They were constrained by horizons and rationalities of the period. There were decisions to increase government spending levels in both the UK and the US in ways that would, just a few years later, be understood as pro-cyclical. At the time, because the business cycle seemed to have been mastered through the judicious use of monetary policy, there was no such understanding. Buoyant tax revenues seemed to provide 'material' confirmation that cyclical swings had indeed been banished and what Colin Crouch has termed 'privatized Keynesianism' delivered on its promises (Crouch, 2011: 114–118). In other words, government spending or the use of tax credits to bolster consumer spending through low interest rates, rising asset prices and the availability of credit to finance mortgages and loans fuelled demand and protected economies from the dangers of an abrupt downturn.

In contrast, some other countries, such as those in the Nordic region, pursued policies that would later reveal themselves to be contra-cyclical. Policymakers in such countries were, to use the US term, 'deficit hawks' and therefore sought, and generally secured, repeated budget surpluses throughout the pre-crisis years.

At the same time, British and US policymakers also sought to meet the demands of particular constituencies or were influenced by electoral considerations. Increases in health provision through the prescription drugs coverage offered by Medicare Part D and introduced by the 2003 Act would, it was widely said, contribute to bringing senior citizens into the Republican electoral fold.

At the same time, a longer-run perspective is also needed. The approaches associated with historical institutionalism that Paul Pierson pursues provide a further part of the answer. Institutional paths are highly resilient. They secure 'increasing returns' to power as they gain an ideational hold, constituencies associated with their preservation and maintenance become entrenched and institutional complementarities begin to form. Expectations begin to adapt and fit around the path, precluding or certainly limiting the possibility of thinking 'outside of the box'. In other words, the costs of path-departing institutional change rise over time (Pierson, 2000). Thus, retrenchment and the cutting back of social provision involves different variables and poses many more challenges to political actors seeking reform than does the initial growth and expansion of such provision. From this perspective, fundamental, path-departing change only takes place during periods of ruptural crisis when there is extensive institutional and ideational flux. Given this, there are short bursts of change and prolonged periods of stability. Put another way, there is a process of punctuated equilibrium.

And, from a path-dependency perspective, some forms of social provision, particularly those tied to entrenched constituencies, have proved particularly resistant to path-departing reforms. As Pierson has noted, institutional arrangements permitted the selling off of council housing stock during the early years of Margaret Thatcher's governments. It was 'a striking example of retrenchment success' (Pierson, 1994: 87). There were also, as noted above, substantial changes to pension arrangements. In contrast, however, health provision and, for example, child benefit remained largely intact. There were institutional complementarities around both that prevented radical reform of programmes or their dismantling.

Similarly, in the US, there were institutional barriers to radical, path-departing reform. Although President George W. Bush successfully secured further tax reductions, his 2004 re-election commitment to partially privatize Social Security, by allowing those aged under 55 to place up to a third of their payroll tax in an individual investment account, had to be abandoned. Fiona Ross argues that while it may have appeared as if Bush, who was at the time flanked by conservative Republican majorities in both chambers of Congress, had a real chance of enacting a partial privatization, the embedded nature of the existing policy regime and the value attached to it by important political constituencies (most notably senior citizens) meant that reform was never feasible (Ross, 2007).[6]

Structural deficits

Government spending thus increased as a share of GDP. In the UK, after Labour's second general election victory in 2001, and despite some faltering around 2006–7 as fears about productivity in the public sector and the burgeoning deficit briefly came to the fore, public spending again rose as a proportion of GDP. This was in part born out of a commitment to raise health spending to the European average and an embedded belief that economic growth levels would not only remain buoyant but grow in the years to come. Spending would thereby fall as a share of GDP while tax revenues would grow. The 'boom and bust' processes of earlier years had, it was ritually asserted by Labour ministers, been consigned to the past.

They were not alone. Although there were differences in emphasis between countries, economic thinking stressed the conquest or at least the subjugation of cyclical economic forces. As former US Treasury Secretary Larry Summers was later to note:

> students now learnt that business cycles were not a hugely important matter. Any output lost during troughs would be made up during booms and, in any case, the 'great moderation' that began in the mid-1980s meant that such fluctuations as took place were not very severe.
>
> (Summers, 2013)

Although experiences during the 1990s led the economics profession to frown on deficits, this ideational setting laid the basis for increased spending and borrowing. In the UK, the centre-Right think tank, Policy Exchange, which was deeply critical of the Blair and Brown governments' spending record, talked of a 'surge' during the first half of the first decade of the new century (Lilico *et al.*, 2009: 1). This led to a 'structural' budget deficit that would, by definition, remain even in periods of economic buoyancy. A report prepared by the Institute for Fiscal Studies later noted that:

> between 1997 and 2007 – prior to the financial crisis – the UK had the 2nd largest increase in spending as a share of national income out of 28 industrial countries for which we have comparable data. Over the period from 1997 to 2010 – including the crisis – the UK had the largest increase. This moved the UK from having the 22nd largest proportion of national income spent publically in 1997 to having the 6th largest proportion spent publically in 2010.
>
> (Chote *et al.*, 2010: 1)

Gradual reform revisited

There is a further reason for the 'return of the state' and rising levels of expenditure as a share of GDP. It rests upon some of the structural weaknesses that characterize gradual change mechanisms. Arguably, in many settings, the impact of gradualism is more limited than it initially appears. This claim requires elaboration.

As noted above, recent studies of change have, in contrast with stricter forms of path-dependency theory, allowed very considerable scope for gradual change processes taking place between moments of profound crisis. Whereas the institutional landscape can prevent radical, abrupt and 'frontal' path-departing reform, it can allow, and perhaps even facilitate, the use by actors of incremental change mechanisms. In other words 'political settings that militate against authoritative change encourage reformers to seek the conversion or erosion of existing policies' (Hacker, 2004: 247). Such incremental or gradual changes can, over the long run and cumulatively, be transformative and path-departing in character.

Approached in this way, the changes wrought by Thatcherism and Reaganomics were much more substantial than they appear when formal institutional structures alone are considered. If the degree of change is considered in terms of social risk that individuals face rather than the structural characteristics of social provision, many are now much more vulnerable to the uncertainties of market forces. From this perspective, there has been a protracted process of 'risk privatization':

> Although most U.S. public social programs have indeed resisted radical retrenchment, the American social welfare framework has also, in crucial areas, offered increasingly incomplete protection against the key social risks that Americans confront.
>
> (Hacker, 2004: 243)

There is much here that it would be difficult to refute or even question. It constitutes a very effective riposte to those who focus on formal structures alone. Nonetheless, if there is to be a realistic appraisal of gradualism and the capacity of gradual change mechanisms to bring about transformative change, accounts also have to consider the limits to that capacity.

In particular, the relative institutional thickness and thinness of the policy structures created by gradual change mechanisms should be brought into the picture. Whereas some policy structures are relatively thin and pliable, others are thicker and therefore have much greater resilience. If structures are relatively thick, they are likely to be enduring and in the longer run cumulatively transformative. If, on the other hand, such structures are thin, those opposed, or broadly resistant, to the reforms that established them may well find opportunities to roll them back so as to restore the status quo ante at a later date.

The extent to which reforms stick and become embedded depends in part upon the character of processes during the enactment phase and the extent to which constituencies of 'winners' emerge and the state apparatus has the capacity to implement and support the measure (Patashnik and Zelizer, 2013). However, other considerations are also involved. In many cases, the institutional structures created by those who pursue gradual change are likely to be relatively thin. This is because gradual change agents (those who pursue such changes) are more often than not taking action from a position of perceived political weakness. Gradualist approaches are pursued in place of more comprehensive or far-reaching forms of change, because the actors promoting them do not feel that they have the capacity to go further and secure more expansive or far-reaching goals or move more swiftly. They are deliberately avoiding a frontal assault:

> actors who wish to change popular and embedded institutions in political environments that militate against authoritative reform may find it prudent not to attack such institutions directly. Instead, they may seek to shift those institutions' ground-level operation, prevent their adaptation to shifting external circumstances, or build new institutions on top of them.
>
> (Hacker, 2004: 244)

Even when reformers initially set relatively ambitious goals for themselves, these may be scaled back as policy proposals pass through the gatekeeping processes to which legislation and other forms of rule-making are invariably subjected. In the US, legislation not only must be negotiated between the executive and legislative branches but also must take into account the constitutional limits imposed upon the measures that the federal government can adopt. In the UK, despite the more centralized and 'sealed' character of its political system, concessions may well be made to particular interests. When the 2012 Health and Social Care Act was under consideration in parliament, *The Economist* noted that 'The health bill survives, but as a messy patchwork of compromises with various interest groups' (*The Economist*, 2012).

Reformers may also be persuaded that they should, in the interests of winning legitimacy through cross-partisan or cross-factional backing, seek more than a simple majority. Indeed, those who perceive themselves to be politically weak or vulnerable often go beyond the numbers required to surmount formal and informal veto points and instead attempt to construct much more than a 'minimum winning coalition' (Pierson, 2001: 418). The formation of such a coalition may have significant consequences for the overall character of the reform. By accommodating the preferences of those whose support for reform is limited and conditional, or at most lukewarm, it will incorporate both path-maintaining as well as path-departing elements.

'Gradualism' has rarely been subject to precise definition. Self-evidently, there is no hard and fast dividing line between gradualism and more ruptural forms of change; they exist on a continuum. Gradualism has, however, been referred to as incrementalism, 'transformation without disruption' or a partial shift in the logics upon which a path rests (Streeck and Thelen, 2005: 4). Nonetheless, if the existing literature is treated as a composite, gradual reforms appear to share some or all of six defining characteristics, although they may also define some forms of more radical and seemingly ruptural forms of change. First, a gradual reform will be limited in terms of its *scope* (in other words, how many actors – sectors, groups or individuals – it affects). Second, it will be limited in terms of its *scale* (that is, the extent of what a reform does or changes). Third, the 'selling' and framing of the measure may be cautious. Indeed, because policymakers are unsure of their position in terms of public opinion, constituencies and interests, the nature of the reform may be consciously 'undersold'. Although developments are not, of course, entirely within the gift of policymakers, the measure may have only a relatively low level of public visibility. Fourth, again because of caution on the part of reformers, or because they perceive a need to construct a broad coalitional bloc so as to secure passage of the reform, they may avoid precision in the drafting of new institutional rules. Indeed, they seek ambiguous agreements so as 'to aggregate different visions and interests' (Palier, 2005: 131). At the least, there may be a reluctance to resolve ambiguities or a hope that such ambiguities may be resolved at a later stage by other administrative agencies or the courts. Fifth, reformers may well fail to include mechanisms in policy changes that might protect them against later amendment or abandonment. There will be little or no 'deck-stacking' whereby there are structures and procedures within institutional designs that would militate against any later attempt to modify the reform and 'establish a structural context that endures long after the enacting coalition has frayed' (Patashnik and Zelizer, 2013: 1074). Such a structural context might incorporate the introduction of new procedural rules or the relocation of political authority so as to make challenges to reforms more difficult or less sustainable (Patashnik, 2008: 26–27). Last, because policymakers see constraints on their ability to act, they will enact only limited or weak enforcement processes. So as to avert or avoid political criticism, or shift the locus of responsibility, such enforcement processes may be weighted towards *ex post* forms. In sum, and in contrast with more path-departing and comprehensive reforms, gradual or limited change is rarely accompanied by what, in arguing for the US Constitution, Alexander Hamilton once termed 'energy in the executive'.

These defining features of gradualism have significant consequences insofar as they shape the perceptions of actors affected by a reform and their understandings of self-interest once it has been enacted. The partial and limited character of gradual reform, its limited visibility, its often loosely defined boundaries, its ambiguities and the weakness of enforcement mechanisms, create openings and lacunae. Put another way, gradual reforms tend to be not only thin but institutionally *porous*. That porosity allows those who define themselves as 'losers' from a reform or those who do not believe that they have an interest in its continuing existence to mobilize, assert themselves, and through this begin a process of reining in the reform or redefining its effects.

Parallel to all of this, the ambiguities and uncertain or ill-defined boundaries of a gradual reform, which may well be more pronounced than those found in more radical or far-reaching measures, permit considerable amounts of institutional 'play' in terms of how the reform is understood and applied in practice. Such 'play' can in some circumstances be the prelude to path-departing shifts (Mahoney and Thelen, 2010: 11–12). However, institutional 'play' can also allow those opposed to a partial reform to rally and mobilize, thereby paving the way for a reversion, or at least a partial reversion, to an original institutional path. Thus, openings and lacunae that characterize gradualism can serve, to appropriate a celebrated phrase from another context, as 'an invitation to struggle'.

That 'struggle' often begins slowly. Amidst initial uncertainty following enactment and implementation, the openings that gradualism can present may not be immediately visible but if they gain visibility it is likely that there will be threshold effects. Actors do not begin to follow the rules until they see that significant numbers of others are abiding by them. Even then, actors cannot assume other actors will respect the rules. There may therefore be a continuing sense of flux.

Two further points should, however, be added. First, categories such as 'losers' and 'winners' are not, of course, set in stone. Although some institutional changes can create more or less unambiguous outcomes, understandings of 'winning' and 'losing' are constructions and may therefore be open to intense contestation. Within this context policy entrepreneurs play a major role in shaping the outcomes of contestation processes and establishing intersubjective understandings.

Second, when individuals or groupings define themselves as 'losers', or probable losers, rather than 'winners' or probable winners, this may well lead to an increase in the intensity of their attitudes and feelings. Kurt Weyland has drawn upon behavioural economics to suggest that individuals and groups react differently to the prospects of a gain and the fear of a loss. When it comes to the prospect of gains, individuals are generally risk-averse. The picture is very different if losses are threatened and if a measure seems, perhaps by virtue of its limited character, open to reversal. The fear of perceived losses can easily trigger significant defiance and resistance as individuals and groups seek out forms of counter-mobilization:

> people who face the prospect of loss tend to take bold, drastic, and risky counter-measures ... people refuse to accept a sure loss of limited magnitude and instead prefer a gamble that holds the uncertain promise of avoiding any loss but also carries the risk of a really large loss.
>
> (Weyland, 2008: 286)

In short, gradual reforms offer openings and gaps that in turn create opportunities and incentives to those who hope to circumscribe the reform or secure their de facto rewriting or the drafting of new institutional rules as well as those who might seek to extend that reform. Within such a context, those who define themselves as 'losers' are likely to be less risk-averse.

Reining in reform

Thus, although some forms of social provision have been vulnerable to what might be termed 'subterranean retrenchment' through the shifting of provision for risk from the state to households ('risk privatization'), some other reforms pursued in both the UK and the US had a thinner character and were thereby reined in or rolled back. This can be illustrated by three examples drawn from the UK.

First, youth training provision can be considered. In the UK, in 1983, the Thatcher government introduced the Youth Training Scheme (YTS) for 16–18-year-olds who were not in a job or education. It included training in 'life skills' to prepare young people for the 'world of work'. Such skills included politeness, 'resisting provocation' and the 'acceptance of authority' (quoted in Gleeson, 1986: 391). It was a marked shift away from the compromise formulae of the post-war years and the traditional role of the humanities within British education. In short, skill training was to displace education. The reform had a firmly neoliberal stamp on it. As Denis Gleeson noted shortly afterwards:

> in a short space of time life skills training has become detached from the wider objectives associated with liberal humanistic education ... teaching young people *about* society has been replaced by a criteria designed to alter their *relationship* with it.
>
> (Gleeson, 1986: 382)

YTS required a very large number of programme providers. Although programme provision was put out to competitive tender, further education (FE) colleges had to be brought in alongside private providers. Staff within further education who had traditionally taught 'General Studies', which had long been a staple part of the FE curriculum and which had in contrast to YTS drawn upon the traditions of the liberal humanities, found themselves teaching 'life skills'. There was some overt but small-scale resistance by both teaching staff and YTS trainees (Gleeson, 1986: 387). However, perhaps more significantly, teaching staff in the FE sector, many of whom still had significant classroom autonomy, drew 'life skills' back towards the General Studies curriculum. They introduced a much broader range of themes and sought to encourage critical reflection by programme participants. Put starkly, training in 'life skills' was to some degree subverted and reincorporated within an older path.

Second, efforts to reform local government taxation provide a further illustration. Although the system of household rates (a graduated property tax) that preceded the poll tax was far from progressive as a form of taxation (although there was an extensive system of rebates), the introduction of the Community Charge (as the 'poll tax' was more formally known) by the Thatcher government in 1989–90 (Scotland) and 1990–91 (England and Wales) also marked a shift towards neo-liberal and market-based approaches. It levied a flat-rate charge (or 'price', thereby making the local government tax regime broadly comparable with the buying of goods and services from a supplier) so as to allow the 'buying' of local authority services and there to be a direct relationship between the tax paid by an individual and the benefit gained. The case for the poll tax went beyond principle. The visibility of the tax would compel local councils to abandon costly social projects and encourage them to contract out service provision to the private sector so as to reduce expenditure levels.

Nonetheless, although the introduction of the poll tax was in many ways a profoundly radical move, the government proceeded with caution. Its introduction was staggered. The tax was first levied in Scotland (1989) and then introduced in England and Wales a year later. Students, pensioners and the unemployed received substantial (80 per cent) rebates. More importantly, the introduction of the poll tax was to some degree a substitute for the large-scale reduction in marginal income tax rates sought by many on the conservative Right who looked, with envy, at the supply-side policies pursued by the Reagan administration during its first year in office.

In the event, the poll tax was rolled back. Its visibility and overtly regressive character (as many observed, under the Community Charge 'a duke pays the same as a dustman') gave anti-poll-tax protests legitimacy. More importantly, the structures within which the tax was embedded had a relatively porous character. The tax was open to evasion and circumvention. Large numbers of people simply ensured that they 'disappeared' so as to escape liability. Some refused to register or pay. In many cases, local councils and perhaps the police do not appear to have had the capacity to pursue evaders and defaulters.

All of this contributed to Margaret Thatcher's political downfall in November 1990. Following her departure from the premiership, tax levels were reduced (by increasing value added tax) and then replaced by the council tax that, like the rates, was levied on the basis of property values. The council tax included some elements introduced by the poll tax. Like the poll tax, it was structured around the idea that the tax was in essence a service charge for the use of local government services. It was also, because of the form that the banding of properties took, regressive. Nonetheless, it also marked a significant step back towards the rates insofar as it was less regressive than the poll tax and represented a tax on property rather than the individual. For many, it looked substantially like the rating system.

Third, attempts to reform health provision also show the limits of gradualism. The passage and implementation of the 1990 National Health Service and Community Care Act was accompanied by claim and counter-claim. The Act created an internal market whereby local doctors (GPs) with larger practices acted as consumers, and as 'fundholders' purchased treatment from hospitals and other providers on behalf of their patients. Simulated market forces and processes of competition would, it was said, provide a measure of choice and encourage cost-effectiveness: 'Fundhol ding greatly increases the bargaining power of GPs, who can take their contracts elsewhere should hospitals, medical consultants, or other agencies show a lack of responsiveness' (Mechanic, 1995: 56). In contrast the Act's opponents charged that the internal market would lead to the neglect of the more 'uneconomic' patients, particularly those who had little hope of recovery. Yet, despite the promise of radical reform, the Act's impact was relatively muted: 'Despite being widely heralded as the most radical change in the NHS since its inception ... the NHS internal market did not produce the degree of measurable change predicted by proponents and feared by opponents' (Mays *et al.*, 2011: 3). Why was this? Again, the Act was characterized by institutional 'holes' insofar as it created opportunities for the status quo ante to reassert itself. First, markets incorporate and rest upon the possibility of failure and indeed bankruptcy. Yet, that could not be allowed in the internal market because the consequences or political costs could not be accepted. Thus 'the incentives were too weak and the constraints were too strong' (Le Grand *et al.*, 1998: 130). The Trusts by the Act (in other words, health providers) knew 'that they could not keep any surpluses if they succeeded and that they would be bailed out if they failed' (Le Grand *et al.*, 1998: 131). Second, although consumers and providers always have imperfect information, it was particularly limited. Consumers (or 'fundholders') had difficulties deciding upon the relative merits of one provider over another. Third, health ranked as such a pivotal national political issue, particularly as general elections began to approach, that central government continued to issue directives and set goals such as the reduction of waiting times. These cut across and ameliorated the quasi-market processes around which the Act had been framed.

Similarly, if the US is considered, reforms are also subject in some cases to roll-back. The marginal tax cuts enacted in 1981 (ERTA) were to some degree reined in by later tax rises.[7] The Tax Equity and Fiscal Responsibility Act of 1982 closed loopholes and cancelled further projected tax reductions. The Tax Reform Act of 1986 broadened the tax base and the lowest tax rate was raised. However, by the time George H.W. Bush took over the presidency in January 1989, the national debt was $2.8 trillion, three times larger than it had been in 1980. And, in an action that was repeatedly used against him, Bush, who had pledged 'Read my lips: no new taxes' during the 1988 election campaign, agreed to increases in individual income tax rates as part of the Omnibus Budget Reconciliation Act of 1990. On top of this, he agreed to a bailout of the Savings and Loan industry that eventually cost more than $100 billion.

Even the 1996 Personal Responsibility and Work Opportunity Act – in many respects a major path-departing reform insofar as it ended Aid to Families with Dependent Children, dramatically limited federally funded welfare and incorporated workfare requirements so that recipients had to undertake a work placement – has, some suggest, been subject to a process of partial roll-back. Thus, a 2013 report compiled for the Cato Institute suggested that despite the 'workfare' requirements in the 1996 Act less than 42 per cent of recipients were undertaking work. Instead, the majority was in different forms of employment training or job search activities (Tanner and Hughes, 2013: 2).[8]

Conclusion

Increasingly, in recent years, there has been a focus on the 'subterranean' forms of change wrought during the years of the Thatcher government and Reagan administration and in the period that followed. Indeed, these 'subterranean' changes are now regarded as more important than the formal shifts in the policy regime through, for example, privatization or trade union reform. Nonetheless, the degree of change that gradualism brought forth should not be overstated. First, efforts to reduce the size of government were limited and government spending (as a share of GDP) quickly increased again, particularly in periods of recession and during the years after 2000–1. Second, gradual change processes, of the type that was often pursued by neoliberal reformers, were, in some instances, vulnerable to processes of containment and roll-back. Established paths thus had very considerable resilience. The next chapter considers the ways in which the British and American Right responded to the dilemmas that all of this posed.

Notes

1 Some commentaries qualified claims that there had been centralization to this degree or that Thatcherism had brought forth a 'strong state' alongside the free market (Gamble, 1988). They suggested that there had indeed been a fundamental change in the overall character of the British state but that it was being 'hollowed out' through processes such as local government reform, the proliferation of agencies, privatization, the transfer of government functions to the European Union and the increasingly limited 'discretion of public servants through the new public management, with its emphasis on managerial accountability, and clearer political control through a sharper distinction between politics

and administration' (Rhodes, 1994: 139). Although relatively cautious about his conclusions, and accepting that there might be countervailing trends, Rhodes suggested that all of this had led to 'the diminished central capability of British government' (Rhodes, 1994: 139).

2 See pp. 50–51 for a discussion of the poll tax.

3 See, for example, the studies of conservatism and school education policy, environmental regulation and Social Security from the 1930s onwards in *Conservatism and American Political Development* (Glenn and Teles, 2009).

4 'Transfer payments' are not straightforward. Often the term is used so as to include contributory and non-contributory benefits. For many on the Right, contributory schemes could be administered more effectively by private-sector organizations and non-contributory schemes constitute 'welfare'.

5 Furthermore, the numbers directly or indirectly employed by the British state had risen to 6.8 million by 2006, 784,000 more than in 1997 when Labour took office (Norman and Ganesh, 2006: 9).

6 Alongside institutional considerations, Bush also faced framing and mobilization difficulties in putting forward his reform proposals. In both the UK and the US, the Right is often associated with 'harshness' and there are therefore political problems addressing pension reform. Furthermore, there was no widely accepted requirement for reform, and projections at that point suggested that Social Security would remain solvent until 2052 (Herbert, 2011: 161).

7 Reagan's critics asserted that taxes were increased eleven times during his two terms of office, although the concept of a 'tax rise' is always subject to contestation. Should, for example, the withdrawal of a particular tax concession be regarded as such?

8 There is often a tension between placing individuals in short-term placements that take up much of a working week and the need for those individuals to seek, and apply for, permanent or longer-term jobs.

3

Embedded neoliberalism

This chapter considers the character of the Right in both the US and the UK and, in particular, its approaches and attitudes towards the contemporary state and the ways in which it responded to the resilience of 'big government'.

The Right, particularly in its Anglo-American form, has, as a defining principle, a commitment to the shrinkage of the state, at least in its role as a social provider, as a mediator between capital and labour and as an ameliorator of perceived market failure.

This commitment has informed and structured successive Conservative election manifestos, campaign statements and Republican platforms, even during the long mid-century period that has latterly been described in terms of 'consensus politics'. Indeed, at certain points, the need to restrain the growth of the state has been framed in dramatic terms. The growth of the state, it was said, placed the market and its virtues, the integrity of civil society and the liberty of the individual in mortal danger. In her foreword to the 1979 Conservative Party election manifesto, Margaret Thatcher wrote:

> No one who has lived in this country during the last five years can fail to be aware of how the balance of our society has been increasingly tilted in favour of the State at the expense of individual freedom. This election may be the last chance we have to reverse that process, to restore the balance of power in favour of the people. It is therefore the most crucial election since the war.
>
> (Conservative Party, 1979)

A year-and-a-half later, the 1980 Republican platform issued a few months before Ronald Reagan secured the US presidency also reaffirmed the case against a bloated post-war state:

> Republicans ... have always taken the side of the individual, whose freedoms are threatened by the big government that Democratic idea has spawned. Our case for the individual is stronger than ever. A defense of the individual against government was never more needed. And we will continue to mount it.
>
> (Republican National Convention, 1980)

Such has been the hold of anti-state sentiments and discourses in recent decades that they have been increasingly embraced and asserted by the social democratic Left and, in the US, many Democrats as well as the Right. At the beginning of 1996, in the State of the Union Address and amidst the budget battles with Congressional Republicans, Bill Clinton proclaimed in a much-cited sentence that 'the era of big government is over'. Across the Atlantic there was both symbolism and realism (as well as resentment by her successor as prime minister) when a year later, shortly before the 1997 general election, Margaret Thatcher reportedly said that Britain had 'nothing to fear' from a Labour government coming to office under Tony Blair's leadership (quoted in Kampfner, 2008).

Nonetheless, although discourses across the Right and much of the Left have come to follow the logic of the 'big government' argument and rest upon commitments to shrink the state, particularly in its role as a social provider, all this has often remained at the level of campaign rhetoric. For the most part there has been a pronounced gap or disconnect between the many denunciations of the state and processes of policy enactment.

Furthermore, as noted in Chapter 2, the policies that had been enacted were vulnerable to roll-back. Indeed, while the Right seemed in both countries to have won sporadic battles, the war was not going well. The post-war state had a resilience that few had anticipated. In particular, overall government expenditure remained obstinately high (as a share of GDP) and threatened to grow again in periods of downturn or at the behest of vote-seeking officials.

Grover Norquist, President of Americans for Tax Reform and a pivotal conservative organizer and coordinator in Washington DC, said in a celebrated comment: 'I'm not in favor of abolishing the government. I just want to shrink it down to the size where we can drown it in the bathtub' (quoted in Peters, 2012). Yet, despite Thatcher, Reagan and Gingrich, that goal remained a very distant prospect.

Strategies and tactics in the US

Against this background, different schools of thought, approaches and strategies emerged within the Right. There were of course significant differences between the two countries, but there were also similarities and overlaps.

Some within the US threw themselves behind calls to 'starve the beast' (the 'beast' being the federal government). The argument had three stages. First, the Right should pursue tax reductions. The relative popularity of such measures would, it was said, ensure that they had an easy passage in Congress and the state legislatures. Second, although some subscribed to the thinking underpinning the Laffer curve and believed that lower marginal tax rates would spur greater economic activity by increasing the incentives offered to both entrepreneurs and employees, there was a recognition that budget deficits would in all probability increase as a consequence of lower tax revenues. Third, in such circumstances public opinion could be mobilized around the need for deficit reduction and there would, it was said, be popular backing for drastic expenditure cuts that would in turn substantially reduce the scope and reach of the state. In July 1978, Alan Greenspan, who had been Chairman of the Council of Economic Advisers under President Gerald Ford, put forward an early version of 'starve the beast' in testimony before the Senate Finance Committee:

> Let us remember that the basic purpose of any tax cut program in today's environment is to reduce the momentum of expenditure growth by restraining the amount of revenue available and trust that there is a political limit to deficit spending.
>
> (quoted in Bartlett, 2010)

There were, nonetheless, challenges, even within the Right, to the logic of 'starve the beast'. It was argued, for example, that there was relatively little empirical evidence to support the claim that tax reductions did indeed eventually lead to public expenditure reductions. Indeed, there were contrary assertions that tax cuts could well be followed by expenditure increases.

There was a second strategy in circulation, although it never gained significant or at least lasting political traction. It was closely associated with Congressman Jack Kemp, who sponsored the 1981 marginal tax cuts and was eventually to serve as the Republicans' vice-presidential running mate in 1996 alongside Senator Bob Dole. Kemp's political 'brand' was structured around the idea of popular capitalism and ways of broadening conservatism beyond its core base among whites and those in the higher-income groupings. He championed supply-side economics, calling, for example, for the elimination of the tax traps that block mobility from welfare to work and the use of subsidies to make work more attractive. Kemp tied much of this to plans for immigration reform and providing illegal migrants with some form of documented status. This issue increasingly formed a fault line among Republicans, many of whom were vehemently opposed to what they regarded as an 'amnesty' for those who were undocumented, and this alone severely limited Kemp's political prospects.

A third strategy, or at a least sense of direction, began to take shape during the 1980s. It was structured around a feeling that much more should be done to hold Republican officeholders to account and limit their scope to make further bipartisan compromises. From 1986 onwards, Grover Norquist and his organization, Americans for Tax Reform, sought to bind election candidates to sign the Taxpayer Protection Pledge. It was not restricted to formal tax rises but also sought to ensure that all the tax credits and deductions that clustered the US tax code remained in place:

> I, _______, pledge to the taxpayers of the _______ district of the state of _______ and to the American people that I will: One, oppose any and all efforts to increase the marginal income tax rates for individuals and/or businesses; and Two, to oppose any net

> reduction or elimination of deductions and credits, unless matched dollar for dollar by further reducing tax rates.
>
> (quoted in Good, 2012)

The pace of efforts to impose checks and restraints upon lawmakers accelerated during the early 1990s. It was driven in part by the belief that conservatism had lost its way after President Reagan had left office and his successor, President George H.W. Bush, had only tepid enthusiasm for conservative principles.

The argument could, and at times did, utilize conservative scholarship as well as simple condemnations of those who were seemingly weak-willed. Public Choice theory pointed at the ways in which elected officials and civil servants sought bureaucratic aggrandizement and the expansion of their own spheres of influence. From this perspective, constitutional or statutory constraints such as term limits or a requirement for the passage of a balanced budget were necessary so as to hold back individual and group ambition.

The drive to curtail lawmakers was at the same time tied to conservative populism insofar as it rested upon an identification with 'citizens' in their struggles against self-interested elites, particularly the 'political class'. However, the argument often went beyond simple hostility to insider 'Beltway' officeholders and bureaucrats and was associated with producerism. In other words, it held up and celebrated the integrity of the productive citizen as opposed to the non-producers who were at the lowest and highest ends of the socioeconomic scale. It condemned the 'underclass' and the illegal migrant while at the same time resenting the educated elites, the politicians and, in some versions, those that drew their income from finance capital or the multinational companies. Although many would say that it was muted, there was therefore opposition within the producerist Right to offshoring as well as many of those who came to American shores.

The drive to limit the freedom of action afforded to elected Republican officials was also brought forth and accelerated by growing partisanship as the parties, which had for a relatively long period in the mid-century years been broad coalitional blocs, increasingly took on fairly sharply defined ideological identities. The defection of the white South, a region that had long been a Democratic fiefdom, to the Republicans and the demise of liberal Republicanism left a Democratic Party that stretched from centrist, 'Third Way' moderation to progressivism and a Republican Party that was resolutely conservative and increasingly brooked no dissenters from conservative orthodoxy. There was bitter, sometimes savage, condemnation of RINOs (Republicans in Name Only) and efforts to purge them as elected representatives. While there were tensions between those who defined themselves as libertarians, social conservatives and 'neocons' (and for a long period groupings such as the Log Cabin Republicans representing gay activists within the party faced major challenges), there were also substantial points of agreement, particularly around economic issues.

The rise of social or religious conservatism should also be brought into the picture. While networks such as the Moral Majority had initially looked for little in the political realm beyond the election of officials who had integrity and faith, growing resentment at increasing secularism and the failure to secure a political transformation of the federal courts, so that earlier rulings such as *Roe v Wade* (1973), which had established abortion as a constitutional right, might be overturned, led religious conservatives to adopt more developed forms of lobbying and campaigning. This had an impact on legislation but also ensured that 'litmus tests' were applied to Republican nominees seeking local, state or federal office on social as well as economic and constitutional questions. Few 'pro choice' candidates secured the party's nominations.

The Contract with America emerged within this context. In the mid-term elections of November 1994, the Republicans secured majorities in both chambers of Congress. Newt Gingrich (until then House Minority Whip) and Dick Armey (Chairman of the House Republican Conference who, after the Republican takeover, became House Majority Leader) co-authored the *Contract*, a commitment to bring eight procedural reforms and ten bills to a vote, which was signed by nearly all the Republican House of Representatives' candidates.

The *Contract* was not a manifesto insofar as it was not a promise to enact legislation. Such promises are tied to the doctrine of the mandate and parliamentarianism and have little or no place in the US political process. Nonetheless, the *Contract* was an effort to rein in Republican Congressmen behind conservative legislation. The measures put forward included the Fiscal Responsibility Act (requiring a balanced budget), the Personal Responsibility Act (reforming welfare provision) and the Citizen Legislature Act, which would have imposed term limits amounting to twelve years on members of both the House and the Senate.

Nonetheless, although some were to see the *Contract* as a significant departure that marked a radical shift in the character of both conservatism and Congressional politics, the 'Gingrich revolution' lost much of its initial impetus within just a few years. Although Congressional Republicans took credit for the passage of welfare reform in 1996 and for measures that contributed to the balancing of the federal government budget later in the year, the élan of the *Contract* gave way to government shutdowns and President Clinton's re-election in November 1996. During his second term, and amidst the long and protracted episode that culminated in the president's impeachment by the House of Representatives, the Republicans suffered electoral reversals in the 1998 mid-term contests, and, in their wake, Gingrich resigned the House Speakership.

Nonetheless, efforts to place restraints upon lawmakers continued, if only because the institutional character of the US political process facilitated and encouraged such a process. The open character of the party nominating process through primaries and caucuses, the relative frequency of elections, the openness of the system to political advertising and advocacy networks, the opportunities given to those with substantial funds and the ability of groups to engage in multi-level lobbying all allow, and indeed invite, campaigns to dislodge incumbents and bring in 'outsider' challengers, as well as efforts to ensure that a lawmaker votes in a way that campaign seeks. These institutional structures also played a major part in bringing forth the Tea Party movement from early 2009 onwards.

A fourth strategy became fully visible by the end of the 1990s. It was structured around calls for 'compassionate conservatism' (a term that was closely associated with George W. Bush's campaign for the Republican nomination in 2000), the provision of assistance to the disadvantaged through voluntary and community effort and the transfer of responsibility for delivery of services from government to the 'third sector'. For much of the Right, it seemed that if the voluntary sector or informal networks could pick up the slack or if it could be opened up to the market there would be ways of progressively reducing the scope and scale of government provision.

Compassionate conservatism had earlier antecedents. Indeed, the 'basic building blocks of compassionate conservatism floated around in conservative circles for over two decades – in the form of "mediating structures" and "empowerment" – before they were rebranded' (Teles, 2011: 179). President George H.W. Bush, who was seeking to place some distance between himself and Ronald Reagan's time in office, had spoken in both his 1988 election campaign and his inaugural address of 'a thousand points of light, of all the community organizations that are spread like stars throughout the Nation, doing good' (CNN, 2009). A White House Conference on Philanthropy was held in October 1999, leading to the creation of an Interagency Task Force on Nonprofits and Government. The Clinton administration built upon this by establishing the AmeriCorps National Service Program in 1993. The 1996 Personal Responsibility and Work Opportunity Reconciliation Act that radically restricted welfare provision incorporated a 'Charitable Choice' provision encouraging states to include religious as well as secular organizations when awarding contracts for anti-poverty efforts.

In part, 'compassionate conservatism' served short-run political purposes. The concept allowed those who used it to distance themselves from assertions that the Right and the policies it pursued were dictated by corporate interests or economic concerns alone. It permitted a move beyond possessive individualism and the marketplace and challenged the claim that concern for those who were disadvantaged was solely the prerogative of the Left. Thus, in seeking the 2000 Republican presidential nomination, George W. Bush had solid reasons to embrace the concept of 'compassionate conservatism'. It enabled him to distinguish himself from Congressional Republicans who by the end of the 1990s had been successfully framed, through the Clinton administration's 'triangulation' strategy, as indifferent to poverty, deprivation and those left behind in the economic race. In particular, 'compassion' provided an opportunity to win over the remaining slithers of genuine independents, make gains among the sizeable number of Roman Catholics in the US electorate and address the gender gap that had defined presidential elections from

1980 onwards.[1] Whereas women (particularly single women) leaned towards the Democrats, men were in the Republican camp. Considered as an electoral strategy, compassionate conservatism offered the opportunity to win votes among women without endangering support among men (Teles, 2011: 189).

'Compassionate conservatism' took shape and acquired substance as the faith-based initiative. It became a commitment to ensure that voluntary, charitable and religious organizations could compete on broadly equal terms with others in tendering to provide social services on behalf of the federal government (providing that government funds were not used for the purposes of proselytizing). These services included provision for substance abusers, advising and assisting at-risk young people, counselling prisoners nearing the end of their sentences and mentoring the children of prisoners. State governments were encouraged to adopt similar policies. So as to ensure this, offices were established within the White House and the different government departments in order to assist groups with the tendering process. Start-up funds for groups were also to be offered. In short:

> Under President Bush's plan, as long as they agree not to use prayer or worship in the programs, faith-based welfare organizations would be free to compete for federal contracts and vouchers from the departments of Justice, Labor, Education, and Health and Human Services to pay for social programs, including child welfare and after-school care, crime prevention, job training, and hunger relief.
>
> (Weiss, 2001: 35)

This partly meant that the regulatory structures governing the award of government contracts would have to be simplified. According to Marvin Olasky, one of the theoretical architects of compassionate conservatism, this meant 'calling off the regulatory dogs'. It also required the deliberate encouragement of voluntary provision and (although this never came to fruition) the giving of government assistance to those who were disadvantaged through tax credits or vouchers so that the recipients or 'consumers' of services could choose between providers. Although it was to be the basis of the faith-based initiative, direct financial aid by government was, according to Olasky, the least desirable policy option (Ashbee, 2003: 41).

Advocates of the faith-based initiative pointed to what they saw as its virtues. Provision through voluntary and faith-based groups would, it was argued, impose less of a financial burden upon the taxpayer. Furthermore, such groups would have a more personal and meaningful relationship with those they were seeking to assist. As Olasky put it, they would not only give material aid but also be able to help transform lives and enable individuals to move towards self-sufficiency. They would have a much greater understanding of need and those who were in distress than an impersonal and bureaucratic government agency. From this perspective, poverty had a spiritual as well as a material dimension. Individuals in need required material assistance but their attitudes, faith in change problem and commitment to personal transformation also had to change. That was much more likely to happen through the efforts of people of faith rather than through administrators and case-workers employed by the government machine. And, furthermore, the faith-based initiative could pave the way for further decentralization, the disengagement of government and the bolstering of civil networks.

Nonetheless, following Bush's eventual election victory the initiative failed to develop and grow in the ways that its most ardent proponents had hoped. Why was this? First, despite the campaigning zeal for compassionate conservatism, the initiative was never a priority of the Bush White House. And its most visible proponent and practitioner, Professor John DiIulio, left the White House as early as 2001.

The late David Kuo, who served as Deputy Director of the Office of Faith-Based and Community Initiatives, charted the course of events. Funds were minimal. There were announcements about social initiatives, such as a later announcement in the 2005 State of the Union Address that there would be a teenage violence prevention programme. But, Kuo recorded, the funds for the programme were simply transferred from elsewhere:

> There was no expansion of anything. There was only the marketing of a new program that sucked money from another grossly unfunded program ... George W. Bush's White House ... was deceiving the public, and in doing so it was mocking the trust of the American people. More disappointing, it was mocking the millions of faithful Christians who had put their trust and hope in the president and his administration.
>
> (Kuo, 2006: 3971)

Second, there were structural ambiguities within the concept itself. Different representations framed compassionate conservatism and the faith-based initiative as a way of supplanting government provision, adding to it or simply using voluntary effort to deliver government provision. There was, furthermore, a lack of certainty about the role of deterrence in social provision. Republicans and the conservative movement rallied around the 1996 Personal Responsibility and Work Opportunity Act that dramatically cut support for claimants and imposed work requirements, thereby compelling many to take entry-level employment. It had seemed, at the stroke of a president's pen, to reduce the reach of the state substantially. Whereas some believed that the voluntary sector would be more likely to operate on the basis of 'tough love' and selectivity and pull back from the blanket largesse offered by government agencies, this was never brought into the open.

Third, core constituencies within the Republican orbit, in particular the Christian Right, were unenthusiastic about the faith-based initiative. There were fears that if religious groupings took federal government funds they would become beholden to government. Other Republican currents, particularly those who were 'economic conservatives' (and stressed the primacy of free market issues) and neoconservatives, who emphasized what they saw as the US's democratic mission in the world, also attached relatively little political weight to the initiative. And, inevitably, the September 11th attacks shifted the agenda towards the neocons.

Furthermore, beyond the Republican Party there were many who saw the initiative as a cover for drastic expenditure reductions and cuts in service provision. It would:

> ultimately replace the remnants of the postwar government safety net with a system of charity appeals, transforming a political right and governmental obligation into an appeal to altruism, dispensed at the discretion of sectarian (and conservative) interests. The shift from the welfare state to neoliberalism converts citizenship into an economic status by transforming entitlements into commodities.
>
> (Weiss, 2001: 36)

Fourth, 'compassionate conservatism' and the faith-based initiative seemed to promise Republican strategists very few votes. The calculus suggested little electoral payback. Although there had been talk of reaching out to independents, the Roman Catholic vote and women in the 2000 presidential election, this gave way to electoral strategies structured more around the mobilization of existing voting bases. The process was fuelled by increasingly intense partisan and ideational polarization. Thus, in 2004, the Bush re-election campaign focused on national security and appeals to traditional morality in an effort to draw increased numbers of core Republican voters to the polls. The 2008 and 2012 elections were also to be highly charged and polarized processes.

Although the faith-based initiative continued in existence for the remainder of the Bush presidency and during the Obama years (becoming the Office of Faith-based and Neighborhood Partnerships), the initiative was in the end little more than a footnote in studies of contemporary history. Presidential candidates, particularly Republicans, made just a brief reference to it. In his 2008 presidential campaign, Senator John McCain, perhaps seeking to bolster his relationships with religious groupings, pledged to maintain the initiative. He would, it was said, extend the range of programmes and increase the choices open to beneficiaries, while at the same time harnessing individual volunteering and private philanthropy (and 'corporate citizenship' so that firms contributed more) to a much greater extent. Mitt Romney, the Republicans' 2012 presidential candidate, had as Massachusetts governor established a faith-based initiative (headed by his wife) to assist religious groups in applying for federal funds and in tendering to provide social services in the state. However, the initiative and 'compassionate conservatism' more broadly barely intruded into either the 2008 or 2012 campaigns.

The British policy 'conversation'

There was far less of a policy 'conversation' among conservatives about options and strategies in the UK. Insofar as it took place, it was for the most part episodic and largely subdued. Inevitably, there were substantial overlaps and exchanges between the different perspectives.

The reasons for this were largely institutional. Outside campaigning groups and advocacy organizations had far fewer opportunities to influence the course of events. Insofar as policy debates took place within the parliamentary party, they were subject to the attentions of the whips and commentators ever seeking signs of disunity. There were, of course, think tanks such as the Centre for Policy Studies (CPS), the Institute of Economic Affairs (IEA) and the Adam Smith Institute, although their charitable status prevented overt campaigning.[2]

Furthermore, although there were discussions about strategy in the wake of the monumental general election defeat in 1997, these were largely tilted towards social and cultural issues. The prospect of 'modernization' led to fractures between 'mods' and 'rockers'. There was less debate about other policy areas. Despite the continuing presence of some high-profile 'Europhiles', a loose consensus formed around an increasingly 'hard' form of Euroscepticism and a belief that the classical liberal faith in the untrammelled market always had to be tempered by the conservative commitment to notions of community, institutions and order. There was a shared recognition that there had to be a retreat, albeit a very partial and limited one, from what some saw as the excesses of the Thatcher era or at least the Thatcherite style. Peter Lilley, once seen as an architect of the Thatcher revolution and at that point deputy leader of the party, announced in April 1999 that 'belief in the free market has only ever been a part of Conservatism'. So as far as health provision, for example, was concerned, the market had 'only a limited role' to play (quoted in Garnett, 2003: 115). The party also pulled back from its earlier policy stances and accepted some of the reforms enacted by the Labour government. There would be no attempt to reclaim the Bank of England's new-found control over monetary policy or abolish the minimum wage (Wade, 2013: 159).

There were other reasons why policy debate was relatively subdued even in the wake of severe electoral setbacks. The Tory Left that had periodically disturbed Margaret Thatcher's early years in government was now extinct:

> There are of course shades of grey, but the main point of ideological contention is clearly between, on the one hand, a substantial minority (possibly bigger in the party in the country than in the party in parliament) who would like to see the Tories adopt a stronger 'faith, flag and family' stance and, on the other, those who consider themselves social liberals.
>
> (Bale, 2012: 88)

The constituency membership seemed to have made the running in pulling the party Rightwards. Constituency associations ensured that those selected for parliamentary seats had few of the sympathies that would in the early 1980s have labelled them 'wet'. In September 2001, Iain Duncan Smith was elected as party leader, securing 61 per cent of the vote among party members even though he had only finished second in the final ballot among Conservative Members of Parliament. While he was removed by a coup among MPs in 2003, the party's Rightward shift was confirmed by the selection of Michael Howard as his successor. Electoral anxieties also played a role in limiting policy dialogue. In the run-up to both the 2001 and 2005 general elections, under the leadership of William Hague and Michael Howard respectively, and fearing electoral meltdown, the party had fallen back upon traditional Conservative themes such as criminality and immigration so as to mobilize its core vote. There were few opportunities to put forward or experiment with new forms of policy that might constitute a 'leap in the dark'.

Options and choices

Nonetheless, although often only partially visible, there were a few echoes of US debates. Some took issue with prevailing orthodoxy in the party and continued to argue along classical liberal lines for more untempered market-led policies. They tied this to an increasingly 'hard' form of Euroscepticism that not only rejected economic and monetary union and regarded the European Union (EU) as a, perhaps *the*, principal source of over-government and excessive regulation, but also increasingly talked in terms of a 'two-speed Europe' that would allow the EU's core nations to move towards 'federalism' if they so desired or at German behest but would let outsiders proceed in ways they themselves chose.[3] Indeed, some were ready to contemplate a British exit from the EU. They tied this to an insistence that the UK could flourish as an independent trading nation. John Redwood, the former Secretary of State for Wales who challenged John Major for the party leadership in 1995, wanted to retain a 'common market' but advocated British membership of the North American Free Trade Agreement (NAFTA) that had brought together the US, Canada and Mexico. He sought to reclaim the UK's control over its own trade policy from the EU: 'If it makes sense to belong to a common market with our Western European partners, it would also make sense to belong to a common market with our American friends and allies' (quoted in McSmith, 2000).

A second approach overlapped with these ideas. There were those who, in an echo of US supply-side thinking, called for radical tax-cutting. The economist Professor Patrick Minford laid out such a strategy at the beginning of 2001. He argued that the Thatcher and Major years had, through the conquest of inflation and the introduction of supply-side reforms, bequeathed a strong economy that, in turn, had allowed the Labour government, through buoyant tax revenues, to increase public expenditure (a process assisted, however, Minford noted, by its imposition of 'stealth taxes'). The Conservatives, Minford argued, should not spend their time looking for signs of economic failure but should instead insist that sustained economic growth provided a basis for tax reductions, although he seemed to move in his arguments between representing tax cuts as an alternative to Labour's expenditure projects and claiming that tax revenues were such that a government could at the same time reduce taxes and continue to spend on public services:

> these huge surpluses should all be given back to the people in tax cuts instead of going into a futile effort to fill the unfillable black hole in the NHS's capacity to run a state monopoly of medicine ... The truth is that the Tories have a once-in-a-generation opportunity: to announce a phased programme of major tax cuts from which there are no losers and which involve no cuts in existing public spending programmes.
> (Minford, 2001)

The Conservative Party leadership seemed to waver around much of this. At times, the leadership appeared to embrace the tax-cutting message but there were also substantial retreats. In the 2001 general election the party called for £8 billion of tax cuts, including the abolition of income tax on pensioners' savings (unless they were in higher-income groups). In the 2005 election, tax-cutting ambitions were more modest and there was a call for tax cuts amounting to £4 billion. Again, there was a fear that a commitment to more substantial reductions would allow the Labour Party to claim, in its campaigning, that the Conservatives would take an axe to social provision. The party thus made a call to 'share the proceeds of growth' so that the revenues accrued from economic growth were shared between tax reductions and public services. Thus, while the tax cuts were therefore limited, the party said that it would devote £23 billion to spending on public services and £8 billion would be used in reducing the budget deficit. All this was to come from £35 billion that was said to be wasteful government spending (Wade, 2013: 161). The emphasis on 'waste' and the savings that they claimed could be made from its elimination thereby allowed the Conservatives to offer something to core constituencies while at the same time reaching out to those in the middle ground who might by this point be tiring of Tony Blair and New Labour, although, as noted above, the party's reliance on traditional concerns such as crime may have limited its capacity to win over those lying outside its core constituencies.

Civic conservatism

The third strategy, the turn to civic conservatism, which was structured around communitarianism, neighbourhood, the integration of the individual and repairs to the social fabric, had much greater significance and important implications for the overall direction of economic policy.

Some of the defining ideas had been in circulation for more than a decade. In 1994 the Social Market Foundation published David Willetts's booklet, *Civic Conservatism*. Willetts, formerly Director of Studies at the CPS and who had become an MP in 1992, looked towards the construction of an institutional framework that would facilitate and foster reciprocal altruism. He hailed the 'little platoons' and called for Britain to become a more institutionally 'lumpy' country (Willetts,

1994: 22). By this he meant that state direction should be reduced and more should be done to rebuild voluntary structures and networks that were responsive to local wishes and at the same time had the capacity to address acute social problems (Willetts, 1994: 36).

All of this corresponded closely with basic Conservative instincts, but the impact of Willetts's arguments during an era when John Major's government was promoting the Citizens' Charters, which implicitly represented the citizen as a consumer, was limited. In contrast with civic conservatism, the Charters had little to say about responsibilities and obligations (Willetts, 1994: 43).

Civic conservatism (although different terms were used at times) was to make more of an impact within the party's collective thinking when the Conservatives were in opposition. The greater attention that civic conservatism secured from the late 1990s onwards had five principal sources of impetus. First, the turn to compassionate conservatism in the US had not gone unnoticed in the UK. In 1999, William Hague, then Conservative leader, seemed at least for a period to embrace George W. Bush's thinking. Boris Johnson, then editor of *The Spectator*, noted the parallels:

> Mr Hague extols the 'little platoons', the churches, the charities which he hopes will step in to the areas of care in danger of state monopoly. Mr Bush talks about the 'little armies' ... Mr Hague speaks of social entrepreneurs; Mr Bush speaks of educational entrepreneurs.
>
> (quoted in Ashbee, 2003: 43)

As noted above, Hague fell back on the party's core vote and was drawn away from policy experimentation and these forms of discourse as the 2001 general election approached. However, in his acceptance speech as party leader in December 2005, David Cameron seemed to invoke the spirit of civic conservatism when said that he sought the pursuit of 'a modern and compassionate conservatism which is right for our times and our country' (quoted in Norman and Ganesh, 2006: 1).

Cameron was not alone. Others in the party rallied to 'compassionate conservatism'. They were not, however, seeking a simple process of policy transfer from the US and they distanced themselves from the approach adopted by the Bush campaign in 1999–2000 and his subsequent administration. In the US, it was argued, compassionate conservatism had been tied too closely to claims (a hallmark of the Christian Right) that moral standards were in decay. It had also remained as little more than a slogan (or even an electoral expedient) and thus there were no credible foundations upon which policymaking could be built (Norman and Ganesh, 2006: 57).

In the UK, compassionate conservatism was to rest upon decentralization to individuals, families, communities and sub-national governments and was to be tied to what was later termed 'localism'. All of this would begin with an 'audit' of government:

> an audit will force us to reconsider the limits of personal and local responsibility. Should individuals bear personal responsibility if they are ill as a result of their own unhealthy lifestyles? Should families bear more responsibility for old age care? Should a given community bear more responsibility for law and order, for education or welfare?
>
> (Norman and Ganesh, 2006: 65)

Second, compassionate conservatism addressed the question of social capital, which had come to the fore in some commentaries and debates. The Organisation for Economic Cooperation and Development (OECD) had increasingly focused on social capital when considering the impediments to economic growth in the developing world, but some of the conclusions that it drew could also be applied to countries such as the UK. There was a growing recognition that Britain was slipping behind in terms of human capital, particularly if the Programme for International Student Assessment (PISA) rankings were considered, in terms of literacy, numeracy and problem-solving skills. The decline in human capital was tied to social capital and social trust, and all three seemed to ebbing away. Some commentators pointed to the 'underclass' in Britain's bigger cities (as well as the decline of traditional village communities) as testimony to this.

Consideration of social capital was not confined to OECD reports or newspaper commentaries bemoaning the decline of civic-mindedness. The concept had been widely popularized through Robert Putnam's 1995 article, 'Bowling Alone: America's Declining Social Capital'. It drew a contrast between the high level of civic engagement and the plethora of voluntary associations described by Alexis de Tocqueville in the 1830s and the high levels of disengagement that, he asserted, characterized the contemporary US. It was evident, the 'bowling alone' thesis asserted, in low levels of voter turnout, the decline in membership of organizations including the labour unions and, for example, parent–teacher associations, the fall in the numbers volunteering, as well as the slump in basic neighbourliness and mutual trust. In a further example that gave the article its title, Putnam also observed that 'more Americans are bowling today than ever before, but bowling in organized leagues has plummeted in the last decade or so' (Putnam, 1995: 70). In other words, solo bowling captured and encapsulated the new disengaged spirit of the age.[4]

For Putnam, at least in his original article, and for this his claims met with significant criticism, the diminution of civic engagement was attributable to the increasing number of women in the labour market (thereby reducing the time available for volunteering), growing mobility rates, the replacement of neighbourhood institutions such as grocery stores by large and remote firms, and the technological transformation of leisure whereby collective activities had been displaced by the television (Putnam, 1995: 74–75).

Nonetheless, although civic conservatism had an affinity with the Putnam thesis, there were reservations about 'Bowling Alone' within the Right. Although there were invocations of the 'little battalions', there was less enthusiasm for the process of developing policy mechanisms that might generate or nurture it. Such an approach seemed all too akin to social engineering.

Third, civic conservatism incorporated and built upon long-established and familiar conservative tropes addressing welfare dependency, the family and the sources of poverty. It therefore had an intuitive appeal. On being deposed as Conservative Party leader Iain Duncan Smith established the Centre for Social Justice (CSJ).[5] While the term 'social justice' is associated with religious faiths and social democratic discourses, the CSJ instead stressed the role of individual effort and the part to be played by family institutions. It talked of community but also of the ways in which the 'underclass' had to be brought back into the ranks of full citizenship. Thus (and this informed government policy from 2010 onwards when Iain Duncan Smith served as Secretary of State for Work and Pensions), whereas the 'Big Society' project stressed voluntary effort, the 'underclass' was addressed in very different terms. There had to be an armoury of incentives and disincentives so as to bring the underclass back into the ranks of what Victorian reformers termed the 'respectable poor'. Those on benefits were represented, in contrast with perceptions of middle England, in terms of *homo economicus*. A 2008 CSJ report on worklessness argued that a reduction in poverty levels required changes to the benefits system so that there were always incentives encouraging upward mobility and asserted that the system fostered and maintained single-parenthood.

> Back-to-work support is failing, and the benefits system is trapping people in poverty and part-time, low pay, low prospect jobs – particularly people with significant and multiple labour market disadvantages. The benefits system also acts as a disincentive to family formation that leads to the best outcomes for children: (married) couple families.
>
> (Centre for Social Justice, 2008: 1)

The CSJ and conservatives more broadly were also influenced by ideas that had crossed the Atlantic. Some took note of Lawrence Mead's arguments that social benefits should be conditional upon the fulfilment of obligations, the basis of workfare schemes whereby a claimant undertakes training or goes on a work placement in return for public assistance. Others were drawn to Charles Murray's claims, spelled out in his 1984 book *Losing Ground*, about the relationship between welfare benefits and poverty and well as illegitimacy by creating perverse incentives that undermined self-effort.

Fourth, civic conservatism assuaged the concerns of those within the ranks of the Right who had reservations about the untrammelled market, valued community and social ties, or sought a shift away from what they regarded as an over-emphasis on the tenets of classical liberalism. To a degree, these sentiments mirrored feelings among some neoconservatives in the US. Irving Kristol's 1978 book, *Two Cheers for Capitalism*, argued that the capitalist order provided economic prosperity and ensured liberty. But, as the title of Kristol's book suggested, he also had significant reservations. Capitalism had many virtues but was at the same time guilty of both amoralism and cultural nihilism insofar as it fostered hyper-individualistic consumerism and immediate gratification. Kristol thus distanced himself from those who stressed economics alone: 'all those Republicans with the hearts and souls of accountants' (quoted in Wrong, 1983).

In Britain, sentiments such as these also gave rise to 'Red Toryism', although it only took shape as such after the financial crisis had broken. Although intellectually successful (insofar as it commanded a wide audience in some papers and periodicals), its political traction was more limited.[6] Red Toryism nonetheless sought to pull the conservative agenda towards civic questions. It incorporated hints of the Tory patrician tradition and its stress upon an organic social order but also employed more contemporary communitarian themes. In his article in *Prospect* magazine, 'Rise of the Red Tories', Philip Blond called for 'communitarian civic conservatism' (it was this that he dubbed 'red Toryism') (Blond, 2009). It brought the idea of popular capitalism together with localism as well as community-based systems and structures. Blond urged, for example, the adoption of policies that would lead to 'relocalising our banking system, developing local capital, helping normal people gain new assets and breaking up big business monopolies' (Blond, 2009).

Fifth, civic conservatism allowed the Conservatives to 'out-Blair' New Labour. Labour and Third Way politics more broadly had also toyed with communitarianism and had structured much of its political message around 'inclusion'. Arguably, community allowed the New Labour leadership to supplant Old Labour attachments such as nationalization and redistribution while at the same time putting some distance between itself and Thatcherism. Indeed community was at times sold 'as the hangover cure to the excesses of Conservative individualism' (Driver and Martell, 1997: 27). However, like the Conservatives' later 'social justice' agenda, Labour often represented exclusion from the labour force in individualist rather than structural terms. Initiatives such as the New Deal (launched in 1998) might have sought to evoke Franklin D. Roosevelt's work projects, but rested on developing the skills, aptitudes and motivation of the individual rather than the provision of employment. As the initiative developed, there were incentives through the Working Families Tax Credit and disincentives insofar as benefits could be withdrawn from those refusing offers of 'reasonable employment'. Indeed, in contrast with some of the ideas that defined traditional social-democratic thinking and twentieth-century liberalism, the 'inclusion' agenda seemed (like welfare reform in the US) to rest on 'the personal deficits of the excluded rather than social barriers and inequalities that systematically exclude' (Roulstone and Prideaux, 2008). Having said this, the continuities between the Blair government and civic conservatism should not be overstated. In contrast with civic conservatism as it later took shape, Third Way politics only paid sporadic attention to charitable and voluntary projects and the third sector.

Sixth, some conservative commentators took note of, and succour from, the technological developments of the 1990s and beyond and the growth of social media to argue that such developments offered a basis for increased connectedness and the recovery of community:

> A smart mathematician improving the Facebook algorithms to enable you to find contacts closer to you could do much more for social cohesion than a Government White Paper ... That powerful image of hundreds of volunteers, their brooms held aloft, coming together the day after the riots to clear things up in London and cities around Britain, shows how social media can be a force for good.
>
> (Willetts, 2013: 31)

Nonetheless, although civic conservatism seemed to hold out considerable political promise, discussion of it remained limited to relatively small groups of commentators. This was partly because the concepts around which it was structured held little appeal for many in the party's grassroots. They were also difficult to translate into press releases. There were also, as when compassionate conservatism was promoted in the US, structural ambiguities.

The concept had some ambivalence to it. It could be an assertion that those on the bottom rungs of the socioeconomic ladder could be brought out of poverty and disadvantage through market processes and that such processes would work much more effectively than the bureaucratic, inefficient and often cumbersome hand of the state. At times, however, it seemed to imply that the resources and capacity of the state could be employed for conservative ends such as the reinvigoration of the traditional family or ensuring that individuals could take a place in the labour market.

David Willetts, regarded as a key party thinker, seemed to share the second of these positions by envisaging a role for government in collectivizing risks such as ill-health or unemployment and also representing the state as a potentially proactive force. It would, at the least, 'nudge' individuals towards preferred outcomes:

> We must limit government, and recognise its failings and inadequacies ... But government has an essential role in a modern advanced economy too, not least as a national pool to share risk and then harness it creatively. And we are doing everything possible to harness the creative power of government to get the economy growing.
>
> (Willetts, 2013: 35)

The Cameron project

David Cameron secured the Conservative Party leadership in December 2005. His time as Leader of the Opposition has generally been understood and represented in terms of a modernization project, an embrace of both cultural liberalism and social inclusion, and a move back towards the centre-ground of British politics (Dorey,

2007). It was thus a repudiation, or at least a partial repudiation, of Thatcherism and its seeming emphasis upon the untrammelled market values and individual advancement personified by Harry Enfield's 1980s character, 'Loadsamoney'.

Cameron's election as leader was hailed as a victory for the modernizers such as those who had been active in C-Change, the modernizing group within the party that had been established by those who had backed Michael Portillo's unsuccessful bid for the leadership in 2001 (Maude, 2013: 2). The Conservatives had long been perceived, in Theresa May's celebrated words (uttered when she was Party Chair), as 'the nasty party'.

Although there was no 'Clause Four moment' (an allusion to Tony Blair's stand against Clause Four of the Labour Party Constitution that had formally committed the party to large-scale nationalization), the Cameron leadership appeared to be consciously aping Blairism. Like Blair before him, Cameron sought to rebrand and reorient, or, as it was sometimes put, 'detoxify' his party.

Under Cameron, and anticipating an extended period in opposition before the next general election, the party leadership sought to make its parliamentary candidates rather more demographically representative and move beyond the traditionally strong issues areas such as crime and immigration on which they had fallen back in 2001 and 2005. At the same time, professionals in the public services were assured that their judgements would be respected, bringing an end to Labour's 'target culture'. Cameron talked in terms of his own personal experience, as a parent, of the health service and state education. They would be safe in his hands.

The modernization initiatives were nonetheless always tempered by steps that might reassure traditionalists. Although slow in fulfilling it, Cameron gave a pledge during his leadership campaign that he would withdraw Conservative Members of the European Parliament (MEPs) from the European People's Party (EPP) that had brought the Tories together with 'federalist' European Conservatives, most notably German Christian Democrats. In 2009, the Conservatives formed a new grouping, Conservatives and Reformists, which relocated the Conservatives within a much more Eurosceptic setting and, following the 2014 European elections, the group was expanded to include Dansk Folkeparti and others much more closely associated with Rightist populism than conservatism. Furthermore, as noted above, the representations of 'social justice' that the party embraced had an authoritarian edge. For his part, Matthew d'Ancona argued that the 'party failed to win an outright majority principally because its "detoxification" was not yet finished' (d'Ancona, 2013: 18).

Nonetheless, although the modernization project was not pursued at a speed or with a consistency that some of the more radical commentators sought, it had a sense of direction. That sense of direction was strikingly absent in the shaping of economic policy. After the 2005 general election defeat and David Cameron's accession to the party leadership there was an understanding that the party had offered modest tax cuts in three successive general elections and had lost on each occasion. Nonetheless, there was little else. Thus, the Cameron leadership was torn between appeasing core constituencies, reproducing Blairism and seeking the votes of 'middle England', and embarking on more ambitious and new policy courses.

The appeasement of core constituencies was evident in two pledges. There was also a relatively traditionalist commitment to protect marriage through the taxation and benefits systems.[7] At the same time there was a promise to raise the inheritance tax threshold to £1 million (2007) and then £2 million (2008), although given the rise in property values it might also be seen as a way of seeking middle-ground votes.[8] There was a deliberate copying of the tactics adopted by Labour in the run-up to the 1997 general election when, in September 2007, George Osborne, the Shadow Chancellor of the Exchequer, gave a commitment on behalf of the party that, if elected, they would adhere to Gordon Brown's plans to increase government expenditure by 2 per cent in real terms over the coming three years.

> Today, I can confirm for the first time that a Conservative government will adopt these spending totals ... under a Conservative government, there will be real increases in spending on public services, year after year ... The charge from our opponents that we will cut services becomes transparently false.
>
> (quoted in Carlin, 2007)

At the same time, and as noted above, some within the party began to talk more openly about civic conservatism (even if the term itself was not employed). Cameron himself sought to reframe the party's claims around the state and its relationship with civil society. In August 2008 he proclaimed: 'I'm going to be as radical a social reformer as Margaret Thatcher was an economic reformer' (quoted in Blond, 2009). Thus, Cameron embraced Thatcherism but also distanced the party from it by focusing on society and the social fabric:

> When my party was last in Government, the main task was to roll back the frontiers of the state. If we get into Government again, I want us to have a different mission. To roll forward the frontiers of society.
>
> (David Cameron, quoted in *The Guardian*, 2006)

Many of these ideas, and certainly discussions around 'Red Toryism', remained limited to periodicals such as *Prospect*. Nonetheless, Cameron remained insistent that civil society had to be bolstered and strengthened if efforts to shrink the state were to be successful. In short, he argued, the state could only be reduced in the medium and long term if civil society had the capacity and vibrancy to take on some of the roles hitherto undertaken by the post-war state. As things stood, in many cases civil society lacked the capacity to do that:

> Yes, there are specific instances where the very act of rolling back the state will serve to roll forward society ... But I believe that in general, a simplistic retrenchment of the state which assumes that better alternatives to state action will just spring to life

> unbidden is wrong. Instead we need a thoughtful re-imagination of the role, as well as the size, of the state.
>
> (David Cameron, quoted in ResPublica, 2009)

The core of the argument was, as Willetts had argued in earlier statements and publications, that the state had to play a proactive role in bringing forth civil society initiatives and projects: 'This means a new role for the state: actively helping to create the big society; directly agitating for, catalysing and galvanising social renewal' (David Cameron, quoted in ResPublica, 2009).

Differential dynamics: the US and the UK compared

On the eve of the 2008 economic crisis those in the ranks of the Right in both the US and the UK who were given to frank statements would have acknowledged the challenges that they faced. There was some room for electoral optimism among British Conservatives insofar as, after a brief honeymoon with the voters, Gordon Brown's government had crashed in the polls. For the first time since the early 1990s New Labour seemed to be struggling. In the US, there was even less of a belief that a Republican candidate could, after President George W. Bush's two terms, secure the White House or that Congress could be retaken. Furthermore, Bush's spending record, his apparent commitment to 'big government' and the seeming quagmire of both the Afghanistan and Iraq wars had caused major fissures among conservatives.

Nonetheless, the Right continued to be torn between contending approaches and strategies. In the US, there were pulls between calls to 'starve the beast', supply-side policies that would extend the boundaries of capitalism, efforts to use political mechanisms so as to ensure that Republican lawmakers adhered to the demands of the conservative movement and, last, a limited turn towards compassionate conservatism in the hope that voluntary initiatives and civic commitment could reduce the burden upon an over-extended state. In the UK, there were parallel tensions between curbing the might of the EU (which perhaps more than Westminster and Whitehall seemed to pose frontal challenges to economic freedom and liberty), tax-cutting strategies (although they were couched as a gain that could be secured from growth or perhaps reducing wasteful government expenditure rather than an assault on the size of the state) and efforts, albeit often largely inchoate in character, to foster social capital through civic conservatism so as to limit the state.

In the US, by the time the economic crisis began to take hold, calls for other and different candidates and the displacement of 'establishment' Republicans were becoming the most common political currency. In the UK, the Conservative leadership seemed to move backwards and forwards between different strategic considerations.

Why was this? What explains the differences? It is a core argument in this book that political outcomes are shaped by the often abrasive interactions that take place as party organizations, constituencies, ideas, institutional frameworks and contemporary economic logic chafe against each other.

In the UK, as a Parliamentary Opposition, the Conservatives faced challenges. Many of these challenges were institutional in character (insofar as 'institutions' are formal and informal rules). The doctrine of mandate has been substantially weakened in recent decades but parties are still constrained by commitments made in the years preceding a general election or in the manifesto. There is a fear that a failure to honour such a commitment might well lead to political penalties. There is therefore a reluctance on the part of all parties in the British system to make a significant number of policy commitments ahead of an election campaign period. Options are kept open.

Furthermore, the broader institutional environment in the UK is markedly different from that in the US. The latter offers countless opportunities and openings to campaigns and groups seeking to hold lawmakers to account. They include primaries, caucuses, quasi-independent campaigning and expenditures, lobbying and litigation. There have been significant changes in the UK over recent decades and party leadership contests have been opened outwards but the political system remains much more closed. Efforts in the Labour Party by the radical or 'Bennite' Left during the 1980s to make MPs more accountable to the membership were largely unsuccessful.

The macroeconomic contexts within which US and British political processes take place were also significantly different and some strategies that were credible within a US context were less feasible in the UK. From the early 1980s onwards radical tax-cutting strategies could play a pivotal role within economic debate and political discourse in the US because the relative strength of the dollar could absorb the short-run or even long-run budget deficits that might accumulate if economic activity failed to increase in the wake of marginal tax reductions to the extent that supply-side economic thinking asserted. The pound was far more vulnerable to the impact of budget deficits. Thus, in contrast with Reaganomics, Thatcherism was far more cautious about tax cuts. This caution continued in subsequent decades.

The Conservative leadership also had to consider its core constituencies, broader swathes of the electorate and popular ideas. Over the decades, the party's voting base has become narrower and more regionalized. Its electoral troubles in Scotland and Wales have been well-charted. Furthermore, YouGov polling suggested that in 2010 only 31 per cent voters in the North supported the Conservatives, 12 per cent less than elsewhere in England (Kellner, 2013). To an extent at least, its electoral future depends upon its ability to secure gains by winning over the marginal voter outside southern England.

Within this context, popular ideas are important. Although political campaigning is concentrated on those in particular segments or niches, surveys of aggregate attitudes and attitudinal changes suggest important long-run shifts that have implications for those seeking election or re-election. Studies by *British Social Attitudes* have charted these. In 1991, after twelve years of Conservative rule, two-thirds of respondents (65 per cent) favoured increasing taxes and thereby spending more on health, education and social benefits. In 2002, after five years of a Labour government, the figure was 63 per cent. After that, however (as public expenditure rose), that number fell and by the time of the 2010 election it was just 31 per cent (Park *et al.*, 2013: x–xi). This was matched by increasingly harsh attitudes towards benefits for the jobless:

> In 1983 nearly half the public (46 per cent) said that unemployment benefits were 'too low' and caused 'hardship'. That figure rose over the next decade, reaching a high of 55 per cent by 1993. Since then, support for this outlook has fallen steadily, and now stands at just 22 per cent.
>
> (Park *et al.*, 2013: xii)

Other studies suggest that different groupings among those dependent on government provision are perceived in markedly different ways. Senior citizens are regarded as the most deserving. Those who are sick and disabled are not far behind. The unemployed are seen as less deserving and immigrants 'as least deserving of all' (Park *et al.*, 2013: 52).

If business interests are considered, although the sway of peak business organizations is limited in both the UK and the US, there was growing disquiet about public expenditure levels as the decade continued. In November 2005, the Confederation of British Industry (CBI) called for a reduction in the pace at which government spending was increasing and to reduce the budget deficit. It talked of a £10 billion 'black hole' in the public finances. The CBI was at the same time fearful that at some point tax rises would be used to bring down the deficit and that such rises would further reduce British economic competitiveness (Seager, 2006).

At any point in time, and in any particular setting, the perceptions of political actors are limited and bound by their perceived horizons. In other words, whereas some models of politics present actors' preferences as exogenous, they are shaped within the art of the possible, which is in turn shaped by prevailing perceptions of the political process at any given point in time:

> a group's actions often will not reveal its preferences but rather its strategic calculations of what is the best that can be accomplished given existing circumstances. An actor's expressed policy preferences may in fact be 'induced' or 'strategic' – that is, they reflect accommodations to circumstances that constrain what can be achieved.
>
> (Hacker and Pierson, 2002: 283)

Thus, during the years preceding the financial crisis, perceptions and the actions that took place on the basis of their perceptions were different in the US and the UK. While American conservatives were drawn to strategies that rested upon holding Republican lawmakers to account, and dislodging those judged to be 'establishment' compromisers, all these cross-cutting pressures and pulls ensured that the Conservatives remained in a state of flux. This flux continued even after the crisis broke and was reflected in the unease and uncertainty of which candidates and party activists complained when canvassing in the run-up to the 2010 general election.

Conclusion

The 'stickiness' and resilience of the state laid a basis for the emergence of different approaches and strategies within the Right. In the US, in 2000, George W. Bush's presidential campaign emphasized 'compassionate conservatism' and ways of building voluntary and faith-based efforts to take the place of government provision, but the institutional openness and porousness of the political system drew activists instead towards mobilization strategies based upon the displacement of those Republican officeholders who seemed to lack commitment to conservative principles. In the UK, there was a weak but more sustained engagement with civic conservatism, but much of the Conservative Party seemed to be pulled between different political poles of attraction. It is difficult, therefore, in looking at the party during much of the period before the 2010 general election to identify a distinct or consistent sense of purpose.

Notes

1 After the 2000 election, a Republican pollster found that just 7 per cent of the electorate had been truly 'independent' insofar as they could have been won by either campaign (Teles, 2011: 205).

2 This was also, of course, the case in the US but they either had nominally separate advocacy arms or there were groupings ready to campaign for the claims that the think tanks made in the political arena.

3 At the time, the Conservative Party opposed Economic and Monetary Union (EMU) for at least two parliaments. This shifted in 2001 when Iain Duncan Smith ruled out membership of the euro (Lynch and Whitaker, 2013: 324). Gordon Brown's opposition to EMU saved the Conservatives from a sustained debate about the issue. Nonetheless, the balance of opinion among Conservatives was overwhelmingly against the project. It was said, with some foresight, that the proposed zone did not constitute an optimal currency area and that monetary union was not feasible without there also being a fiscal union.

4 Despite widely shared assertions that there had been processes of social decapitalization, the empirical evidence for it was at most patchy. Writing at the beginning of the new century, Peter Hall suggests that although there are widening gaps between social groups and young people may have become rather more detached as part of what he terms a 'Thatcher effect', overall levels of social capital in the UK 'have remained relatively robust for the past fifty years' (Hall, 2002: 2). This was confirmed by other studies. In 2007, there were, reportedly, 190,000 voluntary organizations in England and Wales. Across the UK, there were 400,000 community groups. Furthermore, 6,000 new charities were registered every

year, and 600,000 people were employed by charities that were supported by six million volunteers (Powell, 2007: 3).

5 Although the CSJ had a conservative sense of direction, its Advisory Council included Labour figures such as former Home Secretary, David Blunkett.

6 A review in the *Daily Telegraph* noted the impact of Blond's essay on red Toryism: 'It was an immediate sensation. A Blairite think tank, Demos, put him in charge of a Red Tory project. He was feted around town as King Dave's court philosopher, an exciting intellectual with a knack for pithy phrases and the paradoxical conceits beloved of headline writers (Red Tory chief among them) who could both explain and flesh out all that Cameron stuff about the post-bureaucratic age' (Brogan, 2010).

7 It may have been this commitment that forced Cameron to throw his support behind calls for same-sex marriage. If the tax benefit had only been open to heterosexual couples, he would have been open to charges of prejudice.

8 These figures assumed that an inheritance would be bequeathed to a spouse (tax-free) before being passed to children.

4

The advent of crisis and the building of narratives

This chapter looks at the impact of the 2008 financial crisis and its aftermath on the Right. It charts the period of initial uncertainty as the crisis first broke and the construction of a narrative around 'big government' at the end of 2008 and beginning of 2009. It looks, in particular, at the ways in which representations of the New Deal and the 1930s were used to change the terms of debate.

Both the beginnings of the 'Great Recession' and the courses of action that were pursued as events unfolded have by now been very fully charted. The period was structured around an asset bubble, banking crises, a recession, a prolonged economic downturn and subsequent debt crises. If the different histories of the crisis are aggregated, the causal factors included the processes through which mortgages and other loans were securitized and traded, relatively low interest rates, the role of government-sponsored enterprises (most notably Fannie Mae and Freddie Mac) in seeming to underwrite the issuance of loans, and a belief that property prices would continue to rise or, at the very least, ease off so as to provide a soft landing.

Housing prices reached their peak in July 2006 (US) and in the third quarter of 2007 (UK). The consequences of falling property prices, negative equity, growing personal indebtedness and increasing difficulties in selling properties for those who had issued loans remained hidden for a relatively long period, although the demand for securitized mortgages fell. The September 2007 crisis at Northern Rock, which was unable to repay its loans, leading to panic among individual depositors who were fearful of losing their savings, appeared to have been contained. It was, as *The Economist* noted, the first bank run in Britain since 1866. The Bank of England initially provided a liquidity support facility, although this inevitably exacerbated public fears. Then, Alistair Darling, the Chancellor of the Exchequer, announced that Northern Rock deposits would be guaranteed by the British government and the Bank of England.[1] The Bank also abandoned its earlier reluctance to intervene and provided funds for the markets and undertook additional lending against riskier forms of collateral. For a period, this seemed sufficient to calm fears.

The picture in the US was broadly similar. In June 2007, the ratings agencies (Standard and Poor's and Moody's Investor Services) downgraded more than a hundred bonds that were backed by second-lien subprime mortgages. There was, it was acknowledged, a problem or at the least a potential problem with some of the mortgages that had been sold in earlier years to those on low or irregular incomes. Because those who had made the sale were sometimes working on a commission basis, there were systemic incentives to hide or downplay a buyer's ability to repay the loan. Furthermore, when 'teaser loans' had been issued, the buyer appears to have been sometimes unaware that repayment costs might increase over time when an initial interest-only period expired.

There were some more economic shudders at the beginning of 2008. In January, the Federal Reserve reduced the federal funds rate to 3.5 per cent and then eight days later to 3 per cent. This provided the backcloth to the 'Bush stimulus' (the Economic Stimulus Act) of January/February 2008. The Act was passed by Congress on a broadly bipartisan basis (in part because it had both supply-side and demand-side features) and incorporated personal tax rebates as well as tax incentives for business investment.

As the year progressed, the Federal Reserve reduced the interest rate still further and continued to relax its requirements for collateral when extending loans. In March, Bear Stearns, the investment bank that had been heavily involved in the subprime securitization market and was highly leveraged, hit visible difficulties. The term 'toxic assets' entered the popular vocabulary.

The Federal Reserve Bank (FRB) of New York provided an emergency loan to Bear Stearns but the firm was sold to JPMorgan Chase at a price far below its pre-crisis peak. It was supported by further assistance through loans from the New York FRB and the takeover therefore constituted and was widely understood to be a form of 'bailout'. Amidst fears of collateral economic damage arising from the web of interconnections between firms and markets, there was tacit backing from the US Treasury as well as Ben Bernanke, Chairman of the Federal Reserve. There were, however, also warnings of moral hazard at the same time:

> What's going on here is that we're in uncharted territory, a world where the Fed and the Treasury are making up the rules as they go along, where accountability is being ignored and a world where the government bails out Bear Stearns and its creditors rather than letting those who have been reckless learn a lesson for the next time.
>
> (Roberts, 2008)

Although there was a growing realization that market difficulties were widespread, there was still only a limited grasp of their spread and depth. That spread and depth only became evident in mid-September when Lehman Brothers, the fourth largest investment firm in the US, filed for Chapter 11 bankruptcy protection. The US Treasury had sought to arrange a private-sector rescue but, once it became evident that such a rescue could not be arranged, encouraged the bankruptcy to proceed. It had absorbed the admonishments of those who had warned of moral hazard six months earlier.

As the extent to which there was interconnectedness between firms and markets became only too evident, markets fell precipitously and the American International Group (AIG) also seemed about to hit trouble. Indeed, according to Warren Buffett, Chairman of Berkshire Hathaway: 'It became a great silent electronic run on money markets. There was $3 ½ trillion in money market funds and $175 billion of funds flowed out in the first three days after Lehman failed' (quoted in Weisenthal, 2013).

Against this background, the Emergency Economic Stabilization Act of 2008 was passed despite widespread resistance in Congress. The first attempt to pass legislation to allow the purchase of troubled financial assets (a move derided by critics as 'cash for trash') and provide for the direct injection of capital into the banking sector was defeated in the House of Representatives. The bill mustered just 205 votes and was opposed by a third of the House Democrats and two-thirds of the Republicans. For many in the former group, the Act subsidized Wall Street bankers, while for the latter it was government interference with market mechanisms. However, at this point, there was a degree of ideational congruence and some Republicans spoke in tones that would customarily be associated with the Left. For a Texan Republican: 'This legislation is giving us a choice between bankrupting our children and bankrupting a few of these big financial institutions on Wall Street that made bad decisions' (quoted in Isidore, 2008). The market reaction to the House vote was, however, unambiguous. As CNN reported: 'Stock markets reacted violently. Investors who had been counting on the rescue plan's passage sent the Dow Jones industrial average down well over 700 points' (Isidore, 2008). It was the largest drop in a single day and key political and economic figures warned of catastrophe. Against this background, which pitted market logic that required a rescue against conservative zeal for the free market, the Act was passed in an amended form. This time around the voting in the House was 263–171 in support of the measure. A $700 billion Treasury fund was created.

The following week, and just after the FTSE100 index had recorded its largest fall since 1987, the British government also enacted a bank 'bailout'. £200 billion was made available for short-term loans. There was to be government support for efforts by the banking sector to increase their market capitalization and shares would be purchased. For a period the government would underwrite interbank lending, although at this point in time there were hopes on both sides of the Atlantic that if governments responded with sufficient force and conviction (the financial equivalent of the 'shock and awe' doctrine) the markets would regain confidence and that few of the funds that had been allocated would in practice be required.

The 'real economy'

The course of events during September and October 2008 underlined the magnitude of the financial crisis. In the wake of Lehman Brothers' bankruptcy and the ensuing collapse of the markets, and amidst efforts to secure passage of the Economic

Stabilization Act, President Bush reportedly said, 'If money doesn't loosen up, this sucker will go down.' Warren Buffett later asserted that 'In September 2008, we came right to the abyss. If Paulson and Bernanke had not intervened, in two more days it would have been all over' (quoted in Weisenthal, 2013). There were forecasts of widespread bank collapses, ATMs ceasing to issue cash and mass panic. Evocations of the 1929 Wall Street crash and its extended aftermath abounded.

At this point, there was also a sudden and jolting realization that the crisis could no longer be confined to the banking sector but had immense consequences for the wider, 'real' economy. Even if the banking 'bailouts' had forestalled the danger that banks would close their doors, there was still the prospect of a large-scale 'credit crunch' (another phrase that entered the popular vocabulary at this time) whereby loans to both firms and individuals would inevitably be very tightly restricted, jeopardizing both spending and investment.

Against this background, the 'real' economy plummeted. In the US, there was a real negative growth rate of minus 8.3 per cent in the fourth quarter of 2008 and a further 5.4 per cent fall in the first three months of 2009 (Bureau of Economic Analysis, 2014). Although the unemployment figures remained significantly lower than many had predicted given the fall in national output, the US joblessness rate rose from 6.1 per cent in September 2008 (there had been a slow but steady rise from a low of 4.4 per cent in May 2007), reaching 7.3 per cent at the end of 2008 and 10 per cent in October 2009 (Bureau of Labor Statistics, 2014).

The UK went into recession ahead of the financial crisis, although there were still some signs of a relatively soft landing. However, output fell by 2.1 per cent in the last quarter of 2008 and by a further 2.5 per cent in the first quarter of 2009. The economy returned to negative territory or close to it a number of times, subsequently giving rise to talk of a double-dip or even a triple-dip recession (*BBC News*, 2014). Unemployment, however, only hit a peak in the final quarter of 2011 when it reached 8.5 per cent. As in the US, this was a lower figure than might have been expected given the depth and duration of the recession, and its relative 'lateness' (three years after the financial crisis broke) gave rise to claims that it was the consequence of the British government's 'austerity' policies (see Chapter 6) rather than a direct result of the banking crisis and the recession.

Policy responses

As the impact of the crisis became evident invocations of the Wall Street Crash and the Great Depression abounded. Often idealized representations of the New Deal became commonplace. While President-Elect Barack Obama headed towards his inauguration ceremony, *Time* magazine published a front cover merging his image with that of Franklin Roosevelt. Obama was, the magazine was suggesting, about to embark on a recovery programme comparable with the New Deal. Lord Robert

Skidelsky, in a book that was written within months of the crisis breaking, spoke (and this was the subtitle of the book) of 'the return of the master' (Skidelsky, 2009). The 'master' in question was of course John Maynard Keynes.

From this perspective, untrammelled neoliberalism had run its course. The crisis was testimony to the proposition that unregulated markets inevitably give rise to speculation, asset bubbles and, as a consequence, periods of intense recession. Despite assertions in both the 1930s and 1990s by those on the free market Right that markets were inherently self-correcting (a claim that was allied with the 'Treasury View' in the UK), there is no mechanism within the market order that will, in itself, bring forth recovery. Instead, discretionary government action and deficit spending would be required.

From a Keynesian perspective, that action had to rest upon both monetary and fiscal policy. Monetary policy (understood largely at that point in terms of interest rate changes) is necessary but not sufficient. Whereas the interest rate can restrain demand and thereby be used to prevent excess demand and 'overheating', it is much less useful in restoring demand during economic downturns. When consumers and firms are uncertain and fearful about the economic future, even real negative interest rates will not be sufficient to bring forth spending or investment. In such circumstances, and in Keynes's celebrated phrase, the use of monetary policy would be akin to 'pushing on a piece of string'. Tax reductions are more efficacious in terms of stimulating demand but they also have their limits. Again, those who are anxious about a country's prospects and their own economic security (or are perhaps highly indebted) will only spend a relatively small proportion of the additional income that a tax concession extends to them. They may well save instead or pay down debts. And, even if they do spend, much of that may be used to purchase imported goods thereby doing relatively little or nothing to stimulate the domestic economy.

For those who followed the 'master', large-scale government spending was thus essential in periods of crisis. While US unemployment rates had remained high until the outbreak of the Second World War, the New Deal had been accompanied by relatively high growth rates for most of the years during the 1930s. For Keynesians, economic growth was the direct consequence of government spending. Such spending should, it was argued, be directed as it was at times during the 1930s towards projects likely to have a significant multiplier effect across the wider economy. For that reason, those who looked towards Keynesian remedies instinctively thought in terms of public works schemes and, although sections of the environmental Left had early reservations, road construction, repair and maintenance initiatives. There would, furthermore, be spillover effects as infrastructural development laid a basis for development and expansion by private-sector firms (and in this context some not only point to the New Deal but cite the effects generated by the construction of interstate highways during the Eisenhower era).

In arguing the Keynesian case, those who invoked 'the master' could draw upon familiar images such as the Triborough Bridge and the Lincoln Tunnel in New York, both of which were New Deal schemes. In Keynesian thinking, such projects would be funded from deficit budgets and the deficit paid down as and when economic recovery began to take place. Once an economy is again buoyant, tax revenues and the reduced demand upon government provision provides a surplus sufficient for the repayment of the debt incurred earlier.

Caution and restraint

Nonetheless, despite all the invocations of Keynesianism as the crisis first broke, governments only embraced a timid and restrained version of it. It has been described as 'emergency Keynesianism', but even this is perhaps an over-generous formulation (Hall, 2013: 142).

The policy decisions that were taken towards the end of 2008 can be assessed using Peter Hall's celebrated study of economic policy changes in Britain during the 1970s and early 1980s (Hall, 1993). He distinguished between first-order change, second-order change and third-order change. First-order change referred to changes in the settings of existing and established policy instruments. The reductions in the interest rates, which have already been noted, are an example of this. There were also tax policy shifts. The British government reduced value added tax (VAT) from 17.5 per cent to 15 per cent for a thirteen-month period. Although there were some fears that the cut would not be passed on by retailers to the consumer, the government claimed that it boosted GDP by about 0.5 per cent (Edmonds *et al.*, 2011: 20). The measure increased the purchasing power of consumers and, at the same time, encouraged them to bring forward spending that they would, in all probability, have otherwise deferred. The government, furthermore, brought forward about £3 billion of capital spending projects (Edmonds *et al.*, 2011: 21). At this stage, there was, however, little or no second-order change, whereby new policy instruments are introduced. Second-order change only came with the advent of increasingly creative forms of monetary policy as the central banks recognized the limits of interest rate reductions insofar as they alone could not provide a sufficient economic stimulus and turned, alongside a commitment to minimal interest rates, to quantitative easing (QE).

Despite all the talk of neoliberalism or the 'Anglo-Saxon model' being in crisis, there was certainly no short-run or medium-run prospect of third-order or paradigmatic change, whereby the framework within which economic policymaking was being undertaken changed in character. In his 1993 article, Hall had cited the embrace of monetarism at the end of the 1970s as an example of a third-order shift insofar as it represented the formal overthrow of the economic policy paradigm that had governed British policymaking from the Second World War onwards (Hall, 1993). There was nothing comparable in 2008–09. Indeed, as Hall himself noted four years later, change requires 'motivation, means, and a motor', which, to date, have been largely absent (Hall, 2013: 145). Nonetheless, Hall argues, it took about a decade for Keynesianism to unravel and thus the prospect of long-run shifts at a later date should not be precluded.

Why was the Labour government's response so cautious? According to the OECD the measures were equivalent to just 1.4 per cent of 2008 GDP (Organisation for Economic Cooperation and Development, 2009: 110). First, there was uncertainty about the likely severity and duration of the crisis. As noted above, unemployment rose but to a lesser degree, at a slower pace and at a lower rate than many had initially forecast. And, insofar as events challenged entrenched understandings of economic realities, there was a shock and a period of flux. While, such shocks can be, as path-dependency theory suggests, a harbinger of radical, path-departing change, actors may instead cling in a period of crisis to established, familiar nostrums insofar as that familiarity provides a degree of security.[2] Second, as in the 1930s, the institutional architecture of the British state is based upon the structural hegemony of the Treasury. Although Gordon Brown, as prime minister, seems both to have been reluctant to recognize the scale of the crisis during its early stages and to have shrunk from endorsing large-scale expenditure cuts once the agenda shifted towards austerity, the Chancellor of the Exchequer (Alistair Darling) and the 'Treasury View', which invariably emphasizes fiscal restraint and seeks to hold back the 'spending' departments, prevailed. Traditionally, the Treasury has had ties with the City of London and finance capital. It therefore had to consider the exchange rate implications for the pound of large-scale fiscal loosening. Third, the principal or 'peak' business organizations were themselves cautious about a dramatic policy shift. There was little thirst for radical change within organizations such as the CBI. Fourth, although some voters rallied to Gordon Brown's government during the early stages of the crisis, the next general election was not far ahead and Labour was reluctant to be cast again as 'big spenders'. It was a charge that had haunted the party for much of its life. Fifth, there was a degree of faith in the efficacy of the stabilizers offered by state provision. Spending on government services and benefits 'automatically' rose in periods of downturn as needs expanded while tax revenues inevitably fell, thereby providing a reflationary boost. Last, the prevailing 'neoliberal' paradigm had, in its embedded forms, more ideational flexibility and more scope for pragmatic adjustment than its critics often claimed. In the UK, the economic paradigm embraced from the late 1970s onwards had never represented a simple reversion to the neoclassical framework that had prevailed from the late nineteenth century until the Second World War. It had instead accepted a much larger state than in those years, the existence of a social 'safety net' and the belief that government had a responsibility for the common good in periods of crisis. In other words, the Thatcherism and the neoliberal 'revolution' constrained classical Keynesian notions and moved them a long way down the economic policy agenda, but they were not removed altogether. Indeed, the pre-crisis policy regime has been described in terms of 'new Keynesianism' (Hall, 2013: 146). Furthermore, because the government's crisis policy package rested on tax cuts (albeit cuts in indirect taxation) it could be justified on a supply-side as well as a demand-led basis, making it more appealing to the Right.

Against this multifaceted background, the Conservative response was relatively muted. The modesty of the Labour government's package itself cut off criticisms. Therefore, instead of challenging tax cuts (which would have posed significant political difficulties), the Shadow Chancellor of the Exchequer, George Osborne, picked on easier targets and sought to build political capital by pointing to Gordon Brown's earlier bombast. He focused on Labour's earlier claims to have ended 'boom and bust' and the increase in government borrowing that the stimulus measures necessitated. It had, he asserted, created 'a huge unexploded tax bombshell timed to go off at the time of the next economic recovery' (quoted in *BBC News*, 2008).

The 'return of the master' in the UK was therefore a relatively weak and insipid affair. Indeed, it could be credibly argued that he made no genuine return at all. The measures that were adopted were limited in character and framed as temporary expedients rather than a break with established economic thinking. They were forms of 'first-order' change and it was the central bank rather than governments that pursued 'second-order' change through the use of quantitative easing on a large scale.

US bailouts

The story was rather different in the US. As noted above, the Bush administration and a broad bipartisan coalitional bloc in Congress had agreed to a $150 billion stimulus package at the beginning of 2008. The 'Bush stimulus' provided tax rebates of $600 to $1,200 to most taxpayers and $300 payments to veterans with disabilities, senior citizens and other low-income groupings. Again, its passage was facilitated because it rested upon tax concessions rather than spending projects.

At the end of the year, the Bush White House had, as it moved towards its final days, little or no bargaining capacity. The political capital of which Bush had boasted after his 2004 re-election victory had long been exhausted. And, the fractures in the Republican Party had been exposed by the vote on the Economic Stabilization Act. Large numbers of Congressional Republicans simply would not countenance further discretionary government expenditure.

A counter-narrative

As the initial shock of the crisis wore off, and as governments rushed to stabilize the banking sector and prop up demand levels, other actors sought to make sense of changed realities. As has been noted, the response among British Conservatives was muted. In contrast, in the US, there was a large-scale rebellion among Congressional Republicans against the Bush administration's 'bailout' of the financial sector. At this stage, although there was uncertainty about the causes of the financial crisis, there was growing conviction that even 'emergency Keynesianism' would do little to bring about a recovery and would simply enlarge the scope of government still further.

The Right's counter-narrative took a more coherent shape and form in the months that followed, although it initially secured much more political traction in the US than the UK. In its early stage, the narrative was built around some of the claims made by Austrian economics and particular representations of the New Deal and the process of economic recovery during the 1930s.

As the fiscal stimulus (the American Recovery and Reinvestment Act) was gaining Congressional momentum at the beginning of 2009, the Cato Institute gathered about two hundred signatures from economists opposed to the Act. The letter was brief but pointedly argued the case against increased government spending. Such spending, it was said, had not, contrary to the assertions that were being made at the time, brought economic recovery in the US during the 1930s or in Japan during the 1990s: 'it is the triumph of hope over experience to believe that more government spending will help the US today' (Cato Institute, 2009). The letter echoed established supply-side themes by calling instead for the removal 'of the impediments to work, saving, investment, and production'. Thus, to restore growth, tax rates should be lowered and the 'burden of government' reduced (Cato Institute, 2009).

The signatories to the open letter constituted a broad front. Within that front, there were, however, different persuasions. Adherents of the Austrian school, or more narrowly those 'paleo-libertarians' who followed the work of Ludwig von Mises and Murray Rothbard, were among the first to stake out their position on the crisis. They were able to draw upon a long-established body of theory, much of which differs significantly from the broad neoclassical approaches that inform the thinking of many others on the free market Right.

From an Austrian perspective, policymakers who are invariably subject to political pressures are often tempted to stimulate and reflate their country's economy. Thus, central banks (once they had been freed from the constraints imposed by the gold standard and began instead issuing fiat currency) may increase the supply of money and reduce interest rates for political rather than market reasons. This, however, sends misleading signals to those with funds and leads to malinvestment as projects and investments that would under free market conditions prove unprofitable, become profitable. Resources are thereby diverted and wasted. This cannot, however, continue indefinitely:

> The recession or depression is the necessary, if unfortunate, correction process by which the malinvestments of the boom period, having at last been brought to light, are finally liquidated, redeployed elsewhere in the economy where they can contribute to producing something consumers actually want. No longer are wealth and goods diverted into unsustainable investments with inadequate demand and insufficient resources. Businesses fail and investment projects are abandoned.
>
> (Woods, 2009: 72)

For Austrian commentators, events and developments during the years preceding the financial crisis were testimony to all of this. Interest rates had been lowered in response to the end of the dot.com boom at the beginning of the new century, giving rise, in particular, to the housing bubble. The federal funds rate (a key benchmark for other rates of interest) had, for example, been reduced to just 1 per cent between June 2003 and June 2004.

The dangers caused by this were then compounded by the 'Greenspan Put'. The Chairman of the Federal Reserve, Alan Greenspan, had pursued a policy of reducing the federal funds rate if and when stock market prices fell significantly. His critics argued that this created a moral hazard and encouraged risk-taking. Put another way, the Greenspan Put seemed to cushion losses. This distorted the architecture of incentives and disincentives and fuelled speculative activity.

Furthermore, the Austrian critique noted, policymakers responded to periods of economic downturn and crises by lowering rates still further below their market rates, thereby laying a basis for further malinvestment and further recessions. From this perspective, therefore, the monetary and fiscal policies pursued by both the Bush and the Obama administrations intensified the economic difficulties.

The Austrian school won a wider audience through the campaigning efforts of Congressman Ron Paul, who served in 1988 as the Libertarian Party's presidential candidate and went on to make bids to secure the Republican presidential nomination in both 2008 and 2012. On finishing third in the Iowa caucuses at the beginning of the 2012 pre-nomination season, Paul proclaimed 'We are all Austrians now.' It was campaign hyperbole but the crisis won Austrian economics greater attention. And Congressman Paul's calls for the legalization of competing currencies, thereby allowing the market to determine which is sound and putting currencies beyond the whims and designs of policymakers and central bankers, secured new supporters.

Nonetheless, the insistence by Austrian economics that its theory of business cycle (which critics suggested failed to take account of the ways in which firms factor in expectations and consider a broad range of variables in making investment decisions, including the long-run consequences of low interest rates) alone explained crises put its adherents, including Congressman Paul, at odds with others on the Right, including many fellow libertarians. Indeed, Paul himself grouped monetarists and supply-siders together with Keynesians. Despite their differences, their ideas led towards government interventionism and they were, furthermore, all 'compromisers':

> Whether Keynesians, supply-siders, or monetarists, there is always an explanation for deficits, taxes, central banks, fiat money, inflation, and all flavors of interventionism ... it's easily seen that it is the compromisers who are rigid, sterile, impractical, ideological, and egotistical in their defense of the very dangerous system of interventionism and inflation.
>
> (Paul, 2004: 14)

Remembering and representing the New Deal

Although at this point there were some frontal assaults upon the prospect of a large-scale stimulus, most notably by 'Austrians', there were also ideational skirmishes around its edges. The frequent invocations of the New Deal during late 2008 opened the way for some of these.

As noted above, the 1930s have long held an important place in the thinking of the centre-Left. Images of public works abound. These accounts generally acknowledge the limits of the policies pursued by the Roosevelt administration. Unemployment remained high until the advent of the Second World War. The 'first' New Deal, which was centred on the National Recovery Administration and price-fixing, failed. Fiscal expansion was too cautious and the recovery was interrupted by a further recession in 1937–38. Nonetheless, the accounts emphasize and often celebrate the economic growth rates that were achieved during much of the decade. As Christina Romer observed, if 1937–38 is excluded from the picture, 'rates of growth are spectacular, even for an economy pulling out of a severe recession' (Romer, quoted in Rauchway, 2010: 68).

Nonetheless, although positive representations of the 1930s were commonplace in late 2008, they did not go unchallenged. In early November 2008, the columnist and a fellow at the Council on Foreign Relations Amity Shlaes drew upon her 2007 book, *The Forgotten Man*, so as to draw a much more critical portrait of the New Deal years. She directly questioned claims that the New Deal had revived the US and challenged its place in popular economic folklore. First, she argued, federal government spending had crowded out the private sector. The Tennessee Valley Authority (TVA), which is often cited in descriptions of the 1930s insofar as from the Left's perspective the TVA provided employment, stimulated the wider economy and, through hydroelectricity, modernized much of the South, had according to Shlaes killed off the efforts of private enterprise to electrify the region. She argues: 'For every state-relief job created, about half a private-sector job was lost' (Shlaes, 2008a). Second, the Roosevelt administration's words and actions created an atmosphere of uncertainty and anxiety that unsettled the markets and further deterred business investment: 'Everyone feared FDR would regulate or prosecute them next. Businesses refused to invest' (Shlaes, 2008a). Third, New Deal spending created dependency as those forms that were beneficiaries of federal largesse were in effect subsidized:

> As soon as FDR stopped doling out the cash (in 1937, after the election) the economy crashed again. The stock market plummeted. Five years into the New Deal, in the winter of 1937–1938, two in 10 were again unemployed.
>
> (Shlaes, 2008a)

In subsequent commentaries, Shlaes expanded her argument and drew upon a broader range of sources. In arguing against fiscal stimulus measures, she invoked

Milton Friedman's permanent-income hypothesis. Those receiving a tax credit or employed through expenditure projects will not necessarily spend the additional income that they gain. Instead, they consider additional income within the context of their expectations of lifetime earnings (Shlaes, 2008b).

Furthermore, Shlaes argued, as states and districts, and those who represented them, sought to secure the federal government funding that was made available when stimulus programmes were launched, there would be more 'earmarking' and bids for 'pork'. Members of Congress would ensure that projects were initiated for electoral rather than economic purposes. Most importantly of all, the Great Society programmes of the 1960s were 'the ultimate Keynesian experiment' (Shlaes, 2008b). And the expansion of government that this entailed created the persistent economic difficulties, not least the 'stagflation' of the 1970s, that the US presidents who followed Lyndon Johnson had to address and confront (Shlaes, 2008b). Shlaes made a further claim. Increases in taxes, the codes established by the National Recovery Administration and the passage of the National Labour Relations Act (often referred to as the Wagner Act), which strengthened the unions, all pushed wages above market rates thereby reducing the numbers that firms would employ. In overall terms, the New Deal thereby increased rather than reduced unemployment (Shlaes, 2008c).[3]

Reconstructing the crisis

In the US, the Austrian critique and the counter-histories of the New Deal paved the way for the construction of a broader and more comprehensive narrative that identified the causes of crisis while at the same time pointing the way towards particular policy solutions.

Developments at the beginning of 2009 were pivotal. Conservative opinion had begun to harden in the wake of Obama's victory at the beginning of November 2008. Governor Sarah Palin's quasi-autonomous campaign for the vice-presidency had hardened and mobilized attitudes on the Right and encouraged doubts about the legitimacy of an Obama presidency.[4] At the same time, Senator John McCain's campaign had also seemed to illustrate the limits and dangers of restraint and moderation. He, like all the Republicans' presidential candidates since the days of Ronald Reagan, had been drawn from the more moderate and less ideological wing of the party.[5] For many on the Right, McCain's defeat at the hands of Obama confirmed (to adapt the words of Senator Barry Goldwater, the Republicans' 1964 presidential candidate) that moderation in defence of virtue was not only a political and moral vice but an electoral misjudgement.

The Congressional debates and the votes on the American Recovery and Reinvestment Act (ARRA), the fiscal stimulus package, within just a few weeks of Obama taking office, began to establish the defining contours of the conservative economic narrative and at the same time gave it a partisan character by tying it together with the Republican Party's sense of political self-identity. That narrative then took a firmer form during 2009 and 2010 (see Chapter 5).

The Obama transition team had decided upon the broad shape and character of a fiscal stimulus package before the president-elect entered the White House. Indeed, it was settled at a meeting of 'Team Obama' on 16 December (Suskind, 2011: 153). Although there was talk at the beginning of December 2008 about a package costing $300–400 billion, the numbers very quickly increased. Christina Romer, incoming head of the Council of Economic Advisers, began by projecting the size of the likely output gap (the difference between actual national output and the economy operating at full capacity) created by the crisis. The gap that had opened up was, she estimated, about $2 trillion in size (Suskind, 2011: 154). Romer argued the case for a stimulus of $1.8 trillion. Such spending would, she argued, eliminate the gap by the first quarter of 2011, thereby restoring full employment: 'To achieve that magnitude of effective stimulus using a feasible combination of spending, taxes and transfers to states and localities would require a package costing about $1.8 trillion over two years' (Romer, quoted in Scheiber, 2011: 27). Romer later compromised and put forward a proposal for a $1.2 trillion package. Despite Peter Orszag's reservations, there was broad agreement on a figure of about $800 billion.

Even though the Democrats had increased their majorities in the 2008 elections and were close to a number in the Senate that could break filibusters if the party hung together, Obama's economic team were instinctively aware of the political dangers posed by higher figures. Larry Summers, former Treasury Secretary who was to become Director of the National Economic Council, reportedly told Romer that 'one point two trillion is nonplanetary' (quoted in Scheiber, 2011: 41). According to the accounts, only lower options ($800 billion and $600 billion) were presented to the President-Elect (Scheiber, 2011: 40).

While the contents and final character of ARRA (which ran to 1,073 pages) depended upon the institutional prerogatives and uncertainties of Congress, the Act took shape during this initial period. It was markedly more ambitious than the stimulus measures adopted in the UK and in most other countries. It was estimated to be equivalent in size (for the 2008–10 period) to 5.6 per cent of 2008 GDP (Organisation for Economic Cooperation and Development, 2009: 110). Its size and scale owe much to the position of the dollar as a reserve currency and, stemming from this, the capacity of the US to undertake measures that would in other nations jeopardize the confidence of the markets and exchange rate stability. Just as the dollar allowed supply-side economics to secure an intellectual and political foothold during the 1980s, laying a basis for the radical tax cuts of 1981 and the running of deficit budgets (whereas the UK, given the more exposed character of the pound, clung to fiscal rectitude), so it permitted the US to take fiscal risks in early 2009. The attitude of many large firms and peak business organizations in the US also stood in marked contrast to that adopted by their counterparts in the UK. And the relative porousness of the US state apparatus gave considerable weight to business opinion.

The package was far less substantial than figures such as Paul Krugman had hoped, and they quickly pressed for the passage of a second stimulus package. They were of course to be disappointed. The figures in ARRA may furthermore have been around the maximum that could have been secured without significant defections in Congress. Certainly, Larry Summers seems to have believed that $1.2 trillion was politically impractical (Scheiber, 2011: 40–41). There were fears, perhaps expressed most strongly by Peter Orszag, incoming director of the Office of Management and Budget (OMB), that yet further fiscal loosening would be seen as too far from the political mainstream: 'There was the concern that we would look wacko Lefty' (quoted in Suskind, 2011: 154).

Nonetheless, although the size and scale of ARRA were regarded as inadequate by some on the Left (given the magnitude of the crisis), it brought Republicans together. The Act divided Congress along partisan lines and it attracted only three Republican votes. (All three were in the Senate and one, Arlen Specter, defected to the Democrats just two months later.[6])

In sum, at this stage, the conservative narrative had four principal features. First, there was a denial that government spending could create jobs in net terms. The argument, a variant on the 'crowding out' thesis, asserted that government spending was simply a transfer rather than the redeployment, as classical Keynesianism suggested, of 'idle balances':

> Every dollar Congress injects *into* the economy must first be taxed or borrowed *out* of the economy. No new purchasing power is created; it is merely transferred from one part of the economy to another ... Removing water from one end of a swimming pool and pouring it in the other end will not raise the overall water level – no matter how large the bucket.
>
> (Riedl, 2010)

A year or so later, these abstract propositions were bolstered through more empirical claims. White House assertions about the number of jobs created by ARRA were, it was said, unreliable and based upon an outdated model. The Act, a Heritage Foundation briefing paper argued, had created a sixth of the jobs that the administration had claimed and these had to be set against all the jobs lost in the recession (Riedl, 2010).

Second, much of the stimulus spending provided funding for welfare programmes and, many on the Right argued, changed the incentive structure facing those who were out of work and reduced the incentive to secure employment. '[W]hat was labeled a 'stimulus' bill was actually a stimulus to government transfer payments – cash and benefits that are primarily rewards for not working, or at least not working too hard' (Reynolds, 2010).

Third, ARRA not only increased the size and scale of government still further but also extended its reach. Thus, government grew still further if measured through spending as a share of GDP, reaching 41.4 per cent in 2009. And, fourth, much of this spending was said to be a form of 'pork'. In other words, spending projects were being placed in particular districts and states so as to assist in securing the re-election of an incumbent member of Congress.

Nonetheless, there were still some ambiguities and uncertainties in the conservative critique. It was unclear whether deficit spending by government had only a limited impact or, in net terms, no impact at all or if there were differences between short-run and long-term effects. Furthermore, at some points the Right seemed to suggest that ARRA was simply excessive and concentrated on the wrong 'targets', while at other points commentators rejected the claim that government spending programmes could bring forth (or even contribute to) economic recovery. Senate Minority Leader Mitch McConnell noted past Democratic assertions that stimulus measures had to be timely, targeted and temporary. He went on to assert: 'This bill fails on all three points' (Sahadi, 2009). However, John Boehner, the House Minority Leader, seemed to be arguing on behalf of his fellow Republicans that government spending projects could not create employment: 'The president made clear when we started this process that this was about jobs ... And what it's turned into is nothing more than spending, spending and more spending' (Herszenhorn, 2009).

Adding to the narrative

Over time, a further element was added to the conservative narrative. Increasingly, some on the Right began to reconsider the causes of the 2008 crisis and challenge the hegemonic account which, at that point, was structured around the uncontrolled character of the banking sector and claims that predatory capitalism had, in the absence of effective regulation, led to a speculative asset bubble. Increasingly, it was said that government interventionism, the lax fiscal stance adopted in earlier years and regulatory policies had caused the crisis. Thus, excessive government spending was preventing or at the least severely impeding the process of economic recovery.[7]

The dramatic rises in housing prices that preceded the crisis had not, it was argued, been caused by weak regulatory controls or speculative avarice but instead by the determination of both the White House and Congress to ensure that the US became more of a 'property-owning democracy':

> The housing bubble that finally burst in 2007 was driven by a U.S. government social policy that was intended to increase home ownership in the United States and was thus not subject to the usual limits on the length and size of asset bubbles.
>
> (Wallison, 2011: 548)

The Reinhart and Rogoff thesis, outlined in a 2010 National Bureau of Economic Research (NBER) working paper, added a further link in the theoretical chain. The paper was a study of forty-four countries over about two hundred years and considered the relationship between levels of government debt and rates of economic growth. In both emerging and advanced economies, 'median growth rates for countries with public debt over 90 percent of GDP are roughly one percent lower than otherwise; average (mean) growth rates are several percent lower' (Reinhart and Rogoff, 2010: 2). Reinhart and Rogoff seemed to suggest that although there were differences between countries depending upon the composition of debt (and, for example, how much of it is short term or long-term) there is a point at which the overall level of debt can lead the markets to lose confidence (Reinhart and Rogoff, 2010: 23).[8]

The Reinhart and Rogoff working paper, *Growth in a Time of Debt*, and its core findings had a significant impact particularly because they 'fitted' the political conclusions that many on the Right were seeking to draw about the size of government and the levels of borrowing that were being incurred as a consequence of the crisis and, to some degree, in both the UK and the US, the spending decisions that had been made during the preceding years. Certainly, it had much more of an impact than is customary for working papers. Paul Krugman noted in *The New York Review of Books*:

> Reinhart-Rogoff may have had more immediate influence on public debate than any previous paper in the history of economics. The 90 percent claim was cited as the decisive argument for austerity by figures ranging from Paul Ryan, the former vice-presidential candidate who chairs the House budget committee, to Olli Rehn, the top economic official at the European Commission, to the editorial board of *The Washington Post*.
>
> (Krugman, 2013)

Adding to this, those who sought to show that government debt had to be reduced made a further interrelated point. The 'austerians' argued the case for 'expansionary fiscal contraction'. In other words, a reduction in the size of government spending or at the least the rate of growth of government spending would create space for private-sector growth. The concept had been in circulation for a long period but was given new impetus by the increase in public spending levels in the wake of the recession and the fears of the Right that these levels would become the new economic normal (Barry and Devereux, 1995).

For many on the Right, the case for expansionary fiscal contraction was to be confirmed by the course of economic events. By 2011, overall US fiscal policy had moved into contractionary territory as ARRA spending was exhausted. If the period between the second quarter of 2009 and the third quarter of 2011 is taken, public spending fell in real terms by about 1.5 per cent. And yet, as Paul Ormerod noted in a posting for the Institute of Economic Affairs in London, the US economy had enjoyed more than two years of growth:

> How can fiscal contraction be expansionary? But the evidence suggests that this is exactly what has been happening in the United States ... Growth has not been as

> strong as would be desirable, but there has been consistent growth. On any measure, the recession is over ... The lessons for Europe are to have a co-ordinated fiscal contraction.
>
> (Ormerod, 2011)

As the calls for expansionary fiscal contraction were further firmed up, some caveats and nuances were introduced. The argument was put in more developed terms. Writing for the Heritage Foundation, Alberto Alesina and Veronique de Rugy drew conclusions from the European experience that were couched in much more cautious terms than Ormerod: 'we find that fiscal adjustments and economic growth are not impossible' (Alesina and de Rugy, 2014). Indeed, they added that 'fiscal adjustments do not always trigger immediate economic growth'. Second, they argued that if governments made such 'adjustments' through tax increases rather than expenditure cuts, 'the likely result would be deep and pronounced recessions, possibly making the fiscal adjustment counterproductive'. Third, Alesina and de Rugy concluded that expansionary fiscal contractions were 'more likely to occur when accompanied by growth-oriented policies, such as liberalizing both labor regulations and markets for goods and services, in addition to a monetary policy that keeps interest rates low' (Alesina and de Rugy, 2014).

Reasons

Why did this economic narrative, structured around the claim that government policy caused the crisis and the process of expansion depended upon a fiscal contraction, win the allegiance of very large parts of the Right and secure endorsement from some beyond its ranks?

In the US, there was of course a close correspondence between these economic claims and the political claims about the moral necessity of limited, 'constitutional' government put forward from early 2009 onwards by the Tea Party movement (see Chapter 5). It might also be argued that although some federal government programmes (such as Social Security) are widely accepted and indeed institutionalized, American political culture still to some degree embraces and incorporates anti-government sentiments. Government, and government spending at least as a generalized proposition, is widely understood in negative terms. It has also been widely noted that the austerity narrative has a commonsense logic that closely corresponds with accepted psychological notions of morality. It therefore commands a popular resonance. Indeed, as Paul Krugman has remarked: 'Everyone loves a morality play. "For the wages of sin is death" is a much more satisfying message than "Shit happens." We all want events to have meaning' (Krugman, 2013). Furthermore, unfolding events in Europe, particularly Greece, where the country's continued membership of the eurozone appeared at times to be seriously in doubt, had an impact. Representations of the Greek experience, which were couched in terms of reckless government spending, corruption, clientelism and false accounting, all seemed to confirm that government actions were the harbinger of economic crisis. Furthermore, the Left had little, if anything, to bring forth as an alternative course of action. Political debate concentrated on the pace and intensity of the process rather than fiscal contraction itself. Inevitably, that implicit endorsement bolstered the legitimacy of the concept.

The process by which austerity and many of the claims put forward by the Right came to govern political discourse was not, however, purely ideational. 'Material' factors also played a role insofar as fiscal contraction, which in both the US and UK was accompanied by a very loose monetary policy structured around quantitative easing. It was a process that created both winners and losers. Savers with funds that were difficult to transfer faced real negative interest rates. Those with funds that could be transferred into share holdings could make significant gains as the stock markets recovered the ground that they had lost in 2008. While many found it difficult to gain an initial foothold because the credit crunch restricted the availability of loans, those who had mortgages or other long-term loans benefited from relatively low rates of interest. Indeed, there were property bubbles that enabled well-placed or fortunate individuals to gain over a relatively short period.

On the other hand, many wage-earners faced a relentless fall in real income. Indeed, the Office of National Statistics in the UK noted that between 2010 and 2013, real wages were 'falling for the longest sustained period since at least 1964' (Taylor *et al.*, 2014: 1). Once retrenchment programmes were under way, the value of many social benefits also fell in real terms. It was, for example, announced that from April 2013, most benefits for those of working age and tax credits would be increased by just 1 per cent per annum, rather less than the projected rate of inflation (Church Urban Fund, 2013).

Arguably, a programme based around fiscal expansion would have created a rather different set of winners and losers, perhaps enabling those at the lower end of the socioeconomic scale to make more gains and presenting fewer opportunities for making speculative gains. Instead, the use of monetary policy created a sufficient number of 'winners', particularly among those with flexible and transferable assets, to bolster perceptions that overall economic gains had been made and that the austerity strategy had proved a success.

Conclusion

This chapter has tracked the emergence of a free market economic narrative from the point at which the crisis first secured significant political visibility. Initially drawing on Austrian economics and representations of the New Deal era, the narrative gave way, during the period in which Congress considered ARRA and as overall government expenditure levels rose as the recession took its toll, to a rounded and more developed narrative that was structured around claims that stimulus spending could not aid the process of recovery, the federal government's pursuit of social objectives and excess spending had triggered the crisis and that recovery required lower deficit and debt levels.

Nonetheless, this chapter has presented a broad and generalized picture spanning both the US and UK. Processes and events took a different form in the two countries. Chapters 5 and 6 track these in greater depth.

Notes

1 Northern Rock was nationalized in mid-February 2008 following the failure of private-sector proposals.

2 See pp. 43–44 for a summary of the path-dependency argument.

3 Although others dismissed Shlaes's arguments as 'New Deal denialism', her principal protagonist was Paul Krugman. In his *New York Times* columns, Krugman rejected the proposition that the Great Society was an example of applied Keynesianism. It was, he asserted, 'social engineering' and, moreover, President Johnson had followed a policy of fiscal contraction (Krugman, 2008).

4 As the book *Game Change* illustrates very effectively, there was considerable distance between the McCain campaign team and Governor Palin (Heilemann and Halperin, 2010).

5 Having said this, 'moderation' is a relative and moveable concept. It should be set against the overall Rightward shift in the political character of Republicanism.

6 Eleven House Democrats also failed to back the Act.

7 The 'austerity' paradigm and the assertion that government debt constituted *the* defining economic problem was, of course, subject to challenge. Critical commentators stressed, for example, that government debt was very small indeed when set against the levels of debt in the financial sector. Furthermore, much of the increase in debt can be attributed to the financial crisis and its aftermath. Put simply, the deficit is from this perspective largely a consequence of the crisis rather than a cause.

8 The Reinhart and Rogoff thesis was subject to considerable criticism. First, there were methodological questions about the data and the ways in which they were interpreted. Second, there was discussion about processes of causality. Arguably, low growth caused high levels of debt rather than the other way round.

5

Rallying around the Gadsden Flag[1]

This chapter considers events and developments from 2009 onwards. It looks at the emergence and growth of the Tea Party movement, the ideas and constituencies upon which it drew, the impact of the 2010 mid-term elections, the tensions between the movement and Republican Party elites, and the character of the relationship between the Right and the institutional landscape. Following the approach adopted in other chapters, it argues that both policy and policy outcomes were largely shaped by processes of interaction between these different elements.

President Barack Obama was inaugurated, as the Twentieth Amendment to the US Constitution requires, on 20 January 2013. According to Robert Draper, just over fifteen Republican members of Congress and a handful of others, including former House of Representatives Speaker Newt Gingrich, met together that evening to consider the strategies they should adopt. There was broad agreement that they would press some of the more vulnerable White House nominees who were put forward to serve in the new administration, including the Treasury Secretary designate, Tim Geithner. None could expect an easy time in the Senate confirmation hearings. They would, it was agreed, present 'united and unyielding opposition' to the incoming administration's economic policies and, in the longer term, work towards regaining the White House in the 2012 presidential election. Gingrich reportedly said: 'You will remember this day. You'll remember this as the day the seeds of 2012 were sown' (quoted in Draper, 2013: xv).[2]

The beginnings of the Tea Party movement

Nonetheless, although the initial stirrings were on Capitol Hill, the locus of political activity quickly shifted to other terrain. The beginnings of the Tea Party movement are usually dated to the period just after the American Recovery and Reinvestment Act (ARRA) was signed into law by President Obama. This was when Rick Santelli's live and celebrated outburst on CNBC took place. From the time of the 'Santelli rant' onwards, references to 'Tea Parties' or the 'Tea Party movement' became increasingly commonplace. Certainly, for Tea Party activists, the 'rant' quickly secured a defining place in the movement's representations of its own history. By invoking Santelli's spontaneous protest the movement could lay claim to authenticity as a grassroots uprising by citizens protesting against the relentless growth of the state and the incessant provision of federal government largesse to the undeserving. Speaking on a live broadcast from the floor of the Chicago Mercantile Exchange, Santelli asked those gathered around him:

> How many of you people want to pay for your neighbor's mortgage who has an extra bathroom and can't pay their bills? ... President Obama, are you listening? ... We're thinking about having a Chicago tea party in July. All of you of capitalists that want to show up to Lake Michigan, I'm going to start organizing it.
>
> (quoted in McCain, 2009)

As 2009 progressed, individual outbursts, local groups and campaigners began to coalesce into a recognizable movement. Established conservative networks such as Americans for Prosperity, which commanded very significant resources, played a pivotal role in structuring and to some degree professionalizing the movement. The open meetings called by members of Congress during the summer served as a focus for publicizing different initiatives and bringing together hitherto separate efforts (see below).

Actors, representations and frames

Many accounts of conservative opposition to the Obama administration and growth of the Tea Party movement are, as in the movement's own accounts of its origins, structured around actors and agency.

Indeed, the movement's self-representations and the intersubjective meanings around which it was constructed rested on notions of a citizenry reclaiming its rights from oppressive and tyrannical government. Its use of the Gadsden flag (depicting a coiled but ready rattlesnake and the words 'don't tread on me') in rallies, in leaflets and on websites is significant. They drew upon depictions of a bloated governing elite as well as representations of a popular uprising and a citizenry reclaiming its natural rights. Their use of the term 'tea party' is usually understood as an allusion to the Boston Tea Party of 1773, so often celebrated as the beginning of the American colonies' rebellion against a tyrannical government. These representations were tied to more contemporary populist themes. There were, in other words, processes of cultural *bricolage*, whereby old elements are recombined and mixed together with new elements.[3]

The movement's thinking can be understood in terms of Robert Benford and David Snow's threefold categorization of the collective action frames deployed by social movements (Benford and Snow, 2000: 615).[4] The diagnostic frame around which the Tea Party movement took shape was structured around bloated or 'big government' that, it was said, not only posed a threat to the liberty of the citizen but also, through 'crowding out' displaced private sector economic activity, impeded recovery from the recession.[5] The movement's motivational frame (which by definition draws together the reasons to participate in collective action) was built on the seeming weakness and vulnerability of the Obama administration and Congressional Democrats as well as the openness of Republican Party structures to change through, for example, state- and local-level party conventions and primaries. The projected outcome (the prognostic frame) lay in the use of institutional and, more importantly, extra-institutional resistance to the measures being pursued by the Obama administration, most notably its pursuit of healthcare reform.

Such constructions gained credence and traction in January 2010 when Scott Brown won the special Senate election held in Massachusetts following Edward Kennedy's death. The Massachusetts election had a twofold significance. First, the Republicans won through, it was said, the movement's campaigning efforts in a state that had traditionally been solidly Democratic political territory. Second, Brown's victory denied the Democrats a filibuster-proof, sixty-seat majority in the Senate, thereby making the passage of legislation from then onwards very difficult indeed.

Frames must, however, secure adherents and legitimacy if they are to serve as the basis for a social movement. William Gamson has argued that if a frame is to gain adherents and motivate political action, it must incorporate a sense of injustice, identity and agency (Gamson, 1992: 31–109). Each is evident in the Tea Party movement's perceptions and discourses.

There was, first, a profound sense of political, economic and cultural injustice and dispossession. This drew upon the belief that there had been a process of political usurpation as the federal government secured powers that went far beyond its constitutional prerogatives. At times, these notions of usurpation edged towards conspiracy theories and a belief that, for example, hidden government (or United Nations) agencies were transforming the US and liquidating the country's sovereignty. Both Congressman Ron Paul and his son, Rand Paul, who was elected to the US Senate in November 2010, made claims that a NAFTA 'superhighway' was being constructed so as to bring forth a single American–Mexican state (Taibbi, 2010).

These fears of usurpation and loss of sovereignty overlapped with hostility towards the 'new class' that had, from this perspective, captured the machinery of government. In some accounts, it was described as the 'political class'. At times, there was a populist scepticism towards expertise itself (Skocpol and Williamson, 2012: 52–54).[6]

All of this had echoes and resonances. It tapped the anti-intellectualism that, as Richard Hofstadter noted in his 1964 book, informed many movements and was once tied to both evangelical faith and anti-urbanity (Hofstadter, 1996, orig. 1964).[7] The movement's understanding of the 'new class' was also allied, albeit perhaps unconsciously, with the concepts associated with public choice theory insofar as the movement's critiques often incorporated the idea of government expansion and aggrandizement by self-serving bureaucrats and politicians.

Alongside the deep sense of loss and usurpation, there are also *producerist* elements in the movement's thinking: 'The producerist storyline claims that heroic 'productive' middle-class stalwarts are defending themselves against the squeezing vise grip of corrupt parasitic elites above and lazy, sinful and subversive parasites below' (Berlet, 2012: 568).[8] Theda Skocpol and Vanessa Williamson talk in similar terms by referring to the movement's representations of 'workers versus freeloaders' (Skocpol and Williamson, 2012: 64–68). Non-producers (or 'freeloaders') include elites (such as those who are highly educated and, in some accounts, finance capital) as well as those at the lowest end of the socioeconomic scale who were often seen as an 'underclass' or purposively unproductive.

Producerism, in other words the drawing of a structural distinction between producers and non-producers, thus informed the movement's perceptions of federal and state government programmes. As a consequence, despite its defining commitment to 'small government', there is a significant degree of support for, or at least acquiescence in, government programmes that appear to benefit those who are productive and therefore in some senses 'deserving'. In contrast, provision given to non-producers is regarded as far less legitimate:

> Tea Partiers are not monolithically hostile toward government; they distinguish between programs perceived as going to hard-working contributors to US society like themselves and 'handouts' perceived as going to unworthy or freeloading people.
>
> (Williamson *et al.*, 2011)

At times such sentiments intersected with racial discourses. As a group, the poor and those dependent upon 'welfare' (particularly in representations of the 'underclass') includes disproportionate numbers drawn from the ethnic and racial minorities. Thus, dislike of welfare went hand-in-hand with attitudes towards minorities and a sense that white America was in some way under siege. In the 2010 *New York Times* and CBS News survey, 25 per cent of Tea Party respondents said that the Obama administration 'favored blacks over whites' (compared with 11 per cent of the general population) (*The New York Times*/CBS News, 2010: 24). Significantly, rather higher numbers of Tea Party supporters (82 per cent) saw illegal immigration as a 'very serious' problem (compared to 60 per cent of the general population) (Skocpol and Williamson, 2012: 57). There is also evidence that disproportionate numbers in the movement think in terms of negative racially based stereotypes. Some 68 per cent of Tea Party whites agreed with the statement that 'if Blacks would just try harder they would be as well off as Whites', while only 35 per cent of non-Tea Party whites agreed (Zeskind, 2011: 502).

Furthermore, very significant numbers within the movement embraced 'Birtherism', the racially tinged belief that President Obama was not born in the US and therefore was not constitutionally eligible to serve as president. An April 2011 poll found that 45 per cent of Tea Party supporters believed that Obama was born in another country. Indeed, only 34 per cent accepted that the president had been born in the US (Condon, 2011).

There were further ideational overlaps and intersects. Although the movement has sometimes been represented as a repudiation of the Christian Right and a turn towards economic rather than moral issues, there was a significant degree of borrowing from the narratives and discourses that defined contemporary religious conservatism. Indeed, the Tea Party movement's embrace of 'constitutional government' was, perhaps paradoxically, allied with the belief that the state had a part to play in upholding the principles underpinning a 'Christian nation'. This was affirmed as a generalized principle, and when particular moral and cultural issues came to the fore, 63 per cent of movement respondents in the 2010 Public Religion Research Institute study said that abortion should be illegal in all or most cases and just 18 per cent supported same-sex marriage (Jones and Cox, 2010: 4).[9]

The movement's perceptions and understandings of its own identity were also structured by gender. While disproportionate numbers of Tea Party supporters endorsed positions, including an attachment to the traditional family and notions of wives as 'caretakers', associated with social conservatism and the Christian Right, and those who declared in response to pollsters that they were Tea Party supporters were more male than female, women were rather more heavily represented in the ranks of committed activists. As in many other forms of civic activism, women were 'disproportionately active in running the Tea Party ground game' (Skocpol and Williamson, 2012: 43).

Women were not, however, only grassroots activists. Former Alaska governor Sarah Palin, the Republicans' vice-presidential candidate in 2008, was a political lodestar for many. Indeed, she remained such until announcing in October 2011 that she would not contest the 2012 presidential election. Congresswoman Michele Bachmann, who represented Minnesota's sixth district, was a prominent figure within the movement and mounted a bid for the Republican presidential nomination until withdrawing at the beginning of 2012.

Nonetheless, the women who were defined and often defined themselves as 'Mama Grizzlies' were in an ambiguous position. Data suggested that grassroots Republican voters were significantly less likely to support a woman candidate in the party's primaries. Indeed, a 2003 study found that there was a 13.6 per cent drop in support among male Republican voters if the candidate was female. Among Republican women voters, the drop was smaller but still 'quite powerful' (cited in Schreiber, 2012: 553). This may have been because of straightforward prejudice, a belief (particularly among social conservatives) that mothers should be at home with young children, or an assumption that women will hold more liberal positions than men.[10]

Against this background, it may be that Tea Party and Republican women, particularly those who are seeking public office, had to assert their conservative credentials and opposition to 'big government' more vigorously and in a more abrasive way than men. At one and the same time, figures such as Palin and Bachmann highlighted and celebrated their role as mothers but also rejoiced in their muscular capacities, abilities in fending for themselves and their fighting strengths.

The political and personal abrasiveness that Tea Party women were compelled to employ when projecting themselves made them movement favourites. However, at the same time, that abrasiveness limited their broader electoral appeal. In the November 2010 mid-term elections, Sharon Angle and Christine O'Donnell, Tea Partiers who were the Republicans' Senate candidates in Nevada and Delaware respectively, secured enthusiastic backing within the movement but went down to defeat in the general election. Both had a long record of injudicious statements that secured acclaim within the movement but were used in the general election to discredit them and cast significant doubts upon their credibility within the political arena.

Perceptions and the American state

Perceptions, beliefs and understandings such as these are not, however, free-floating. They are informed, shaped and structured by particular institutional settings. The beliefs and perceptions of Tea Party activists and supporters were shaped, in particular, by the defining characteristics of the American state. Those characteristics informed the ways in which many, particularly those on the Right, perceived and understood processes of governance and the nature of social provision and regulation.

Those characteristics require explanation. Drawing upon the literature associated with American Political Development (APD), Lawrence Jacobs and Desmond King contrast the sprawling character of the American state apparatus with the state forms customarily found in the countries of Europe (Jacobs and King, 2009: 6). The latter, they argue, are much closer in terms of their structural character to the Weberian ideal. Seen in this way, the European states are staffed by professionalized bureaucracies that are organized on rational and hierarchical lines and there is a relatively clear dividing line between the state and civil society. That line has, of course, been blurred in recent decades as the state in many countries, most notably the UK, has been 'hollowed out' through the dispersion of services and processes of competitive tendering. Nonetheless, there is still a discernible line and the concepts of 'the state' and 'civil society' retain their analytical legitimacy.

In the US, the demarcation lines between the state and civil society are blurred and indistinct.[11] This is only too evident if the housing market is considered. The state has long been involved in shaping a structuring the market through tax concessions, efforts to maintain low interest rates so as to promote a property-owning democracy and the securitization efforts of government-sponsored enterprises such as Fannie Mae and Freddie Mac. Healthcare provision tells much the same story. Long before the 2010 Affordable Care Act was passed, the state was heavily involved not only through Medicare and Medicaid but also through tax credits (sometimes dubbed 'tax expenditures') and different state programmes. Some commentators have therefore talked in terms of a dispersion of 'stateness'. Others refer to the American 'welfare state' but stress that in contrast with systems that rest upon direct assistance through government programmes, it relies in significant part upon indirect provision through tax credits or through private providers alongside some direct delivery systems.

The dispersed and fragmented character of the state and the indirect character of state provision hide and obscure both the sheer size of the state and the extent to which it is interventionist. Christopher Howard refers to both the 'hidden welfare state' and 'the welfare state nobody knows' (Howard, 1997, 2007):

> In short, the American welfare state may be unusual, but less for its small size than for its reliance on a wide variety of policy tools to achieve what many European welfare states do primarily through social insurance ... we should be highly suspicious of anyone who declares that the United States has a small welfare state.
>
> (Howard, 2007: 19)

In a similar vein, Suzanne Mettler invokes the 'submerged' state (Mettler, 2011). Kimberley Morgan and Andrea Louise Campbell refer to 'the delegated welfare state' (Morgan and Campbell, 2011). In particular, whereas some of the programmes that provide assistance for those facing the most serious forms of disadvantage take a direct form (such as food stamps or Medicaid), those that benefit higher-income groupings generally rest upon 'tax expenditures' and are as a consequence far less obvious. In many cases, they are not perceived and understood as 'benefits' or a form of government provision.

Degrees of visibility and invisibility are not, of course, fixed. Indeed, they fluctuate. Critically, the policies pursued by the Obama administration and the 111th Congress and the ways in which they were framed by opponents heightened the visibility of those forms of provision that were provided directly and openly by the federal government. This, *ceteris paribus*, pulled attention from the less visible forms of provision, most notably tax expenditures, thereby rendering them still less visible. Whereas many supporters of the Tea Party movement gained from and acquiesced in the less visible and indirect government programmes (whether they were tax expenditures or those such as Medicare and Social Security that were widely perceived to be largely detached from government), they were viscerally hostile to the more direct and highly visible programmes that were directed at the lower end of the economic scale.

Constituencies

Movements can also be assessed in terms of the groupings and constituencies upon which they draw. Despite the extensive press coverage that some Tea Party women secured, the movement, like much of the grassroots Right more broadly, rested disproportionately upon white males. Many had above-average incomes. The movement's ranks were furthermore disproportionately drawn from the older age cohorts. In April 2010, a poll found that just 7 per cent of Tea Party supporters were in the 18–29 age bracket. Some 75 per cent were aged between 45 and 64, and 29 per cent aged over 64 (*The New York Times*/CBS News, 2010: 41). The *New York Times* concluded: 'The 18 percent of Americans who identify themselves as Tea Party supporters tend to be Republican, white, male, married and older than 45' (Zernike and Thee-Brenan, 2010).

The growth of the movement can in part be explained by considering the impact of political, economic and cultural changes upon those constituencies that were disproportionately represented in its ranks. Many of the policies pursued between 2009 and 2011 by the White House, Congress and the Federal Reserve seemed likely to adversely affect the perceived interests of these constituencies. They feared both relative and absolute losses. Those losses that were relative seemed to pit these groupings and constituencies against other groupings and constituencies that were largely regarded as, in one way or another, less deserving competitors.

Thus, the holding of interest rates at a minimal level that was negative in real terms redistributed wealth from savers, who tended to be older and in higher-income groupings, to borrowers who tended to be younger and in middle- or lower-income groupings. The American Recovery and Reinvestment Act (ARRA) of February 2009 incorporated extensive tax concessions (amounting, depending on the form of calculation used, to between 28 per cent and 36 per cent of the total), but because these were largely phased over time (so as to encourage recipients to spend rather than save the additional income, which might happen if they suddenly received a fairly large sum) they inevitably lacked visibility. The spending components that appeared to benefit lower socioeconomic groupings, including the unemployed, through, for example, the provision of employment (on 'make work' projects) had far greater visibility. There were also claims that whereas the recession had adversely hit male workers (leading some conservative commentators to call it a 'mancession'), women gained rather more than men from ARRA (Perry, 2010).

The Affordable Care Act also seemed to create winners and losers. Healthcare reform was structured around the extension of insurance coverage to lower-income groupings (who were disproportionately drawn from the minorities) and inevitably appeared to increase the demand for medical services while doing little or nothing to affect the supply. In simple terms, if more were insured or enrolled in Medicaid (and assuming supply remains loosely constant) doctors would be compelled to meet the needs of significantly more patients. In other words, there were fears among seniors that Medicare would be 'diluted' if health provision was extended (through 'Obamacare') to other groupings (Saad, 2010).

Some within the American Right already saw themselves as losers long before the onset of the 'Great Recession'. Although relatively few mid-century white men had the ability to serve as the sole breadwinner, they progressively lost out in relative terms during the decades that followed as women and minority applicants increasingly secured more senior employment positions. Indeed, traditional male occupations faced a cycle of decline as foreign competitors gained more and more of a foothold. At the same time, the new industries that emerged, most obviously in information technology, appeared to offer remuneration (at very high rates) only to those who were young and in many instances seemed to be products of the counterculture. Repeatedly, middle, male America appeared to lose out.

Thomas Frank's 2004 book, *What's the Matter with Kansas? How Conservatives Won the Heart of America*, which attributed the defection of male, manual workers to the Republicans to the pervasive influence of moral issues such as abortion and homosexuality and the Democrats' associations with cultural liberalism, has been subject to criticism (Bartels, 2006). Nonetheless, while the electoral impact of abortion may have been relatively limited, gay rights, the prospect of same-sex marriage and a broader, more generalized sense of cultural decay do appear to have added still more to the anger of the 'angry white man', and that anger certainly had associations with long-run economic shifts and the ways in which they undermined traditional representations of male work and the man's relationship with his family.

There were other cleavages. Skocpol and Williamson have pointed to the divide between generations. While the 'baby boomers' gained much from rising property prices and the long post-war economic boom, there were mixed feelings towards the young. Indeed, they suggest that the Tea Party movement rested in part on concerns that younger people were to some degree also workshy: 'young people feature prominently in the stories Tea Partiers tell about undeserving freeloaders, and anecdotes about people in their own families sometimes stand in for larger generational tensions' (Skocpol and Williamson, 2012: 72). Arguably, such sentiments are tied to the growing numbers of young people who live at home or remain financially dependent upon their parents (Shah, 2013).

Institutional architecture

As has been noted, the deliberations of actors, ideas, and constituencies all interact with each other and the institutional features of the settings within which they are located. The ways in which the defining characteristics of the American state informed and moulded Tea Party ideas were noted above. And, as Chapter 4 argued, broader institutional structures shaped the different political strategies that were adopted in the UK and the US. In providing opportunities while closing off others, those structures led conservative activists in the US towards approaches and campaigns based upon efforts to change the character of the Republican Party and the political complexion of those who held public office in the party's name.

In recent years, the impact of 'old', formal institutions upon political processes has been overshadowed in accounts and studies by the new institutionalism's focus upon policy legacies and rules. Nonetheless, despite this shift in focus, 'old institutionalism', which concentrates on formal structures and arrangements, has a significant part to play in explaining the development and character of the Tea Party movement.

The open and porous character of the party system (as well as the often empty character of the Republican Party at precinct level) offers opportunities to outsiders and quasi-outsiders that are not conceivable in the relatively closed and structured European parties. During 2010 in particular, the system of primary contests to decide upon election candidates allowed activists to mobilize and put forward alternative candidates to those seen as too closely allied with the Republican 'establishment'. The fragmentation of authority and the multiple loci of the policymaking processes within the executive, legislative and judicial branches of government invite and encourage those opposed to a measure to repeatedly harry its passage and enactment. There is rarely, if ever, a point at which a reform is settled and agreed beyond dispute. Often, because of this, the rules surrounding policy debates are far from certain:

> American politics are often and rightly described as conflictual. But the conflict is of a certain kind: not a prize fight, but a bar fight – a fracas with no real bounds on who can participate, no rules regarding tactics or weaponry, and no settled end point. Just when it seems quiet, it starts up again in the alleyways outside, pulling in new combatants with new energies.
>
> (Rudalevige, 2011: 21)

At times, the vagaries and uncertainties of contingency gave the movement further traction, although they could only do so within particular institutional settings and logics. The sense of distance between lawmakers and their constituents and widespread disdain for 'Beltway' politics led many members of Congress to convene 'townhall' meetings in their districts and states during the summer months of 2009. Members of the public were invited to attend so as to question their congressman or senator. These gatherings became a rallying point for those opposed to the Democrats' reform programme (in particular healthcare reform) and accelerated the growth of the movement. Six months later, the special election in Massachusetts for Ted Kennedy's US Senate seat not only allowed the movement to campaign among a mass electorate but, through Scott Brown's victory, denied the Democrats a filibuster-proof majority in the Senate and placed the entire reform process in very serious jeopardy. The Affordable Care Act only secured legislative passage through the use of the reconciliation process that allowed the House of Representatives to pass the version of the bill passed earlier by the Senate, although it continued to remain under legislative assault and was vulnerable to judicial challenges. The primary season and the Republicans' subsequent general election victories in 2010 and again in 2012 (despite Mitt Romney's eventual capture of the nomination) allowed Tea Party supporters to mobilize and organize. They also set the stage for the ensuing battles between Congressional Republicans and the administration, including the federal government shutdown of October 2013.

The Ryan Plan

The book has sought to show how outcomes are shaped through the processes of interaction between those levels or tiers described in the different literatures outlined in the Introduction. In particular, there have been tensions between the constituencies that came together in the Tea Party movement, the Republican elites (particularly those in Congress), the sometimes ambiguous logic of neoliberalism that periodically found expression in the policy positions adopted by corporate interests, and the highly cluttered institutional landscape that characterizes US politics.

Policy and strategies emerge from the stresses between these levels and the different ways in which actors seek to navigate, manage and at times circumvent them. All this is evident in the character of both the policy proposals put forward by leading Republicans during the recession years and some think tank reports. They constituted efforts at *brokerage* between contending forces.[12]

Congressman Paul Ryan, who became Chairman of the House Budget Committee in January 2011 and served as Mitt Romney's vice-presidential running mate in the November 2012 election, established himself as a principal Republican strategist. He played a significant part in drafting the Republicans' budget proposals for Fiscal Years 2012 and 2013, both of which were entitled as variations on *The Path to Prosperity*. The budget resolutions were duly dubbed the 'Ryan Plan'.

Although it became a target for repeated Democratic attacks, the Plan struck an ideationally cautious note if considered against the character of the American Right at the point when it was published. Ryan employed frames associated with *layering*, insofar as the Plan represented the policy proposals that it put forward as a way of protecting and extending an existing policy legacy. Rather than invoking the constitutional claims made by the Tea Party movement, the Plan instead focused on Medicare provision for senior citizens (as well as Social Security) and attempted to claim the mantle of President Lyndon Johnson's 'Great Society'. The adoption of the Plan would, it was argued, ensure that seniors would be guaranteed, as Johnson had pledged, 'the healing miracle of modern medicine' while at the same time their families would not have to make excessive contributions to finance this. Thus: 'To fulfill Johnson's pledge in the 21st century, America's generations-old health and retirement security programs must be saved and strengthened' (House Budget Committee, 2012: 7). The Plan also co-opted a slogan customarily associated with the Left (and some libertarians) by calling for an end to 'corporate welfare'. It attacked subsidies to the energy sector, the practice by which government picked 'winners' and 'losers', political favouritism and 'taxpayer bailouts' (House Budget Committee, 2012: 12).

At the same time, however, there were pledges to repeal the Affordable Care Act and reconsider the Dodd–Frank reform of the financial sector. The budget proposals also devolved responsibility for 'public assistance' programmes to the individual states (so that Medicaid would be funded through block grants) and imposed budget cuts. The overall effect, the Plan asserted, would reduce federal government spending 'from its current elevated level of 24 percent of the economy to 20 percent by 2015' (House Budget Committee, 2012: 75). This was tied to steps that would put the budget 'on path to balance' (House Budget Committee, 2012: 5). Indeed, the federal government budget deficit would, the Plan promised, be reduced to below 3 per cent of GDP by 2015.

There was an inevitable commitment not to raise taxes and this was linked to tax reform proposals. The corporate tax rate was to be reduced to 25 per cent. The personal income tax system would be consolidated and rationalized so that there were only two brackets of 10 and 25 per cent. The Alternative Minimum Tax was to be repealed. Alongside this, however, despite the focus on tax rates, there was a parallel commitment to broaden the tax base so as 'to maintain revenue growth at a level consistent with current tax policy and at a share of the economy consistent with historical norms of 18 to 19 percent in the following decades' (House Budget Committee, 2012: 66).

Medicare, the system of health provision for seniors, was to be reformed so that it would become, in effect, a voucher scheme. While the current system would remain in place for those approaching retirement, younger age cohorts would be allowed to choose between different and competing private coverage options. In other words, there would be a process of market liberalization. In a deliberate echo of the Affordable Care Act that incensed many on the Left, there were to be exchanges thereby facilitating the process of choice by those who were enrolled and subsidies for those facing financial hardship or in significant medical need. All of this would, it was promised, constrain the spiralling growth of Medicare costs that had such significant repercussions for the overall federal budget: 'The competitive market for Medicare choices would foster innovation and quality, while ensuring that the program is financially stable' (House Budget Committee, 2012: 53).

The Ryan Plan was inevitably subject to extensive criticism. Questions were asked about the basis for tax revenue projections and where the projected cuts in discretionary spending would be made. It was, Paul Krugman charged, only 'a set of assertions' (Krugman, 2012).

Nonetheless, it was, as noted above, an ambitious form of brokerage between the demands posed by the Tea Party movement and those seeking a return to 'constitutional government', corporate interests and anxieties of broader constituencies about the future of long-embedded programmes such as Social Security and Medicare, and the institutional landscape that imposed countless veto points and opportunities on those promoting radical reform. So as to do this, the Plan rested upon *layering*, *conversion* and *drift* rather than frontal assaults upon structures of the contemporary American state.[13] Medicare reform was framed as a way of strengthening the legacy of the Great Society. Direct cuts would be limited but government expenditure levels would fail to match either inflation rates or the projected increase in population.

The Tea Party movement: a scorecard

Despite the élan of the Tea Party movement particularly during 2009 and 2010 and the Republicans' success in winning back the House of Representatives at the end of 2010, there were also very significant losses.

Although frayed at the edges, all three major reforms enacted by the 111th Congress (ARRA, the Affordable Care Act and the Dodd–Frank Wall Street Reform and Consumer Protection Act) survived sustained legislative and judicial challenges. Furthermore, whereas both the Tea Party movement and the Republican 'establishment' had sought President Obama's eviction from the White House, he won re-election. After the internecine battles of the 2012 presidential primary season, former Massachusetts governor Mitt Romney emerged as the victor. However, he never secured the enthusiasm or the undivided loyalty of party supporters and was always seen as a relatively weak nominee. There were, nonetheless, hopes shared by much of the Right, and expressed most vocally by some *Fox News* contributors, that the coalitional bloc that had secured Obama's victory in 2008 could not be sustained. In particular, there were forecasts that turnout among the younger age cohorts and minorities would be lower in 2012, thereby enabling Romney to seize the White House. In the end, of course, and although Obama's margin of victory was smaller than in 2008, the judgements made by conservative pundits were shown to be mistaken. At the same time, the Senate remained in Democratic hands. Indeed, the party made a net gain of two seats.

And the repeated clashes between the Obama White House and Congressional Republicans, once they had regained the House, seemed to end either in a draw or in defeat for Republicans. The first of these clashes and the flashpoint for later battles took place around the Continuing Resolutions (CRs) necessary, in the absence of a formally agreed federal government budget, to maintain government operations. The Republicans' Congressional leadership resisted protests from Tea Party groups and conservative advocacy organizations such as the Club for Growth who hoped to make the passage of CRs conditional upon the inclusion of steps to remove budgetary provision from Obamacare and 'defund the Left' by withdrawing financial aid from Planned Parenthood and public broadcasting. Representative Michele Bachmann posed these as issues that divided those in Congress who sided with the Tea Party movement from the Republican 'establishment': 'If a member votes for the continuing resolution, that vote effectively says, I am choosing not to fight' (quoted in Weigel, 2011). Nonetheless, despite these words, only limited numbers of Congressional Republicans were ready, at this point, to defy the leadership or provoke a political crisis.

The second clash was structured around the federal government debt ceiling, the total borrowing that could if necessary be incurred. Although the ceiling had long had the potential to secure political traction, if only because the budget deficit itself had emerged as a pivotal political issue during the 1980s and 1990s and drove Ross Perot's independent campaign for the presidency in 1992, it only intermittently came to the fore. Indeed, although the Congressional Republicans had threatened not to raise the ceiling in their fights with President Clinton during the mid-1990s, it had often been regarded as only an administrative or technical issue rather than a political weapon. There was a broad understanding that even the rhetorical threat of a US government default (because in the absence of a debt ceiling increase it might no longer be able meet all its obligations) could well cause very severe repercussions in the financial markets.

By 2011, however, once the issue had been amplified by Tea Party organizations and conservative news outlets, the debt ceiling had been reframed as a defining political question. It stood as a cipher for the expansion of the federal government and its unending profligacy. It chimed with commonsense notions of individual or household borrowing and the old adage that a debt crisis cannot be resolved by incurring yet more debt. Tea Party activists quickly made the ceiling a defining principle and insisted that there should be no increase. An observer at a February 2011 meeting involving Congressional Republicans and Tea Party representatives recalled:

> The marching orders were ... you must not, under any circumstances, vote for an increase in the debt ceiling. Period. No conditions ... the debt ceiling was going to be a lot more trouble than anyone realized. They did not want a negotiation there. There was a religious-like fervor on that point: Voting for the debt ceiling was a sin, and you can't just sin a little.
>
> (quoted in Klein, 2011)

Nonetheless, in place of a simple refusal to agree to the increase in the debt ceiling, the Republican leadership in Congress again adopted a more restrained approach as a basis for negotiations between the parties and with the White House. They linked an increase in the ceiling to the imposition of budget cuts. On 31 July, two days prior to the point at which the existing ceiling might be exceeded and amidst forecasts of dire consequences for the nation's credit worthiness and claims that the White House might resort to extraordinary measures by, for example, invoking the Fourteenth Amendment (which, for some, rendered the debt ceiling unconstitutional), an agreement was reached.

The Republicans made gains from the episode. The debt limit was to be increased but there were, in exchange, cuts of $917 billion over ten years. Nonetheless, the Budget Control Act of 2011, which was passed on the basis of the compromise, can be considered a draw. Agreement beyond the initial tranche of cuts was deferred and delegated by creating a bipartisan Congressional Joint Select Committee (dubbed a 'supercommittee') that would consider different options and on the basis of these propose debt reduction measures by 23 November. To avoid charges from both sides that the compromise was simply postponing tough decisions and 'kicking the can down the road', the plan incorporated what was regarded at the time as a deterrent mechanism. Indeed, comparisons were drawn with the 'doomsday machine' that brought the world to a close in Stanley Kubrick's 1964 film, *Dr Strangelove*. If Congress was unable or unwilling to pass a deficit reduction bill including at least $1.2 billion in cuts, there would be a process of 'sequestration' whereby cuts were 'automatically' made in equal proportions to the federal government's defence and non-defence programmes stretching between 2013 and 2021. Some areas of spending were exempted. Although Medicare would be subject to cuts, both Social Security and Medicaid were protected. Sixty-six Republicans felt that it conceded too much and voted against. However, the proposal gained the backing of 174.

The formula would, it was argued, compel lawmakers to agree upon fiscal retrenchment measures so that the automatic sequestration mechanisms did not come into play. Republicans would be spurred on by their anxieties about the prospect of cuts to defence budgets. By the same token, Democrats would fear cuts to domestic programmes. Under the terms of the formula, the cuts would be across-the-board and would hit programmes favoured by lawmakers as well as those to which they were much less committed. Republican and Democratic members of Congress would thus be compelled to compromise and agree upon an ordered and balanced programme of deficit reduction measures.

The third clash came at the end of 2012 during the 'lame duck' session of Congress that falls between the early November elections and the beginning of January when the new members take their seats and a further Congress begins proceedings. At this point, the 'Bush' tax cuts enacted in 2001 were set to expire. Both the Obama administration and Congressional Democrats were committed to ensuring that the cuts were renewed for couples earning under $250,000 per annum and individuals earning $200,000 (amounting, it was said, to about 98 per cent of the American population) but reimposed on those earning above that threshold. It was one of the relatively few Left populist policy positions that had a totemic value in bolstering Democratic Party identification. By making a gesture towards more progressive forms of taxation and their redistributory effects, Democrats could not only distinguish themselves from the Republicans but also reassure core constituencies that they remained, albeit loosely, associated with a loosely progressive form of politics.

For the Tea Party movement and many Republicans, the prospect of a de facto tax increase raised a point of principle. The movement had been formed on the basis of claims that the tax burden was already such that it threatened both liberty and growth. Although there were tactical drawbacks in seemingly defending low rates of taxation on the highest-income groupings, both the party in Congress and the wider conservative movement had coalesced and defined its political identity around opposition to tax increases.[14]

In the absence of legislation, the US faced a 'fiscal cliff' insofar as the tax rises and scheduled expenditure cuts would have significant deflationary consequences. (There were, however, those who argued that the staggered impact of the changes constituted much less of a drama and a process more akin to a 'fiscal escalator'.) Barring agreement between Congress and the White House, the Bush tax cuts were set to expire (for all income groupings) on 31 December 2011 together with temporary payroll tax cuts and some business tax concessions. There would also be shifts in the Alternative Minimum Tax, adversely affecting significant numbers. At the same time, budget cuts totalling about $1.2 trillion and affecting more than a thousand programmes, agreed upon as part of the 2011 Budget Control Act, would come into effect. This would, it was said, at least among those who described all of this as a 'cliff', cause a dramatic drop in the already frail and tenuous growth rates. According to the Congressional Budget Office, if the US fell off the 'cliff', real (inflation-adjusted) GDP would fall by 0.5 per cent and unemployment would rise to 9.1 per cent by the last three months of 2013 (Congressional Budget Office, 2012: 1).

In the event, the US did not, of course, fall off the 'fiscal cliff'. The eleventh-hour agreement between Congressional Republicans and the White House provided a respite from crisis. It was, however, only temporary and thereby set the stage for a fourth clash.

Amidst all of this, and despite the hopes that accompanied the creation of a 'supercommittee', the inability of Congress to agree upon long-run measures to reduce the government deficit became only too evident. Thus, although designed as a deterrent mechanism that would ensure a bipartisan compromise, the budget sequestration process came into operation at the beginning of March 2013. There were significant exemptions but defence and non-defence spending were affected in equal proportions. About $1.1 trillion was to be cut from projected levels of spending over the period from 2013 to 2021. Forecasts about its overall economic impact varied depending upon the estimated value of the multiplier, but were generally between 0.5 and 1 per cent (Boesler, 2013). With hindsight, there were reasons why efforts to forge a compromise failed and the 'supercommittee' was relegated to the political sidelines. Although it had been designed as a threat to bring forth a bipartisan compromise, there were political advantages for both sides in allowing the sequester to take its course. Sequestration reduced deficit and debt levels while allowing both Democrats and Republicans to attribute fault to their opponents. Neither had to take responsibility or answer to their constituencies.

By early autumn, partisan tensions had again risen. There were three principal reasons for this. First, many Republicans remained committed to unwinding and unravelling the Affordable Care Act ('Obamacare') and were seeking out any and every political opportunity to do so. Second, the passage of a federal government budget or continuing resolutions necessary to maintain government operations had to be passed by 1 October. In other words, a deadline was approaching. Third, in mid-October, as debt had risen and some forms of debt had 'retired', the federal government again needed to raise the 'debt ceiling' (which had been set at $16.7 trillion). Under pressure from Tea Party supporters, the House Republicans decided that they would only agree to the continued funding of government if the Democrats consented to a one-year delay in the imposition of healthcare reform. For their part, the Democrats (who have a majority in the Senate) and President Obama refused to countenance a compromise on this. It had become central to the Obama legacy and the Democrats' identity as a party.

The failure of the House to agree a continuing resolution triggered a government shutdown from 1 October. Services apart from those deemed essential (a relatively broad category) were suspended. As part of the process, national parks and monuments were closed. Many federal government employees remained unpaid and unable to work.

Even at the beginning of the fight there were, however, signs that those seen as Republican 'establishment' figures by the Tea Party movement were both unenthusiastic and pessimistic about the confrontation with the White House. They continued to oppose Obamacare but believed that the shutdown strategy would inevitably fail and end on terms that would favour the Democrats. Karl Rove, who had served as President George W. Bush's principal electoral strategist, also warned that the party would lose the support of independent voters who had backed the Republicans in large numbers in the 2010 Congressional elections. There were also memories of government shutdowns in the 1990s when the Congressional Republicans had lost the battle to win public opinion in their fights with President Clinton. They were held responsible for the withdrawal of government services:

> The desire to strike at ObamaCare is praiseworthy. But any strategy to repeal, delay or replace the law must have a credible chance of succeeding or affecting broad public opinion positively. The defunding strategy doesn't ... It is an ill-conceived tactic, and Republicans should reject it.
>
> (Rove, 2013)

In the end, after sixteen days when much of the government had ceased to function, the accuracy of comments such as these was confirmed. John Boehner, the Republican Speaker of the House of Representatives, and some other less hardline Republicans backed down. Eighty-seven House Republicans and all of the Democrats voted to restore government funding without any concessions of consequence to Obamacare's opponents. The Senate backed the bill by 81 to 18.[15]

Shifts, changes and impact

Nonetheless, although there were successive defeats and Republicans and Tea Partiers often seemed to secure little from the politics of the period, the Tea Party movement had a significant impact on political processes that went well beyond the ranks of those who defined themselves as 'activists' or 'supporters'.

All in all, the movement had four different forms of impact. First, and most obviously, its campaigning efforts led to a shift in character of Congressional representation. In the 2010 mid-term contests, almost half of the seats gained by Republicans in the House of Representatives were won by candidates that Tea Party organizations had endorsed. Once those elected had taken their seats, sixty-four members of the Republican conference in the House of Representatives (which totalled 242 members) joined the Tea Party caucus that had been formed in July 2010 by Michele Bachmann (Miller et al., 2012: 365).[16] Furthermore, as Clarence Lo notes, the political impact of the movement will be evident in the years to come through the election to the US Senate of Tea Party favourites such as Marco Rubio and Rand Paul, although the positions that they may be compelled to adopt as they reach out to broader constituencies may fray their subsequent relationships with committed Tea Partiers (Lo, 2012: 118).[17]

Second, the movement changed the character of the conservative agenda. It ensured that Republican members of Congress stood more or less firm against the legislation pursued by the Obama administration and the Congressional Democrats. While it could not prevent the eventual passage of healthcare reform ('Obamacare') in 2010, movement activities contributed to a climate that required the dropping of its more radical components, most notably the 'public option' that would have created government health insurance that operated in competition with private-sector provision. Some Democrats had believed that, if introduced, the 'public option' would over time have squeezed private companies out of the health insurance market. Certainly, the movement compelled Republican leaders to back away from the idea of a 'grand bargain' between the parties to address the deficit and debt through which the Democrats would have agreed to reductions in 'entitlement' programmes: Medicare, Medicaid and Social Security. For their part, the Republicans would as their side of the bargain have accepted increased tax rates on some higher-income wage-earners.

Third, the movement also had an impact on other political actors and public opinion more broadly. At times, the movement's candidates and issues created backlash effects. As in the 1990s, militant Republicans were held responsible for the federal government shutdown in October 2013. At the same time, however, the efforts of Tea Party activists, as well as other conservative organizations and outlets, contributed to shifts in public opinion on healthcare reform during 2009. The movement highlighted the extent to which there would, they claimed, be government direction of health, the cost burden imposed on the business sector and the threat to liberty posed by mandates. In February 2009, according to a poll conducted by the Kaiser Family Foundation, just 11 per cent of respondents felt that they and their families would be 'worse off' if healthcare reform was enacted. By August the figure had risen to 31 per cent (PollingReport.com, 2013a).

The movement also seems to have swayed opinion through its emphasis upon government expenditure, the deficit and the debt. It gave these issues a salience that they would not otherwise have had. Large swathes of public opinion embraced the calls for significant spending reductions (although, that having been said, there was support for tax increases alongside budget cuts). In February 2013, large majorities (81 per cent of Republicans, 65 per cent of Democrats and 70 per cent of independents) asserted that 'major' deficit reduction legislation was an 'essential' priority for the president and Congress during the coming year (Pew Research Center for the People and the Press, 2013). From the beginning of 2011 onwards (when the Pew Research Center began asking the question), a plurality asserted that cutting the federal government budget deficit was more of a priority than the adoption of measures 'to help the economy recover' (PollingReport.com, 2013c).[18]

Fourth, the movement's activities and the ways in which they reshaped the Republican Party had an impact upon the Obama White House. They shifted the administration's policy stances, or at least halted their evolution in particular directions, and ensured that retrenchment and the austerity agenda were embraced. The Obama administration and many Congressional Democrats accepted calls for fiscal rectitude and, at least in loose terms, the assumptions underpinning notions of 'expansionary' fiscal contraction. While not endorsing the specificities of the Reinhart and Rogoff thesis, they shared a generalized belief that the state had become too bloated and had reached a point where it could constrain economic growth and stifle the long-run recovery process.[19] As President Obama put it: 'doing nothing on the deficit is just not an option. Our debt has grown so large that we could do real damage to the economy if we don't begin a process now to get our fiscal house in order' (The White House, 2011).

There were, of course, differences between the parties, particularly when it came to the assignation of responsibility for the country's difficulties. In his statements Obama stressed the dilemmas posed by the ageing of the population and the demands imposed by retirees. The president stressed that about two-thirds of the federal government budget was spent on Medicare, Medicaid, Social Security and national security. The problems had been, he said in comments that created a partisan dividing line, exacerbated by revenue loss as well as expenditure increases, and in particular the Bush administration's tax reductions:

> But after Democrats and Republicans committed to fiscal discipline during the 1990s, we lost our way in the decade that followed. We increased spending dramatically for two wars and an expensive prescription drug program – but we didn't pay for any of this new spending. Instead, we made the problem worse with trillions of dollars in unpaid-for tax cuts – tax cuts that went to every millionaire and billionaire in the country; tax cuts that will force us to borrow an average of $500 billion every year over the next decade.
>
> (The White House, 2011)

The president also stressed the need to protect social provision and 'investment' in the nation's future. He emphasized the responsibilities of higher-income groupings and thereby made the case for allowing the tax cuts enacted a decade earlier by the Bush administration and Congress expire for those at the upper end of the scale. However, Obama added a qualification. He was, he said, adopting 'an approach that puts every kind of spending on the table – but one that protects the middle class, our promise to seniors, and our investments in the future' (The White House, 2011).

2012 and beyond

The Tea Party movement seemed, however, to have reached an impasse by the end of 2012, and President Obama's second-term election victory gave renewed impetus to those on the Right who questioned the movement's strategy, character and direction. Indeed, as 2013 progressed, there were increasingly visible tensions between the movement and 'establishment' Republicans as party elites sought to put some political distance between themselves and the movement. They increasingly mobilized in their own interests and by doing so passed a threshold that gave them strength in numbers.

For the party 'establishment' there were growing fears that identification with the movement could impose significant political costs. In 2012, some closely associated with the movement went down to defeat in seats that might otherwise have been won by the Republicans. Christine O'Donnell's defeat in the Delaware Senate race has been widely cited. Tea Party supporters and the character of inter-candidate competition during the primary season may have pulled former Massachusetts governor, Mitt Romney, the Republicans' 2012 presidential candidate, towards political positions that were later to dim his prospects of winning the presidency.

Although limited in character, there were parallel ideational shifts as median opinion seemed to shift away from positions associated with Tea Party thinking. The Gallup Organization asked in its polls: 'do you think the federal government today has too much power, has about the right amount of power, or has too little power?' There was a fall in the proportion of respondents believing that the federal government had 'too much power' (from 59 per cent to 54 per cent) between September 2010 and May 2013 (PollingReport.com, 2013b).

There was, furthermore, a process of movement exhaustion after four years of campaigning and at the same time fractures as, amidst uncertainties in the Middle East, national security and foreign policy issues again came to the fore. Whereas some talked of foreign policy realism and the hazards of embroilment in foreign wars and stressed the threat that surveillance systems posed to individual freedoms, others emphasized the continuing dangers posed by terrorism and militant Islam.

It seemed therefore as if the movement had lost ground. Nonetheless, although the 2014 primary season lent considerable credence to this claim, a question mark has to be placed against it. In June 2014, House Majority Leader Eric Cantor lost his primary in Virginia's 7th district. He was defeated by a little-known Tea Party activist whom he had massively outspent during the course of the campaign. As *The Atlantic* commented:

> No one thought Eric Cantor, the House majority leader, could actually lose. His primary challenge in his suburban Richmond district, from a local economics professor named David Brat, was thought to be nominal. No sitting majority leader has lost a primary since the position was invented in 1899.
>
> (Ball, 2014)[20]

Conclusion

The chapter has considered the emergence and development of the Tea Party movement and the character of its relationship with the Republican Party 'establishment'. It has assessed the movement's growth in terms of the frames within which it perceived Washington politics, government social provision and 'entitlement' programmes, the constituencies on which it drew, and the ways in was shaped and given traction by the defining characteristics of the American state. It has argued that despite the Republicans' and Tea Partiers' many setbacks and losses, the movement played a significant part in shifting the centre of political gravity in the US towards fiscal retrenchment.

Notes

1 See p. 98 for a discussion of the Gadsden flag.

2 In contrast, David Horowitz, the often combative editor of *FrontPage* magazine, offered relatively conciliatory comments on inauguration day. He noted Obama's avoidance of overt partisanship and hailed the symbolism of the nation's first black president (Horowitz, 2009).

3 The concept of *bricolage* has been discussed (within the context of institutional change) by John L. Campbell (2004: 69–74).

4 Although social movement studies have for the most part focused on movements broadly associated with the Left, and sometimes only considered Rightist movements as 'counter-movements' or as 'astroturf' (in other words, not a legitimate movement), the analytical frameworks that are used (for example, resource mobilization approaches) can be used to study Tea Party activism.

5 The 'crowding out' thesis, along of course with many other claims, was challenged by critical commentators. They argued that instead of displacing private-sector investment, government spending (particularly capital expenditure) encouraged and facilitated private-sector economic activity. In other words, it corrected market failure (Lee, 2011: 59).

6 The term 'populism' should, however, be used with a degree of caution. Although populism can take Left- and Right-wing forms, it often incorporates hostility to financial as well as political elites. There has, however, been only limited evidence of opposition to Wall Street among Tea Party activists and supporters.

7 Charles Postel questions accounts that describe the Tea Party movement as 'populist'. The US populist tradition, he argues, has long been tied to progressivism and calls to 'spread the wealth' (Postel, 2012: 28).

8 Postel offers a different perspective. He rejects the application of the concept of 'producerism' to Tea Party thinking. It, he argues, 'sends only occasional barbs toward the corporate executives, bankers, and lobbyists, who in the past were the systematic targets of "producerist" movements. Instead, today's Tea Party usually celebrates the corporate elites as heroes of the market' (Postel, 2012: 33). The contrast with past movements is, of course, valid, but movements often redraw the boundaries (in this case between producers and non-producers) and redefine the character of the 'Other' that exists within particular ideational traditions.

9 Chip Berlet suggests that religious conservatives (and other more radical Rightist strands) came to the fore once the movement had become established: 'At first much of the energy for organizing the grassroots portion of the Tea Party movement came from libertarians and supporters of Ron Paul. Over time, participants in the pre-existing Christian Right and Patriot Movements emerged as playing an increasingly significant role in local units and chapters of the Tea Party movement' (Berlet, 2012: 566).

10 There is evidence that Republican voters were particularly reluctant to back childless women candidates (Schreiber, 2012: 553).

11 US state 'exceptionalism' also takes other forms. In sum, it is, to use Stephen Skowronek and Karen Orren's phrase, a 'hapless giant' (Orren and Skowronek, 2004: 12). Indeed, the entire state apparatus is riddled with cross-cutting jurisdictions and indistinct or uncertain lines of authority. The relationships between the different departments, agencies and regulatory commissions are often fraught and uncertain. All of this seemed to be brought into sharp relief by Hurricane Katrina and the multiple crises that arose in New Orleans. While President George W. Bush said, in words that he doubtless regretted subsequently, 'Brownie, you're doing a heck of a job', others argued that Michael D. Brown, a political nominee appointed to head the Federal Emergency Management Agency (FEMA), was unprepared for the demands of the post. The flooding and the breakdown of authority in the city and the seeming abandonment of the country's most disadvantaged citizens cruelly exposed the fundamental incapacities of the American state. It could wage foreign wars but did not have the structural ability to provide domestic relief and assistance. Furthermore, in place of a professionalized bureaucracy organized on a rational and hierarchical basis, political appointees who often secured posts because of political debts or personal loyalty occupy many of the most senior positions.

12 For the most part, the think tanks of the Right were not involved in policy initiation. Intense partisanship created too febrile a political climate. Instead, they concentrated on the development and extension of policy ideas that had already been accepted or endorsed by movement gatekeepers.

13 See p. 37 for a discussion of *layering, conversion* and *drift*.

14 It remained (and remains) a point of argument whether the expiry of a tax cut constitutes a tax 'increase'.

15 The crisis further weakened the 'Hastert Rule'. This informal rule has governed the House Republicans since the 1990s and asserts that the Speaker should not allow a

vote in the chamber on a bill unless a majority among the House Republicans supports the measure.

16 At the beginning of January 2013, the caucus had forty-nine members.

17 Few would contest the claim that the movement also had a negative impact on the Republicans' electoral fortunes. Christine O'Donnell's capture of the Republican Senate nomination in Delaware, and her subsequent defeat in the general election, has been widely noted. In a race that the Republicans might have expected to win, Sharon Angle failed to dislodge Senate Majority Leader Harry Reid in Nevada. In the 2012 presidential election, some attribute Mitt Romney's defeat to the Rightward positions that he was compelled to adopt during the long primary season.

18 The question was: 'If you were setting priorities for the federal government these days, would you place a higher priority on spending to help the economy recover, or a higher priority on reducing the budget deficit?'

19 See pp. 92–93 for an outline of the Reinhart and Rogoff thesis.

20 However, despite a closely fought primary race, long-time Senator Thad Cochran of Mississippi beat off a Tea Party challenger shortly afterwards.

6

Britain, retrenchment and the 'Big Society'

The chapter considers events and processes in Britain during the recession years. It looks at the Conservative Party (as well as the exigencies of coalition politics) and the fortunes of UKIP, the different core constituencies to which the Right was tied, economic logics and the character of the institutional structures within which British policymaking was undertaken. In particular, the chapter surveys two ideational shifts. First, the Conservative leadership committed itself to radical and sustained fiscal retrenchment. This was, however, rationalized on largely pragmatic grounds. Then, second, it reframed retrenchment so that it became an explicit commitment to shrink and restructure the British state, thereby reconfiguring its relationship with both the economy and civil society.

In the UK, radical fiscal retrenchment had been foreshadowed. It was, as noted in Chapter 4, anticipated by the Labour government's commitment to an early switch away from fiscal stimulus policies and the early paying back of 'bailout' expenditure. According to the projections agreed by the Chancellor of the Exchequer, Alistair Darling, 93 per cent of the stimulus would take place in 2009 and fiscal policy would be deflationary by 2010. (Thus, the costs of earlier measures, most notably the temporary reduction of VAT, would be quickly recouped.)

This marked out Britain in terms of its fiscal projections from many other nations. Nearly all of the crisis-hit countries planned to allocate a substantial proportion of their overall stimulus expenditure to spending in 2010. Indeed, Italy expected to devote 85 per cent if its expenditure to projects in 2010. The figure for the United States was 42 per cent (Organisation for Economic Cooperation and Development, 2009: 110).

As noted in Chapter 4, Labour's fiscal caution owed much to the pending general election and the party's persistent fear that it would again be represented as profligate, as well as the ambivalence of business interests towards stimulus policies, the anxieties of the City of London and the long-run institutional privileging of the Treasury (which was traditionally allied with the City) within the structures of the British state.

Thus, by the time of the May 2010 general election the austerity narrative went largely unchallenged, although few spelled out the extent and scale of the retrenchment measures that it implied. Labour's manifesto sought to rally the party's core constituencies by pledging to protect 'frontline public services' but there was also a commitment 'to halve the deficit over the next four years'. As the Institute for Fiscal Studies (IFS) noted in a survey of the three principal parties' plans, Labour's 2010 budget (delivered in March) was premised on beginning the process of fiscal tightening in 2011–12, continuing until 2016–17, with 'the pain front-loaded in the earlier years' (Chote *et al.*, 2010: 1). Although Labour's 2010 budget measures included items that cheered the party's backbenches, it looked ahead to 'tough choices on welfare: our reforms will increase fairness and work incentives, including £1.5 billion of savings being delivered' (Labour Party, 2010: 0:6). Labour's plans foresaw a ratio of spending cuts to tax increases of 2:1 (Chote *et al.*, 2010: 2).

At first sight, the Conservatives' plans were not radically or substantially different. As the IFS remarked, their proposals at the time of the 2010 general election 'would make a relatively modest difference to the long-term outlook for government borrowing and debt' (Chote *et al.*, 2010: 2). Government debt would, according to their projections, fall to a figure below 40 per cent of GDP in 2031–32, the same year that Labour envisaged.

Nonetheless, despite these similarities, there were some important differences between the parties. The Conservatives established their credentials as more aggressive budget-cutters. They announced that if they formed a government they would begin fiscal tightening a year ahead of Labour with a cut of £6 billion of 'wasteful' spending in 2010–11. The process, they asserted, would be completed in 2015–16, a year ahead of Labour. The Conservative election manifesto also included attacks on Labour's spending levels and its plans to increase National Insurance contributions, which, it claimed, would lead to the loss of 57,000 jobs in small and medium-sized businesses alone (Conservative Party, 2010: 8). Furthermore, whereas Labour, as noted above, thought in terms of a 2:1 ratio between spending cuts and tax increases, the Conservatives envisaged a 4:1 ratio (Chote *et al.*, 2010: 2). There were also differences of scale. Although Labour (and the Liberal Democrats) committed themselves to far-reaching cuts in public services that would, taken collectively, constitute 'the deepest sustained cut to spending on public services since the four years from April 1976 to March 1980', the Conservatives' proposals went further. They would, the IFS noted, represent the biggest cuts to expenditure on public services over a five-year period since 1945: 'in real terms the Conservatives would need to cut public services spending in their unprotected areas by £63.7 billion, Labour by £50.8 billion and the Liberal Democrats by £46.5 billion between April 2011 and March 2015' (Chote *et al.*, 2010: 2).

There were some ancillary proposals. These included a plan to create (and this built upon claims that Gordon Brown had manipulated the figures) an 'independent' Office of Budget Responsibility so as to 'restore trust' in the government's management of its own finances (Conservative Party, 2010: 7).[1] There would be an emergency budget within fifty days of a Conservative government taking office. Despite the cuts in 'wasteful spending', there would, year-on-year, be real increases in health expenditure levels and at the same time the Conservatives would 'honour our commitments on international aid' (Conservative Party, 2010: 7).

Some other pledges were also made. There would be a one-year freeze in public-sector pay excepting the one million employees on the lowest pay levels. There would be a 'review' so as to advance the point in time at which the state pension age would increase to sixty-six (although the party pledged that it would not be until at least 2016 for men and 2020 for women). There was also a commitment to bring in some means-testing of social benefits by, for example, ending tax credits for 'better-off families with incomes over £50,000' (Conservative Party, 2010: 8).

Nonetheless, all this having been said, although the Conservatives proposed deeper and faster cuts, they were not framed in terms that challenged the prevailing economic paradigm. The party argued that Labour had overspent during its period of office thereby creating a structural deficit (that would remain even in periods of sustained growth), and there was a danger that if this went uncorrected Britain would as a consequence be punished by the financial markets. There were, it was said, significant amounts of unnecessary government spending that could be targeted. There was thus an emphasis in the Conservative election manifesto on the upward pressure upon interest rates that a loose fiscal stance can create and the need to accommodate the anxieties of the credit ratings agencies. Expenditure cuts would, the manifesto insisted, be directed towards 'wasteful spending':

> We will safeguard Britain's credit rating with a credible plan to eliminate the bulk of the structural deficit over a Parliament. Our fiscal policy will seek to help keep interest rates lower for longer … Urgent action is needed if we are to avoid the higher borrowing costs that would inevitably follow from a credit rating downgrade. So we will cut wasteful government spending to bring the deficit down and restore stability.
> (Conservative Party, 2010: 5–7)

There were just a few hints of path-departing or at least path-shifting plans if broader macroeconomic policies are considered. There was a recognition in the manifesto that British economic growth had had an unbalanced character. In part, these imbalances were regional in character. As the manifesto noted, many regions outside London and the South East were heavily dependent upon public-sector provision and the key to a more geographically balanced national economy lay in policies that would stimulate further private-sector economic activity. This was in turn tied to the Conservatives' plans for public transportation and the, perhaps at first sight surprising, emphasis that they placed upon the railways. As the manifesto noted: 'A rebalanced economy requires an extensive and reliable infrastructure' (The Conservative Party, 2010: 23). While Margaret Thatcher famously disliked the railways and instead embraced the car, the manifesto promised that a Conservative government would 'begin work immediately' upon the high-speed railway line (HS2) linking London with Birmingham, Manchester and Leeds. There was also a pledge that 'Stage Two' would extend the high-speed network to Scotland and Wales and that proposals for the construction of additional runways at Heathrow, Gatwick and Stansted would be scrapped in the hope that air passengers would transfer to the new railway network (The Conservative Party, 2010: 23).

The Conservatives' commitment to rebalancing not only had a regional character but also took other forms. There were sectoral imbalances. Recent economic growth, the manifesto argued, had been heavily dependent upon government spending and irresponsible credit expansion. A year later, in February 2010 at the annual Mais Lecture, George Osborne, then Shadow Chancellor of the Exchequer, built upon this by speaking of the need for policies that would 'contain credit cycles' (quoted in Lee, 2011: 62). Savings levels had plummeted. The country had become 'dependent on unsustainable inflows of capital from abroad' (The Conservative Party, 2010: 12). More resources had to be channelled towards productive investment and the winning of overseas sales: 'A sustainable recovery must be driven by growth in exports and business investment, and through a better environment for wealth creation' (The Conservative Party, 2010: 11). A year later, Osborne spoke explicitly of 'a new model of economic growth that is rooted in more investment, more savings, and higher exports' (quoted in Lee, 2011: 60).

Coalition

In the confused aftermath of the 2010 general election, the coalition agreement forged between the Conservatives and the Liberal Democrats (who had, prior to the election, pursued a policy of equidistance from both the major parties) that formed the basis for the new government reproduced much of the Conservatives' earlier economic thinking (although deficit reduction policy was relegated to Section Nine of the programme). The Liberal Democrats shifted from a 'softer' to a 'harder' austerity narrative.

The coalition agreement reaffirmed the concept of a 'structural deficit' at the core of Britain's economic difficulties, committed itself to making 'modest cuts of £6 billion to non-front-line services within the financial year 2010/11' and promised a 'spending review' (HM Government, 2010: 16). Indeed, there were later suggestions that the Governor of the Bank of England and the Permanent Secretary at the Treasury had given tacit backing to the Conservative position during the negotiations between the parties that preceded the formation of the coalition (Wintour, 2010b).

The coalition agreement not only bound the Liberal Democrats to the defining features of the Conservatives' thinking. It also took the fiscal retrenchment process a stage further by structuring it around reductions in the overall size of government. The reasoning was not given in the agreement but it seems that the coalition negotiations not only changed perceptions about the scale of the fiscal challenge but also convinced the Liberal Democrats that the deficit could not be reduced through tax increases or a policy mix that incorporated significant tax rises. Such rises would, it was argued, jeopardize investment, economic activity and the prospect of recovery. The agreement stated that 'the main burden of deficit reduction' should be 'borne by reduced spending rather than increased taxes' (HM Government, 2010: 15). There were other echoes of the Conservative manifesto. There was a commitment to reduce the number and cost of quangos (HM Government, 2010: 16). There were some, albeit opaque, references to outsourcing. And, in the education sector, the pledge to increase the number of self-governing academies and create 'free schools' survived the process of coalition formation: 'We also believe that the state should help parents, community groups and others come together to improve the education system by starting new schools' (HM Government, 2010: 28). In their study of the coalition agreement, Thomas Quinn, Judith Bara and John Bartle conclude that on the issue of deficit reduction agreed coalition policy was consistently 'Right' (in terms of the Left–Right spectrum) and 'the Conservatives won that particular argument' (Quinn *et al.*, 2011: 16).

Why did the Liberal Democrats embrace Conservative thinking so readily? First, as noted above, there was a sense of crisis during the coalition negotiations and increasing sensitivity to the mood swings of the financial markets. Indeed, as the talks proceeded the deficit and the pace of deficit reduction began to be regarded as increasingly pressing. Reportedly, Gordon Brown (who at that point remained in Downing Street) stated that Labour would accelerate the process if a Labour–Liberal Democrat coalition was formed. A document was issued stating that there would be cuts in 2010–11: 'In light of market concerns, tough action will be taken to reduce the deficit' (quoted in Laws, 2010: 145).[2]

Second, although Andrew Adonis has argued otherwise in his account of Labour's post-election negotiations with the Liberal Democrats, the electoral arithmetic (and perhaps Labour's exhaustion) seemed to demand a coalition or at least a 'confidence and supply' arrangement between the Liberal Democrats and the Conservatives (Adonis, 2013). In such circumstances, the Liberal Democrats had only limited space within which they could extract concessions and deficit reduction could not be a negotiating item.

Third, while the Liberal Democrats had indeed wished to move more slowly on deficit reduction during the election campaign, it had not been a manifesto priority (Quinn *et al.*, 2011: 16). Indeed, according to the IFS, although the Liberal Democrats had endorsed Labour's plans for fiscal tightening this had been done 'informally' (Chote *et al.*, 2010: 1).The party leadership therefore had a significant degree of flexibility on the issue when the negotiations opened.

Fourth, although the Liberal Democrats (and their predecessor parties) had long been seen as leaning to the Left, the emergence of 'Orange Book' Liberalism (with which Nick Clegg, who became Liberal Democrat leader in 2007, was associated) marked a shift towards a more classical and market-based economic liberalism, or at the least its incorporation within the Liberal Democrats' ideational mainstream.

And, fifth, there were early ripple effects from the crisis in Greece. By May 2010 press reports increasingly spoke of serious difficulties with the Greek government's accounts, that the scale of its overall indebtedness had been underestimated and that loans would be required. The defining features of the crisis had been firmly and unambiguously defined in terms of a structural deficit and the need to impose drastic retrenchment measures. Tales of corruption, clientelism and government largesse abounded. At the urging of the European Union (EU) and the International Monetary Fund (IMF), and as a condition for loans, the Greek government introduced some austerity measures. Representations of the Greek experience thereby served as a 'bridge' lead to a move away from perceptions of the crisis structured around banking and the unaccountable irresponsibility of the financial sector and towards understandings based upon 'big government', public debt and the spending projects of politicians who had been weak, dependent upon the patronage of particularistic interests, corrupt or perhaps ideologically driven. In these circumstances lessons were drawn that extended far beyond Greece but were also applied to the UK.[3] The shadow of Greece hung over British political deliberations.

The June budget

The incoming coalition government's first major economic move came with the June 'emergency' budget. The measures that were adopted were framed in terms of a necessary and proportionate response to an acute crisis. As George Osborne, Chancellor of the Exchequer, said in delivering the budget:

> The coalition Government has inherited from its predecessor the largest budget deficit of any economy in Europe with the single exception of Ireland. One pound in every four we spend is being borrowed. What we have not inherited from our predecessor is a credible plan to reduce their record deficit. This at the very moment when fear about the sustainability of sovereign debt is the greatest risks to the recovery of European economies.
>
> (quoted in *The Daily Telegraph*, 2010)

The budget won backing and an endorsement from the Organisation for Economic Cooperation and Development (OECD) that had by then, together with the IMF, firmly associated itself with calls for fiscal retrenchment:

> The comprehensive budget announced by the government on 22 June was courageous and appropriate. It was an essential starting point. It signals the commitment to provide the necessary degree of fiscal consolidation over the coming years to bring public finances to a sustainable path, while still supporting the recovery.
>
> (Organisation for Economic Cooperation and Development, 2010: 3)[4]

The 2010 Spending Review

The 2010 Spending Review, promised in the coalition agreement, the details of which were announced in October 2010, covered the years from 2011–12 through to 2014–15. As the *BBC News* announced it: 'Chancellor George Osborne has unveiled the biggest UK spending cuts for decades, with welfare, councils and police budgets all hit' (*BBC News*, 2010). Over four years, £81 billion was to be cut. The budgets for government departments aside from health and overseas aid, which were ring-fenced, were to be cut by an average of 19 per cent over four years (HM Treasury, 2010: 5).[5]

Nonetheless, despite the scale of the cuts, the Cameron government continued to pursue the case for deficit reduction on largely pragmatic grounds. The Spending Review cited the backing of international bodies such as the IMF and OECD and pointed to the long-run macroeconomic consequences of public debt. The call for fiscal retrenchment was structured around the Labour government's alleged profligacy and the assertion that high debt levels would have a 'crowding out' effect leading to upward pressure on interest rates. This, it was said, would increase the costs of servicing public debt and reduce investment and, as a consequence, productivity rates and overall economic growth. Even at current levels, debt servicing reduces the capacity of government to undertake other forms of public spending: 'It is unproductive and unfair to spend more on debt interest payments than, for example, on schools in England' (HM Treasury, 2010: 3). High debt levels also threatened a government's ability to cope with significant economic shocks that might arise in the future. And, last, government borrowing inevitably imposes a burden on future generations because it will, at some point, have to be repaid together with interest. Simple claims about profligacy and excessive spending came together with the claims and arguments associated with 'expansionary fiscal contraction' whereby significant reductions in government expenditure lead to corresponding increases in private-sector economic activity (see Chapter 4).

Reframing retrenchment

In the years that followed, and despite frequently heard claims that the Liberal Democrats were playing a restraining role, the character of political discourse shifted and the retrenchment process was increasingly framed by the government, or at least its Conservative members, in far more radical terms. There was a shift away from pragmatism and the framing of retrenchment in terms of appeasing the markets.

The key statement of policy came towards the end of 2013. Speaking at the Lord Mayor's Banquet in the City of London, David Cameron gave some important insights into government thinking after three-and-a-half years in office. Although the speech surveyed different areas and paid particular attention to City interests, it had five core components.

First, Cameron's speech to the Lord Mayor's Banquet incorporated a reaffirmation of the 'balancing' that had been stressed back in 2010. He spoke of 'a new kind of economy where the benefits of growth are shared by all, north and south alike' (Gov.uk, 2013). This was to be backed, as in 2010, by infrastructural investment that would ensure greater balance and bind the nation more closely together:

> We can't have an economy for all if people in the parts of the North or in some rural communities are left without the transport links or the superfast broadband they need to take part. So we are investing in infrastructure that serves the whole country. £680 million to ensure we have the best superfast broadband in Europe by 2015. The biggest investment in road since the 1970s. The biggest rail investment since Victorian times. With Cross-rail, the biggest construction project anywhere in Europe. And with High Speed 2, the first new train line running north out of London for 120 years.
>
> (Gov.uk, 2013)

Second, there was a reaffirmation of the importance of welfare reform. Whereas others would be drawn in, persuaded and enticed, those on the bottom rung of the socioeconomic ladder would be subject to a much stricter set of financial incentives and disincentives. Deterrence would draw welfare dependents (the term 'Benefits Street' was introduced into the vocabulary two months later when, in January 2014, a television series of that name highlighted the lives of long-term claimants in Birmingham) into the labour market and full citizenship:

> We know the most progressive way to tackle poverty is through work. And yet for generations, people who could work have been failed by the system and stuck on benefits. So we're putting an end to the poverty and wealth traps that have plagued our welfare system for too long. We're capping welfare, so that no family is better off on benefits than in work. And through universal credit, we're ensuring that for every extra hour you work and every extra job you do – you should always be better off.
>
> (Gov.uk, 2013)

Third, the defining features of the 'Big Society', as it had been represented in 2010, were restated. The project was represented in terms of voluntary and neighbourhood effort so as to give a greater vibrancy to civil society, though, at the same time, Cameron pointed to the proactive role government should play (although the character of that role was, as always, never subject to close scrutiny) in facilitating such an effort:

> I'm also very focused on supporting the voluntary sector to work alongside the state in fighting poverty and building this economy where everyone can take part. For example, one of the best answers to payday lending is the credit union movement. As a government we have invested £38 million to double the membership of credit unions, a shining example of the Big Society in action.
>
> (Gov.uk, 2013)

Fourth, Cameron restated the shift made at the beginning of the year when he declared that the Conservatives would, if they formed a government after the 2015 general election, and after negotiations with other EU nations to secure 'a more competitive and flexible European Union', hold a referendum to decide upon continued membership (Gov.uk, 2013).

Last, and it was at this point that the shift became evident, Cameron's speech to the banquet incorporated the argument that there could be no return to the status quo ante. Macroeconomic policy should no longer be concentrated on undoing the damage that, through the prism of the austerity narrative, Labour had wrought. Instead, the character of the British state was to be restructured. Cameron committed the party to shrinkage:

> We can't simply try and rebuild the same type of economy that we had before the crash. We can't just go back to how things used to be. We need to build something better ... that doesn't just mean making difficult decisions on public spending. It also means something more profound. It means building a leaner, more efficient state. We need to do more with less. Not just now, but permanently.
>
> (Gov.uk, 2013)

Reasons

How and why did the Cameron leadership make the shift? After all, although Orange Book liberalism had embraced competition and choice, it had not won the hearts and minds of many Liberal Democrats, and a Conservative commitment to the fundamental restructuring of the state and a redefinition of its role could only be expected to put further strains upon coalition arrangements and relationships.

The answer lies partly in the political character of the 2010 generation of Conservative MPs. Their ranks included individuals such as Dominic Raab, MP for Esher and Walton, and Mark Reckless, MP for Rochester and Strood. On economic issues they joined forces with 'old Right' figures such as John Redwood, Peter Lilley and David Davis, as well as Daniel Hannan in the European Parliament, but there were some differences of tone and at times substance on social and cultural issues. As Tim Montgomerie of *Conservative Home* noted,

> most of the new intake are Thatcher's children, having cut their political teeth when she was prime minister, but they are more than that. They share her Euroscepticism. They want to cut taxes. They think that serious offenders should go to jail. They believe in competition in the public services. But unlike many who kept their safe seats during the Blair years, the Class of 2010 are seasoned door-to-door campaigners, who have heard and absorbed where voters stand on the NHS. They understand that voters want a Tory party with a heart as well as a head. They are fully behind Iain Duncan Smith's social justice agenda. They are respectful of gay relationships.
>
> (Montgomerie, 2011)

Furthermore, the requirements of coalition government (whereby substantial numbers of Liberal Democrats had to be accommodated) and the entrenched position of senior cabinet members (including George Osborne as Chancellor of the Exchequer and William Hague as Foreign Secretary until July 2014) severely restricted the prospects for upward mobility by those on the backbenches, thereby fuelling resentment and discontent. Those in the 2010 intake who might reasonably have hoped to join the very lowest rungs of government within the lifetime of the parliament (and then had their loyalty ensured once they became part of the payroll vote) found their way upwards blocked.

There were other reasons for discontent. Again because of the exigencies of coalition politics, Conservative MPs had to vote for legislation that had not been included in the Conservatives' 2010 election manifesto. And, as noted above, because of Labour's successive general election victories many in the new intake were experienced political campaigners with established network associations. They did not, therefore, prove as pliable as the whips might have hoped. Thus, by May 2013, it was reported that 85 per cent of the new intake had at some point rebelled against their government (Simons, 2013). A significant proportion joined the 301 group (representing the number of seats the Conservatives appeared to require in 2015 during the period when it was expected that the total number of parliamentary constituencies would be reduced to 600). The group sought to change the 'narrative' among Conservative MPs, but also reform the mechanisms within the parliamentary party so that backbench opinion had more of an impact.

At the same time, the commitment to the restructuring of the state provided an opportunity to rally the party. Significant elements within the political project that the Cameron leadership promoted were only thinly embedded within Conservative ranks and the party's collective thinking. Although some of the issues that 'Cameronism' brought to the forefront, most notably the promises that the National Health Service (NHS) would not only be maintained but strengthened, were highlighted by significant numbers of Conservatives in their 2010 constituency campaigns, there was less enthusiasm for some of the leadership's civic reform plans as well as geographical and sectoral 'rebalancing'.[6] There were also fractures. In particular, the introduction of same-sex marriage and the construction of HS2 provoked profound divisions. While 123 Conservative MPs supported same-sex marriage on its Third Reading in the House of Commons, 134 opposed it (while Cameron had declared his support for the measure, MPs were given a free vote).

The 'knowledge regime' associated with the British Right exerted Rightward pressures on the Cameron leadership. Whereas the Thatcher government had, in its early days, to contend with and surmount the fears of 'wets' (those more patrician Conservatives who sought to ameliorate the logic of monetarism), in the cabinet the Cameron government had, at least within its own ranks, no such inhibitors. Instead, while populist calls were often also heard when the EU, immigration or cultural issues came to the fore (which were often tied to calls for restrictions on the transnational mobility of people and products), Conservatism's economic thinking was pulled towards a 'purer' form of neoliberalism.

In particular, the think tanks associated with the British Right lobbied (insofar as their status allowed) for the intensification of retrenchment processes and the move from pragmatism to restructuring. Indeed, the Institute of Economic Affairs (IEA) offered a free market critique of government policy throughout the crisis period. The ring-fencing of the NHS budget and the commitment to increase foreign aid were 'simply indicative of politically-motivated profligacy and not good economics' (Booth, 2011). IEA representatives criticized the rise in VAT at the beginning of 2011, called for the opening up of public services to market forces, the scaling back of regulations and, at the least, far more drastic spending cuts so as to create a framework that would foster economic growth. Such cuts would have hit sectors that the Cameron government regarded as politically sacrosanct:

> it will prove impossible for the government to deliver the necessary spending cuts whilst maintaining its commitment to ring-fencing. David Cameron's promise to increase pensions in real terms, more or less no matter what economic conditions prevail, is irresponsible and completely at odds with the Chancellor's rhetoric. Areas such as health, schools, foreign aid, HS2, pensions and other benefits for older people should all be considered as areas in which savings can be made.
>
> (Booth, 2014)

The critique offered by the IEA was endorsed to a greater or lesser extent, and in a strident or subdued form, by many across the British Right, including think tanks (including the Adam Smith Institute, which was ranked as the highest-placed UK domestic policy think tank by *Foreign Policy* magazine), advocacy organizations, Conservative members and the party's elected officials. Their ranks included, for example, figures such as John Redwood MP, the former minister who had, over a long period beginning during John Major's premiership, distanced himself from successive party leaders by putting forward market-based and resolutely Eurosceptic arguments.

In its more developed forms (and it drew upon the changing representation of the economic crisis and its causes outlined in Chapter 4), the critique had eight principal planks. First, although events and developments in the US and beyond had played a part, the severity of the crisis in the UK could in very large part be explained by domestic variables. Second, in an echo of Austrian arguments, there was an emphasis on UK monetary policy during the years preceding the crisis. The Bank of England had, it was said, pursued a lax monetary policy that fuelled credit expansion in place of sustainable growth. (Redwood has argued that interest rates were then, in 2007, increased to a rate that hastened the crash.) Third, although there was an acknowledgement that monetary policy had contributed to the crisis, the emphasis was upon the role of government spending and the real increases that took place from 2001 onwards. Indeed, as the crisis progressed the focus quickly shifted from monetary to fiscal issues. Fourth, there was a firm belief that recovery required the freeing up of market forces by shrinking the state and processes of deregulation. Fifth, there was anxiety, to a degree greater than that found in many other critiques, about the dangers of inflation and the likelihood of bubbles (resulting either from minimal interest rates, quantitative easing or schemes designed to stimulate the housing market such as 'Help to Buy'). Sixth, there was also concern about the continuing burden of government debt and the scale of borrowing that was necessitated by it. Seventh, it was argued that the spending reductions that the Cameron government had implemented and promised for the coming years were relatively limited and that much more retrenchment was required. Only this could reduce government borrowing still further and untether market processes. And, eighth, and most visibly, there was a commitment to 'hard' Euroscepticism. There was little faith in renegotiating processes, a distaste of continental European liberalism and conservatism and a belief that the UK should make its own way as a trading nation.

There were further reasons why the narrative shifted towards state restructuring. There was no evident enthusiasm for a dramatic shrinking of the state or radical restructuring. Business organizations opposed regulation and supported retrenchment, but generally backed infrastructural spending. Often business organizations were pulled in different directions on the same issue. The Confederation of British Industry (CBI) argued that 'the benefits of EU membership to British business have significantly outweighed the costs', but at the same time stressed the regulatory burden and placed the issue of continued membership towards the bottom of its agenda (Confederation of British Industry, 2013: 11). Nonetheless, the ambivalence of business interests and the peak organizations that represented them about many core economic policy issues gave the British Right a freedom of political manoeuvre that it might not otherwise have had.

Furthermore, even if business interests had spoken loudly with one voice then it may well not have been heard all that clearly by those within Conservative circles. If the distinction that defines the approaches associated with the Varieties of Capitalism framework is employed, there are sharp differences between coordinated market economies (CMEs), such as Germany, and liberal market economies (LMEs), such as the UK and the US. From this perspective, countries are primarily identified as LMEs and CMEs on the basis of the relationships between individual firms and the extent to which they are coordinated or rely upon market processes. Whereas, within CMEs, collective employers' organizations at either a sectoral or cross-sectoral level play an important part in, for example, wage setting, training policies and presenting a collective viewpoint to both government and the unions, such organizations are far weaker and less encompassing in LMEs (Hall and Soskice, 2001: 24–25). Thus, collective organizations such as the US Chamber of

Commerce, the National Association of Manufacturers and, in the UK, the CBI and the Institute of Directors are often bypassed by individual firms and government (as well as policymakers and legislators more broadly), which only pay limited attention to their views. In other words, policymakers and legislators in LMEs are subject to fewer concentrated, centralized and collective pressures and constraints than their counterparts in CMEs. Lobbying, at least so far as economic policymaking is concerned, takes a more diffuse form.

There is another consideration regarding the role of business interests and their relationships with the political process in the UK. The US state apparatus is not only structured around a multiplicity of overlapping jurisdictions and blurred lines of authority but is relatively open and porous. Indeed, Lawrence Jacobs and Desmond King argue that 'the internal deliberations and independent decisions of civil servants and authoritative policymakers are persistently compromised by the interference of outside interests' (Jacobs and King, 2009: 6–7). At the same time election candidates are heavily dependent upon financial contributions. However, in both cases, the diversity of those seeking to secure influence and the disparate character of donor bases may act as a check upon one sector securing a disproportionate hold over public officials. In contrast, the British state has a more sealed and centralized character, thereby limiting the direct access of outside interests including peak business organizations or directing them through prescribed channels.

The creative use and deployment of monetary policy also played a part in shifting the political agenda towards a smaller state. Once the limits of minimal interest rates were believed to have been reached, the Bank of England along with many other central banks (most notably the Federal Reserve) engaged in large-scale purchases of financial assets. Although it stoked fears of inflation among some in both the British and American Right (whereas others had a fear of deflation and its likely effects upon investment), Quantitative Easing (QE) increased the money in circulation and, it was argued, staved off the most severe consequences of the financial crisis and contributed to British economic recovery. Indeed some, including Sir Mervyn King, then Governor of the Bank of England, argued for the greater use of QE. The apparent successes of QE in sustaining economic activity strengthened the claims of those who argued that an activist fiscal policy or even the use of the automatic stabilizers offered by extended government social provision were no longer required. Put another way, the successes offered by the judicious application of monetary policy allowed the post-war state to shrink.

Furthermore, although the picture was far from unambiguous, there were indications of economic growth enabling the government to talk in terms of a 'recovery' and giving the Conservative leadership the confidence to expand and extend their political vision. Put another way, although more critical commentators pointed to bubbles in the housing market and the continued dependence of the British economy on a very lax monetary policy, 'Plan A', the commitment to an 'expansionary fiscal contraction', seemed to have worked. Between the spring of 2010 and May 2012, about 381,000 public-sector jobs were lost but during the same period 634,000 private-sector jobs were created (*The Economist*, 2012).

There were, alongside this, processes of cross-national knowledge and policy transfer. The Canadian experience was cited by both the British and American Right. Whereas Canada had, in 1994, a federal government budget deficit of 9 per cent, Prime Minister Jean Chrétien's 'bloodbath budget' cut departmental spending by an average of 20 per cent. This, it was said, had put Canada on the road to economic recovery (Porter, 2010).

The Conservatives also looked at policy ideas from closer to home. After Cameron took office, there were policy summits with leaders from the Nordic and Baltic states. As Michael White noted in *The Guardian*: 'More than the French or Germans, they are open-market economies. It helps Tories relax knowing that of the seven only two – Finland and Estonia – are full eurozone members' (White, 2012).[7]

Last, the ideational processes through which the Cameron leadership moved from pragmatic austerity to state restructuring had a logic and dynamic of its own. A form of path dependency was at work. The concept of path dependency is usually understood in terms of self-reinforcing sequences. Once established, perhaps because of a chance event or chance decision, paths are strengthened and bolstered and so the costs of abandoning the path and pursuing an alternative course become prohibitive. Nonetheless, as James Mahoney records, path dependency may be understood and represented in a very different way. There can be a chain of reactive sequences (rather than self-reinforcing sequences) as one action, event or decision lays the basis for, or triggers, a subsequent action, event or decision: 'These sequences are "reactive" in the sense that each event within the sequence is in part a reaction to temporally antecedent events' (Mahoney, 2000: 509). In other words, in the absence of significant countervailing pressures, calls for fiscal retrenchment and the belief that state spending inhibited economic growth (and thus fiscal contraction would expand overall economic activity) moved through to their own conclusion. From this perspective, that conclusion held that expansionary contraction was not only a set of theoretical propositions that applied to nations in moments of acute crisis, when deficit and debt levels threatened market perceptions of sovereign debt, but applied at all times.[8]

Restructuring the British state

The projections issued by the Office of Budget Responsibility (OBR), which was created in 2010 to monitor public finances, seemed to confirm that talk of shrinking the state was far from being mere rhetoric and the British state was indeed becoming much 'leaner'. They suggested that by 2018–19 (when the OBR foresaw a budget surplus), government spending on public services and administration would have fallen to its smallest share of national income since 1948 (the year from which comparable National Accounts data are first available) (Peston, 2013). As commentators broadly associated with the Left noted, it seemed that the economic and social history of the post-war era was being rewound. Little would be left:

> The work of three generations in building the sinews of a state that support systems of health, transport, education, environment, policing, science and the rest is to be summarily withdrawn over the next five years. It is a landmark moment in our national life.
>
> (Hutton, 2013)

The process of state restructuring was based not only on the shrinking of social provision but also on the extension of outsourcing and privatization. Writing in *The Daily Telegraph*, the prime minister argued that it should be assumed, unless it could be shown otherwise, that government provision should be delivered through the private rather than the public sector. In other words, the state should have to justify its right and ability to offer a service. Where it failed to do this, there should be private delivery. The onus of justification was shifted from the private to the public sector:

> We will create a new presumption ... that public services should be open to a range of providers competing to offer a better service. Of course there are some areas – such as national security or the judiciary – where this wouldn't make sense. But everywhere else should be open ... This is a transformation: instead of having to justify why it makes sense to introduce competition in some public services – as we are now doing with schools and in the NHS – the state will have to justify why it should ever operate a monopoly.
>
> (Cameron, 2011)

Certainly, the pace of privatization and outsourcing accelerated dramatically after a relatively long period in which both John Major's government and the Labour administration that followed pursued the private finance initiative through which public projects were funded by private capital. By early 2013, it was being reported that the UK public sector was 'the biggest outsourcing market outside the US'. In 2012, the number of outsourcing contracts valued at £3.4 million or more that were awarded by government bodies increased by 16 per cent on 2011 (Leach, 2013). In May 2013, reports indicated that there had been a 168 per cent increase (if measured in terms of value) in the value of public-sector outsourcing contracts during the first three months of 2014 compared with a year previously. Some 30 per cent were new contracts rather renewals (Plimmer, 2014).

The breadth of outsourcing and privatization processes is very striking. Privatization initiatives included the Tote (a bookmaker), the Channel Tunnel rail link, the Royal Mail, medical services, work programmes for the unemployed, the training of RAF pilots, prisons and detention centres and the probation service. The prime minister looked ahead to more private road schemes.

> Why is it that other infrastructure – for example water – is funded by private sector capital through privately owned, independently regulated, utilities ... but roads in

> Britain call on the public finances for funding? ... We need to look urgently at the options for getting large-scale private investment into the national roads network, from sovereign wealth funds, pension funds, and other investors.
>
> (David Cameron, quoted in *BBC News*, 2012)

Furthermore, although representations of the Big Society conveyed images of small-scale enterprise and voluntary groups were sometimes involved, the tendering process was largely structured around large firms, four in particular, that had the capacity, knowledge and networks to mount a credible bid. Indeed, the *Financial Times* was struck by 'the speed at which the coalition is pressing ahead with plans to outsource more services and the government's reliance on a small number of big companies' (Plimmer, 2014). And, as some commentators pointed out, about a quarter of outsourcing contracts were awarded to offshore companies, which, they noted, added little or nothing to UK employment or tax revenue figures.[9]

The extent and pace of change was also striking in the education sector. As noted above, the government was committed to the creation of independent (but non-profitmaking) 'free schools'. This was drawn, albeit loosely, from a similar policy pursued in Sweden that, paradoxically, had long been regarded as a model for the social-democratic Left in earlier years.

> Since the free schools programme was established in Sweden, over 1,000 new schools have opened. They have been founded by foundations, charities and others – and they have attracted pupils by offering better discipline and higher standards. Because any parent can take the money the Swedish Government spends on their child's education and choose the school they want, standards have risen across the board as every school does its best to satisfy parents.
>
> (The Conservative Party, 2010: 50)

As Peter Taylor-Gooby and Gerry Stoker note, the goal was to remove all schools from direct local authority control:

> In education, the move to expand the number of self-managed academies – ultimately to include almost all state schools – will erode the role of local education authorities. Private providers will again be encouraged to enter the market, managing individual schools or groups of schools.
>
> (Taylor-Gooby and Stoker, 2011: 9)

There were also reforms to the structural character of public administration. There was a targeting of quangos (partially independent and unelected public bodies) that were said to have added a costly and inefficient layer to sub-government and seemed to have proliferated. The coalition government conducted a study shortly after it came to office and 200 bodies were listed for abolition, 120 for merger and 176 for substantial reform. By 2012, it was reported that although some new bodies had been created, the number of 'non-departmental public bodies' (another definition of quangos) had fallen by 220. And, in many cases, they had rather less decision-making autonomy (Tonkiss and Dommett, 2012).

The pace of change continued even as the coalition government neared its end. The Queen's Speech for the final year of the 2010 Parliament was delivered at the beginning of June 2014. Despite claims that the government had exhausted its programme and had few other legislative reforms to put forward, the Speech included a commitment to radical pensions reform that would enable retirees to take a lump sum rather than an annuity.

Transformational change

As the Cameron government continued in office, and on the basis of the changes described above, commentators increasingly stressed its transformative credentials and the radicalism of the restructuring process that was taking place.[10]

Of course, there is a case for caution in drawing conclusions. The restructuring project may well face significant obstacles (see Chapter 8). Nonetheless, this having been said, the coalition appeared to be taking steps, in terms of restructuring the state, where both the Thatcher and Major governments had feared to tread. Even if the pace is at some point softened, the trajectory has been set. Peter Taylor-Gooby has few doubts about the scale of the change:

> The 2010 Coalition has set itself the challenge of combining an unprecedentedly rapid and profound retrenchment with a fundamental restructuring of the public sector, both to be accomplished within five years. The immediate justification is a presumed need to reduce national indebtedness. The longer-term goal is to shrink the state, free up the market and set British political economy on a new course.
>
> (Taylor-Gooby, 2012: 61)

Concepts such as 'radical' or 'transformative' are, of course, difficult to define with precision or confidence. As Paul Pierson notes, quantitative indicators are, at least over the short run, limited in terms of their usefulness. Public spending levels, for example, may remain at a certain level or indeed rise because of an increase in unemployment or its duration, 'even as social rights and benefits are significantly curtailed' (Pierson, 1996: 157). Furthermore, reforms might have a long-run or lagged impact that is not visible in a particular year's expenditure figures. In his comparative study of welfare retrenchment during the Thatcher and Reagan years, on the basis of disaggregation between policy sectors as well as 'applied path dependency' he drew the conclusion that retrenchment had been limited in character. While council housing provision was vulnerable to dismantling, the NHS, pension provision and much of the post-war welfare state remained intact. Furthermore, as Chapter 2 recorded, the fall in the size of the state (if measured as a proportion of GDP) was limited and increased again once the 1991–92 recession took its toll. And, real (inflation-adjusted) expenditure increased during nearly every year of Margaret

Thatcher's premiership (there were just two exceptions, 1985–86 and 1989–90) (Emmerson and Frayne, 2005: 3).

> Even in Thatcher's Britain, where an ideologically committed Conservative Party has controlled one of Europe's most centralized political systems for over a decade, reform has been incremental rather than revolutionary, leaving the British welfare state largely intact. In most other countries the evidence of continuity is even more apparent.
>
> (Pierson, 1996: 173)

The recent shift in the scholarly literature from path dependency to cumulative and gradualist theories of change has been noted elsewhere in this book. As Wolfgang Streeck records, 'gradual change may have profound enough consequences to justify considering an institution or a social system to be fundamentally transformed by it' (Streeck, 2009: 9). In many ways, this adds to the difficulties encountered in seeking to identify radical, transformational or path-departing change.

Nonetheless, it has been usefully said that partial or gradual reform is that which fails to change the overall character of institutional logics. As a corollary, it follows that researchers should attempt to establish whether there has been a 'tipping point' when institutional 'logics' change in character.

Assessed in these terms, there is every reason to think that when the final balance-sheets are drawn up, the Cameron government will be considered a very radical project. Some tipping points have been passed and institutional logics have shifted markedly. In the Thatcher years, debt interest and high unemployment limited the extent to which departmental spending could be cut. The Cameron government has reduced overall expenditure in real terms by an average of 0.4 per cent annually. Whereas there were 'set piece' privatizations of public utilities during the 1980s, outsourcing has grown relentlessly and dramatically under the coalition and has become a norm. Child benefit, long exalted as a universal benefit and left in place by the Thatcher government, became subject to means-testing. There was a commitment to far-reaching reform of welfare provision and increased labour market flexibility. A single Universal Credit would ensure that there were always incentives to move into employment. Welfare reform had redistributional consequences. Many of the benefit cuts that the Cameron government enacted had regressive effects. They were equivalent to a loss of about 2 per cent of income for the three poorest quintiles in the British population, 1.5 per cent for the next fifth and 1 per cent for the highest quintile (Taylor-Gooby and Stoker, 2011: 8).

Although health provision was ring-fenced from cuts by the coalition government, health costs were rising at a faster rate than inflation, thereby imposing cost pressures. And, at the same time, population growth and demographic shifts, in particular the ageing of the population, implied further demands upon government budgets, thereby leading to substantial policy drift. Furthermore, the Health and Social Care Act (2012) still brought forth important changes. It extended the role of the market, at least in delivery, by seeking to award contracts to 'any willing provider' who might be drawn from either the private or third sector, permitted a form of denationalization through mutualization and created 'clinical commissioning groups' or consortia. They inherited the funds that had previously been the responsibility of Primary Care Trusts and 'bought' services on behalf of their patients from hospitals and other providers. Price could play a role in such a process, leading the British Medical Association to state that it has 'concerns over the use of ... deregulated tariffs in the NHS, because this system brings with it price competition, which can risk basing decisions on price rather than on clinical need' (quoted in Edwards, 2011).[11]

The fate of the 'Big Society'

Nonetheless, despite the scale of these reforms, a proper balance-sheet also has to consider the areas and sectors where change had a more limited or muted character.[12] In other words, the picture of change has to be disaggregated and qualified. In particular, both the localism project and the 'Big Society' faced significant obstacles.

Some elements in the localism agenda were fulfilled. Police and Crime Commissioners were elected, albeit on low levels of voter turnout. Nonetheless, the agenda also hit difficulties. In April 2013, efforts in the Growth and Infrastructure Bill to relax the requirement to secure planning permission for limited extensions to properties were quickly reined in. Although the government saw the relaxation of planning controls as an important part of its 'localism' agenda, a shift away from the bureaucratic state and an extension of homeowners' rights, many Conservative MPs were fearful that neighbours would be unable to prevent unsightly or intrusive building projects. Eric Pickles, the Secretary of State for Communities and Local Government, backed down in the face of the parliamentary revolt and promised an amendment to the proposals so as to incorporate a 'light-touch neighbours' consultation scheme' for building work (*The Huffington Post UK*, 2013).

The 'Big Society' also appears to have lacked sufficient institutional resources and capacity. By 2012, Big Society Capital had been established so as to loan funds to social enterprises but it was in large part drawn from dormant bank accounts and its reserves only totalled £600 million. Such enterprises had to show credit-worthiness and were thereby subject to market considerations. Furthermore, as a critical observer noted: 'it is a bit of a drop in the ocean, given what is happening to the sector, with the deficit-reduction programme really hitting the sector' (*BBC News*, 2012).

Nonetheless, although the localism projects and the 'Big Society' lack traction, the Conservative-led government is pursuing a broader 'inclusion' agenda. That agenda informs, underpins and permeates different initiatives. Some of these initiatives seem to be directly and starkly counter-posed to the government commitment to austerity economics and the rolling back of the state. Others have provoked waves of political anguish from the Conservative Party's traditional supporters and appear to have triggered calls for Cameron's resignation as well as defections to the United Kingdom Independence Party (UKIP). They have nonetheless been pursued because they express and reflect, albeit in a heavily mediated and refracted way, the neoliberal imperatives noted above.

The inclusion agenda draws on efforts both to reconcile the UK socially, spatially and sectorally (thereby addressing the need to both bolster social capital and balance the British economy) and to redraw the boundaries of civil society. Whereas Thatcherism was informed by a 'two nations' perspective and spoke, during the 1984–85 miners' strike, of 'the enemy within', and insofar as it embraced a social agenda by bringing forward Section 28 (of the 1988 Local Government Act), which prohibited the 'promotion' of homosexuality in schools, 'Cameronism' sought an expansion of its boundaries through, for example, same-sex marriage and HS2.

Yet, if the Conservatives reached out in terms of both 'lifestyle choices' and the English regions lying beyond London and the South East, 'inclusion' had its boundaries. There was a striking contrast between the promise of community participation, localism and inclusion (which were structured, as the title of the 2010 Conservative manifesto sharply conveyed, around 'an invitation to join the government of Britain') and the more coercive approaches employed in addressing welfare dependency.

This dualism took a more explicit and rigid form in early 2012 when David Cameron, alongside others in the government, defined the Conservatives through a message that was popularly understood as 'strivers versus skivers'. The party, he said, 'cares about the strivers, the battlers, the family-raisers, the community-builders' (quoted in *Metro*, 2012). The Chancellor of the Exchequer, George Osborne, put it in starker terms:

> Where is the fairness, we ask, for the shift-worker, leaving home in the dark hours of the early morning, who looks up at the closed blinds of their next door neighbour sleeping off a life on benefits? When we say we're all in this together, we speak for that worker. We speak all those who want to work hard and get on. This is the mission of the modern Conservative Party.
>
> (*Channel 4 News*, 2012)

Explaining change

While the 'Big Society' itself made only a limited impact, the Cameron government has for the reasons considered above proved far more path-departing than many had predicted. Those in the Conservative Party's ranks and beyond who saw the Cameron 'modernization' project as an accommodation to Blairism, the centre-ground or metropolitan relativism and expected the formation of a coalition to lead to hesitancy and indecision have been wrong-footed. Many on the Left have perhaps been quicker to recognize this. Cameron 'exploited the crisis to carry out a conservative transformation possibly more radical than that of his model Margaret Thatcher' (Purtill, 2013).

A question arises from this. Given the institutional obstacles and the resilience of paths, in what circumstances can far-reaching change take place? While Paul Pierson emphasizes the 'stickiness' of paths, he also identifies four variables that may influence the likelihood of radical change being enacted. (Nonetheless, these variables are, as Pierson stresses 'only tentative and would need to be subjected to sustained comparative scrutiny'; Pierson, 1996: 176.) First, he considers the extent to which there is 'electoral slack' whereby governments feel confident enough to withstand the electoral fallout that may arise from decisions (such as a decision to withdraw or reform a benefit). Second, he notes (with some prescience) that 'moments of budgetary crisis' (although, and this is difficult to secure, there has to be widespread agreement that there is indeed a crisis and a broad consensus about its character) may allow governments or an administration to make cutbacks but at the same time frame those cuts as efforts to maintain or even rescue a particular programme. Third, opportunities for retrenchment may arise if programmatic cutbacks have only low levels of visibility. This in turn, Pierson argues, may depend upon the structures of government, as policymaking processes may be more difficult to track and it may be more difficult to pinpoint responsibility for measures in federal or separated systems of power. Last, the institutional 'rules of the game' may matter in other ways insofar as they 'can restructure the ways in which trade-offs between taxes, spending, and deficits are presented, evaluated, and decided' (Pierson, 1996: 176– 177). At other points in his account, Pierson also considers, in assessing the opportunities open to potential reformers, the extent to which programmes are strongly or weakly institutionalized, the degree to which a government might gain political credit for a retrenchment measure (which is rare, although the sale of council housing by the Thatcher government in its early days offered opportunities) and the forms of 'political planning' that a government may or may not undertake (Pierson, 1996: 162).

Pierson's variables have certainly stood the test of time. The Cameron government was very aware of its need to exploit the 'electoral slack' offered in 2010. Indeed, there was a conscious decision to frontload the passage of the government's economic reforms so as to maintain the political momentum and take advantage of the 'honeymoons' that incoming governments enjoy. In the case of the Cameron government, the dynamics of coalition also had to be considered. The formation of a full coalition (as opposed to, for example, 'confidence and supply' arrangements between the Conservatives and Liberal Democrats) gave the government greater legitimacy and (despite the reservations of some Liberal Democrats and among rather greater numbers of Liberal Democrat voters) an added layer of support, but there was also an awareness that relationships between the two parties might fray during the years that followed. At the same time, senior Conservatives felt that the Thatcher government had failed to exploit early opportunities and that the Cameron government should learn from this. Francis Maude, who following the 2010 general election became Paymaster General and Minister for the Cabinet Office, was emphatic:

> If you look at the last transitions of governments and the way they came in, I would say one of the things that Thatcher regretted was not pushing ahead vigorously enough, and quickly enough, in terms of reform. The big reforming Thatcher governments were not until 1983 and 1987.
>
> (quoted in Wintour, 2010a)

Furthermore, there was self-evidently a moment of acute budgetary crisis. All three major political parties agreed upon its severity, although there were differences about the pace of austerity measures. All three also agreed that the bulk of the deficit would have to be recouped through expenditure reductions rather than tax rises that, it was argued, would, if imposed, choke the supply side of the economy. While visible measures such as the rise in VAT came early (at the beginning of 2011), the expenditure cuts were spread across most departments and staggered across the years. And, political responsibility was not only shared between the Conservatives and Liberal Democrats (and to some extent Labour, insofar as it had also foreseen the necessity of austerity policies) but distributed between central government and the local councils that had to administer many of the cutbacks. At the same time, the extent and impact of local government cuts varied very considerably between areas. At the beginning of 2014 it was reported that councils in the ten most disadvantaged areas of England faced cuts averaging 25.3 per cent between the financial years 2010–11 and 2015–16, whereas the cuts were only (on average) 2.54 per cent in the ten least deprived areas (Watt, 2014).

All these variables opened the way for the enactment of the radical shifts to which the Cameron government was committed in a way that they had not been during the Thatcher years. Nonetheless, the retrenchment programme was also facilitated by both the framing tactics and the change strategies that the coalition government pursued. As noted above, although real living standards had fallen, perceptions that the Conservatives' economic policy was 'working' contributed much to its political legitimization. Moreover, many of the changes were forms of layering, conversion and drift rather than frontal assaults. Free schools were introduced 'on top' of existing provision while academies represented the conversion of established institutional forms. The NHS reforms were constructed around, and indeed framed as a strengthening of, GPs' practices rather than constituting their displacement. Although there were cutbacks in real (inflation-adjusted) terms, much of the contraction in provision was secured through policy drift. Expenditure failed to keep pace with inflation, the increase in the overall size of the British population and the country's changing demographic composition.

All of this (and the perceived weaknesses of the other parties) enabled the Conservatives to remain electorally competitive. Despite the cuts, support for the

Conservatives in the opinion polls dipped from late 2010 onwards but rarely fell below 30 per cent (UK Polling Report, 2014). While Labour had a poll lead it always appeared to be fragile and tenuous and there were persistent questions about Ed Miliband's leadership. For Conservatives, the challenge posed by UKIP was significant but containable (see below).

There were further reasons why retrenchment was not necessarily accepted and certainly not embraced but tolerated. As John L. Campbell notes, when change is being pursued, elite narratives must connect and resonate with 'public sentiment' (Campbell, 1998). Liam Stanley has, through the use of focus groups, charted perceptions of the crisis and the ways in which austerity was legitimized. Retrenchment policies, Stanley argues, were perceived and understood as a form of penance for over-indulgence by both individuals and government during the pre-crisis years.[13] There was:

> a cultural disposition towards viewing the cutting of the large fiscal deficit as a necessary solution to a moralised crisis of state over-spending, reflecting wider societal experiences of perceived over-spending and related feelings of guilt concerning pre-2008 excessive consumption and financialisation. As one focus group participant put it: 'we're reaping what we sowed'.
>
> (Stanley, 2014)

Often, sentiments such as these overlapped with resentments about welfare expenditure and welfare claimants who were seen as the beneficiaries of government largesse. Polling showed that 44 per cent of respondents said that the total spent on benefits was 'too high', while only 35 per cent said that the figure was 'about right' or 'too low'. Of those who felt it was 'too high', 54 per cent blamed Labour. These findings appear to chime with longer-run studies of attitudinal change that appear to show a swing towards individualism and a shift against collective provision. Whereas, in 1994, 15 per cent attributed economic disadvantage to laziness or lack of willpower, the figure had by 2013 risen to 23 per cent (Meagher, 2013). The Conservatives' framing of the issue in terms of 'strivers' and 'skivers' resonated closely with all these sentiments. Nonetheless, having said this, although retrenchment rallied adherents, there are relatively few indications that the long-run Cameron project, which emerged into the open in late 2013 and looked forward to a permanently shrunken state, had won popular backing. Certainly, there was continuing support for specific programmes and forms of government provision.

Amidst all of this, there is a case for bringing class back into accounts of change during what is often termed the neoliberal era. As early accounts within historical institutionalism stressed, institutions and institutional structures mediate interests. They do not in themselves and in isolation explain political outcomes. Class is not, of course, the only variable in play. As the history of the Tea Party movement in the US highlights, other perceived sources of identity and social cleavages interact with class (see Chapter 5). They include age, gender, race, ethnicity as well as broader and more diffuse perceptions of interest that give rise to self-defined 'winners' and 'losers'. Nonetheless, class and understandings of class also matter. Much of the political caution and hesitancy evident in Margaret Thatcher's first term of office to which Francis Maude referred (see above) can be attributed to her government's fears about the organized labour movement. In 1981, government plans to close a number of coal mines were withdrawn. However, as Colin Hay and Stephen Farrall note, the temporality of Thatcherism is contested. Although some authors, perhaps most notably Peter Hall in his discussion of the paradigm shift as monetarism displaced Keynesianism, focus on the period immediately after Margaret Thatcher took office in 1979, others consider the pace of change at later points (Hall, 1993). Arguably, it was only after the defeat of the prolonged 1984–85 miners' strike (as well as the electoral boost that had already been extended by the Falklands War, the Labour Party's troubles and the Conservatives' resounding election victory in 1983) that Thatcherism took a more radical form. Both the radicalism of the 1987 election manifesto and the later intensification of the reform process can be cited as evidence (Hay and Farrall, 2014: 15).

Populism and populists

A history of the British Right during the crisis years cannot, however, be confined to the Conservative Party, those in its orbit, its allied constituencies or even, for that matter, the institutional framework within which it has sought reforms. The role of the radical Right, most notably UKIP, should also be considered.

In recent years, Rightist populism has been a pan-European development. Parties established or formed through regrouping processes around assertions of national identity and immigration as opposition to the European 'superstate' have made significant electoral gains, particularly in the wake of the economic crisis. Governments and established opposition parties, particularly in the most indebted countries, have had little room for manoeuvre or fiscal flexibility when faced by demands for assistance from even the most vocal constituencies. They have instead committed themselves to the austerity narrative. At the same time, public trust in political institutions has fallen and electoral turnout has been in decline (Schäfer and Streeck, 2013: 2–3). Alongside these factors, the growth of Rightist populism also owes much to 'the accelerated pace of Europeanization' (most notably through economic and monetary union), the removal of long-established social safety nets and perhaps to the changed character of terrorism (as well as perceptions of its associations with Islam and thus immigration) (Berezin, 2013: 241).

Given all of this, it is tempting to group UKIP together with the Front National (France), Dansk Folkeparti (Denmark) or Lega Nord (Italy). All exist on the borders between mainstream politics and the outsiderism that gives them their élan. They have all played a part in reshaping the character of the mainstream. Indeed, some of the sentiments that they express are now shared across much of the political spectrum. As Mabel Berezin notes: 'nationalist rhetoric and policy proposals that are usually the purview of the European populist Right have become part of the centre-Right and, in some instances, Left political discourse' (Berezin, 2013: 239).

There are also, however, similarities between UKIP and its populist counterparts across Europe if its voting base is considered. They all tend to be more male than female. Although UKIP retains some Tory elements (and many of their voters had formerly backed the Conservatives, a process accelerated once the Conservatives entered government, and lived in non-urban southern England), it draws disproportionately upon the white working class, many of whom have lost out in both absolute and relative terms from the economic and cultural changes of recent decades. Studies of UKIP's 2010 vote found that voters were, when compared with supporters of other parties, slightly older and more likely to be white, male, in social classes C2, D and E and less likely to be a graduate (Lynch *et al.*, 2011: 8). They had a sense of displacement and loss that had been hastened by the economic crisis. Real income had fallen precipitously. In short:

> Already disillusioned by the economic shifts that left them lagging behind other groups in society, these voters now feel their concerns about immigration and threats to national identity have been ignored or stigmatised as expressions of prejudice by an established political class that appears more sensitive to protecting migrant newcomers and ethnic minorities than listening to the concerns of economically struggling, white Britons.
>
> (Ford and Goodwin, 2014: 125–126)

Nonetheless, UKIP has its political specificities. In contrast with many other European populist parties it does not have a social-democratic edge to its thinking. It emphasizes the free market and has more of an Atlanticist outlook and a greater commitment to free trade. At times, it has described itself and is described as libertarian. UKIP was also slow to embrace the ideas that define European populism. In its early days, the party had a single-issue character focused on membership of the EU alone as it vied with the Referendum Party. This gave way to 'civic nationalism' as the party sought to distinguish itself very clearly from the British National Party (BNP) and others on the far Right. It only then moved beyond single-issue politics and sought to capitalize upon shifting public sentiments. Increasingly, it offered Rightward populist discourses around immigration, multiculturalism, criminality and hostility to the 'political class' in both Brussels and Westminster.[14]

UKIP's growth was fully evident by the time of the 2009 elections to the European Parliament where the use of the *d'Hondt* system of proportional representation (in the UK) encouraged the rational voter to back minor parties (including the BNP as well as UKIP) and thereby allowed them to make gains. UKIP increased its share of the poll to 16.6 per cent and, perhaps more significantly, secured a significantly broader voting base. Although there were also drops in support, UKIP made gains in the North (Euroscepticism had initially seemed to be a largely southern preoccupation). It also won growing support in working-class and socially disadvantaged areas (Ford and Goodwin, 2014: 77).

Although UKIP's share of the vote fell to just 3.1 per cent a year later in the 2010 general election (although not all seats were contested), the party continued to embrace a broader populist message while maintaining 'hard' Euroscepticism as its primary defining feature. Like the Right populist parties of continental Europe, it spoke in increasingly strident terms about Islam, often going beyond attacks upon those who were 'fundamentalists' and instead putting forward a critique of the Muslim faith itself. All of this seemed to pay off in the 2014 European Parliament elections when UKIP outgunned the other parties by securing 27.5 per cent of the votes and twenty-four seats.

As other sections of the book have argued, tensions and abrasion bring forth shifts. The friction between the Conservatives and UKIP and between government policy and the constituencies upon which UKIP drew, as well as tensions within the Conservative Party itself, was a driver of policy. While the Cameron government held steady on issues such as same-sex marriage (a matter of some, although not overwhelming, importance to UKIP voters, according to a May 2014 poll), it embraced the call for negotiations and a referendum on Britain's continued membership of the EU (ComRes, 2014: 34). Prominent Conservatives, including Boris Johnson, the Mayor of London, began to argue that British withdrawal was to be preferred to membership of an unreformed EU.

The challenge posed by UKIP may also have influenced the Conservative decision in June 2014 to back the broadening of the Conservatives and Reformists group in the European Parliament, to which the Conservatives belong, to include Right populist parties such as Dansk Folkeparti (Denmark) and Perussuomalaiset (The Finns Party) and the decision a few weeks later to make a forthright stand that served as a rallying point against the nomination of Jean-Claude Juncker, former Prime Minister of Luxembourg, as President of the European Commission.

Conclusion

The chapter has put forward four principal points. First, it considered the Conservative-led government's embrace of fiscal retrenchment as a necessary but pragmatic response to the preceding Labour government's alleged over-spending and then, by 2013, fiscal retrenchment as a means by which the long-run shrinkage of the British state could be secured. It has argued that the Conservatives changed their representations of the retrenchment process because of path-dependent logics, the absence of opposition, internal political processes within the Conservatives' parliamentary party and the structural character of British business interests. Second, the chapter noted the relative weakness of the 'Big Society' and localism projects and their failure to secure political take-off. Third, it looked at the extent and scale of the changes ushered in by the Cameron government and the reasons why it was able to bring them into effect. Last, the chapter considered the ways in which the crisis accelerated the growth of UKIP and the ways in which this may have contributed to the reshaping of Conservative politics.

Notes

1 Much of this had been foreshadowed by George Osborne's Mais Lecture in February 2010. It marked the Conservative Party's embrace of austerity as the defining element in its economic thinking (Lee, 2011: 62). There was an understanding that, perhaps paradoxically, the reduction of public expenditure could provide the basis for an effective electoral strategy. As Andrew Gamble notes: 'Osborne in particular sensed that the crash had given the Conservatives a remarkable political opportunity, because for the first time since the exchange rate mechanism debacle in 1992 the Conservatives had an opportunity to take back the mantle of economic competence from the Labour party' (Gamble, 2014: 3).

2 According to David Laws, however, Ed Balls gave a rather different message during the negotiations and asserted that Labour intended to maintain its original deficit-reduction plans (Laws, 2010: 146).

3 The claim that the UK could be compared to Greece was directly challenged by many on the Left. Nonetheless, such was the potency of the comparisons that many chose to accommodate or acquiesce in the lessons of Greece. Labour was, after all, seeking to re-establish its economic management credentials.

4 The IMF's positions seemed to change over time. Together with the European Union and the European Central Bank, it demanded severe austerity policies in Greece as a condition for loans (Blyth, 2013: 79). However, subsequently, the IMF's chief economist stated that the British government was, by imposing cuts on the scale that was being undertaken, 'playing with fire' and called for more government spending. By 2014, the IMF backtracked and, while warning of a housing bubble, acknowledged that the retrenchment programme was 'appropriate' (Armitstead, 2014).

5 This was, the Spending Review noted, the same pace that the preceding Labour government had planned (HM Treasury, 2010: 5).

6 Other calls for 'rebalancing' secured only limited backing among Conservatives. In a 2012 report (*No Stone Unturned in the Pursuit of Growth*), commissioned by Downing Street, Lord (Michael) Heseltine called for the shifting of funds from central government to the regions, more infrastructural projects and the devolution of power so as to reinvigorate the bigger cities (Wintour, 2012).

7 The British government sometimes looked to other countries if policy is considered more broadly. As policy towards immigration toughened, it drew upon Australian initiatives. It was announced that a pilot scheme would be introduced requiring visitors from seven countries (including India and Pakistan) to pay a £3,000 cash bond before being allowed to enter the UK. This would be forfeited if the individual failed to leave the UK by the date when his or her visa expired (Leppard, 2013).

8 Nonetheless, although sequencing processes have their own logic and dynamic, they do not of course take place in a vacuum. Paths always and invariably interact with other paths (and the different tiers introduced in Chapter 1). And, as a consequence, they change in character, and the pace of their development accelerates, decelerates or remains broadly constant.

9 There were also claims that the proposed Transatlantic Trade and Investment Partnership (TTIP) liberalizing trade between the US and the European Union would 'lock in' privatization measures by allowing firms that might be later be taken back into public ownership to seek legal redress (Taylor, 2014).

10 See Chapter 8 for a discussion of reform processes and the character of transformations.

11 Julian Le Grand, who served as an advisor on health issues to Tony Blair, challenged those who saw the Act as a ruptural break. The reforms, he argued, 'are evolutionary, not revolutionary: a logical, sensible extension of those put in place by Tony Blair, which in turn developed the internal market set up by John Major' (Le Grand, 2011).

12 Chapter 8 considers some of the other political obstacles facing reform efforts.

13 Retrenchment was widely framed and understood, as Chapter 5 noted, in terms of a 'morality play'.

14 UKIP was, however, slow to mobilize around growing resentment about immigration from Eastern Europe. It remained focused on EU membership and was fearful of being identified with organizations such as the BNP. The party was still at times described as 'the BNP in blazers' (Ford and Goodwin, 2014: 64–66).

7

Chafing, abrasion and the contemporary Right

This chapter returns to the concept of 'intercurrence'. It surveys the different components of the contemporary Right, the points at which they abrade, the character of the 'chafing' that take place and the political outcomes that emerge from all of this.

The Introduction to the book surveyed the different literatures charting the history and development of the Right over recent decades and suggested that each of these literatures focuses on and captures important processes within a particular political level or tier.

In the UK, scholars have for the most part considered the personality clashes and policy disputes within the Conservative Party and within government during the periods when the Tories have been in office. Their accounts emphasize agency and accord primacy, implicitly or explicitly, to the discretion of political actors. Responsibility for the Conservatives' general election defeats in 1997, 2001 and 2005, for example, was laid at the door of successive party leaders and their weaknesses or miscalculations. Many accounts of Margaret Thatcher's political downfall in 1990 attribute it to her clashes with both Michael Heseltine and Geoffrey Howe. Put another way, there is an emphasis upon the choices made by political actors and an implied assertion that such choices go a very long way in explaining the character of political outcomes.

Much of the US literature has been different in terms of both tone and character. Although there have been many accounts of campaign efforts and personal battles on Capitol Hill or in the higher echelons of the executive branch that have been informed by the exhaustive, although almost always unattributed, briefings given by leading participants, scholarly studies of American conservatism have tended to focus on broad constituencies and the processes of electoral alignment and realignment that periodically take place, particularly those that lend themselves to quantitative analysis. Swing groupings, be they 'soccer moms' or 'NASCAR dads', have attracted close attention.

It is an approach that gives much less weight to agency. Indeed, it might be argued that processes of causality suffer from a degree of neglect. However, insofar as they are brought into the picture, the literature considers settings and contexts. At times, for example, it has surveyed the ways in which changing socioeconomic contexts have paved the way for shifts in partisan allegiances or changes in the relationships between political elites and public opinion.

The third relevant literature, which is drawn from historical institutionalism, considers policy legacies, processes of long-run change and the obstacles that neoliberal reformers have had to face in seeking to transform the institutional landscape. Although not explicitly institutionalist in character, a further related sub-field has sought to assess the degree of change wrought in the UK during the Thatcher years and the points in time during the 1980s at which it took place (Hay and Farrall, 2014). Was, for example, the crucial moment of change in 1979 when the Thatcher government first took office or at a later point, perhaps after the Falklands War, once the 'Thatcherite' faction had firmly established its hegemony within the senior ranks of the Conservative Party?

Within the neoliberalism literature, there has been an emphasis on the logic of particular socioeconomic processes and the application of what Naomi Klein aptly describes as a 'shock doctrine'. While there is usually an acknowledgement that neoliberal regimes are embedded differently and take markedly different forms within contrasting settings so that the character of applied public policy varies from country to country, there is a stress upon the determinate role of capital and the seemingly globalized nature of the drive towards freer markets, decommodification and the roll-back of state social provision.

Last, there is the literature that considers 'Thatcherism' in ideational terms. The literature grew up around the phrase 'authoritarian populism', which was used to describe the form that Thatcherite hegemony appeared to take as it mobilized around particular representations of order, the state, the people and the nation. The literature surveyed the ways in which hegemony was renegotiated and reconfigured and, in turn, provoked a debate about the degree to which Thatcherism was at root cultural or political in character. There was a further divide among those who saw it as largely the latter about its class basis. The discussion took place within a Marxian framework. Did Thatcherism represent a particular class fraction or convey the interests of the bourgeoisie more broadly? Did it enjoy a degree of relative autonomy from class interests or was it a loyal servant of those interests?

Chapter 1 built upon these literatures by introducing the concept of *intercurrence*. It is, as the chapter noted, employed in some studies and surveys of American Political Development (APD). Whereas many other approaches within the social sciences suggest or at least imply that there are institutional complementarities holding together the elements within an economy, a society and political order, intercurrence and APD rest upon the proposition that there is for the most part a lack of 'fit' between different institutional and ideational orders. This is because such orders emerge in different settings, amidst different political configurations and for different purposes. While there may at times be fits, these arise for the most part from contingency or the skills of well-placed actors. In the absence of fits, there will be friction and chafing between orders as they abrade against each other. This, from an APD perspective, is a primary driver of change.

The book argues that the relationships between the levels or tiers captured in each of the literatures surveying the Right are akin to the 'orders' described by APD scholarship. Like an 'order', each tier has its own dynamics and logics and each to some extent develops independently at its own time and pace. Thus, the character of their interactions is akin to intercurrence. There will be friction, chafing and abrasion between them.

Intercurrence, the 'Great Recession' and the contemporary Right

How should the history of the Right during the recession years be interpreted if considered through the prism of the different literatures? If the first of these literatures, which stresses the role of individual and group agency, the ideas they embrace and pursue and the strategies they subsequently employ, is used as a framework for analysis, the development of the Right during the 'Great Recession' should be understood in terms of policymakers, ideational entrepreneurs and the character of their relationships with formal institutional structures.

Thus, from this perspective, the changes made to policy regimes by the Conservative-led coalition government should be described through the Cameron leadership's ideas and beliefs and its capacity to translate these ideas and beliefs into practice. From this perspective, policy was shaped by the belief that the 'structural deficit' was *the* defining economic problem of the immediate period (thus requiring a full coalition rather than a Conservative minority government maintained in office by a 'confidence and supply' agreement), the parliamentary arithmetic that demanded a coalition, the pace and dynamics of the coalition talks between the Conservatives and the Liberal Democrats coupled with the personalities of the principal players during the days that followed the general election in May 2010, Cameron's personal commitment to the third sector and the 'Big Society', and an increasing understanding that the financial markets required the speedy formation of a stable government. As David Laws of the Liberal Democrats later recalled, there was, as the talks between the parties progressed, a growing fear that a loss of market confidence would put upward pressure on interest rates with all the consequences for the broader economy and government debt that would bring (Laws, 2010: 146).

Similarly, seen in this way, the subsequent failure of the 'Big Society' to reach a point that might be described as a 'take-off into self-sustained growth' and the lack of interest in civic conservatism is, from this perspective, largely attributable to an absence of sufficient political will and the displacement of the project, in subsequent years, by other priorities. And, if the course taken by the Right in the US during the recession years is considered, attention would focus, as it does in, for example,

Robert Draper's account, *When the Tea Party Came to Town*, on the deliberations of Republicans in Congress and their relationships with Tea Party activism:

> The protagonists of this story are a few of the 435 American men and women on both sides of the aisle who love their country and who showed up to the Capitol with every intention of leading, or at least serving, the people who voted them into office.
>
> (Draper, 2013: xvii)

Alongside the study of individual protagonists, agency can, however, also be represented, as it has been in a significant proportion of studies, in group-based or collective terms. The Republican 'establishment' (or at least the party's elites), the different funding groups and the organizations around which the Tea Party movement was structured can be understood as conscious and deliberative actors. From this perspective, both the rise of the movement and the different responses of 'establishment' interests can be understood as the product of choices made by those groups and networks in the wake of President Obama's election in November 2008 as they sought to give political expression to their ideas, ideals and values.

Seen through the prism of agency, these choices largely shaped the outcomes that followed. For a significant proportion of those who adopt an agency-led perspective, the movement was much more the product of elite-structured and elite-led activity than the spontaneous citizens' uprising that was depicted in the movement's self-representations. Even those who in other settings embrace a more structural approach have, when considering the Tea Party movement, stressed the role of particular political entrepreneurs and funding organizations. Thus, Americans for Prosperity (AFP) and the Heritage Foundation played an important part in training movement activists (Meagher, 2012: 482). Indeed, it was particularly quick on the uptake. By April 2009, so as to build the Tax Day protests, AFP employed thirty-four national office employees and thirty-five state-level employees (Formisano, 2012: 69). Together with Freedom Works and American Solutions for Winning the Future, an advocacy organization established by Newt Gingrich, the former House of Representatives Speaker, AFP played an important role in establishing the Tea Party Patriots (Brant-Zawadzki and Teo, 2009).[1] The Tea Party Express was created in the summer of 2009 through the efforts of a political action committee and a Republican-leaning consulting and public relations firm. It went on to raise and donate more than $2.7 million to election candidates during 2009 and 2010 (Skocpol and Williamson, 2012: 106–107).

It has also been widely noted that the movement's growth and expansion also owed much to *Fox News* and individual conservative commentators such as Glenn Beck and Rush Limbaugh. Indeed, survey data suggested that Tea Party supporters were more likely to rely on *Fox News* as a source of news than not only the general population but also other Republicans (Disch, 2011: 128). Put another way, *Fox News* and conservative talk-radio outlets served as both 'cheerleader and megaphone' (Skocpol and Williamson, 2012: 121).

Nonetheless, while both individual and group agency-based perspectives are very helpful in establishing an overall picture, some significant caveats should be entered. Although the Tea Party movement was not entirely spontaneous (although there were elements of spontaneity in the story) and certainly not governed by the efforts of volunteer activists alone, it was also not pure 'astroturf' in the way that some accounts and figures, such as then House of Representatives Speaker Nancy Pelosi, have suggested. In other words, the movement was much more than the plaything of outside interests, organizations and individuals. At the very least, as Clarence Lo notes, the movement's decentralized character enabled the different factions and social movement organizations to secure 'marginal autonomy' from both conservative organizations and Republican Party constituencies (Lo, 2012: 99).

Groupings and constituencies

The fate of the Right during the 'Great Recession' can also be considered in terms of the demographic groupings and broad constituencies upon which it drew. As Chapter 5 noted, the Tea Party movement was disproportionately based upon white, older age cohorts with above-average incomes. From this perspective, its politics were shaped by the perceived interests, which were structured around class-based, racial and generational fears, of these groupings. Class and racial fears were particularly pronounced. In an April 2010 poll of Tea Party supporters conducted by the *New York Times* and CBS News, 56 per cent of respondents said that the Obama administration's policies favoured 'the poor'. Some 25 per cent stated that they favoured blacks over whites (*The New York Times*/CBS News, 2010: 24), and 52 per cent said that in recent years 'too much' had been made of the problems facing African-Americans (*The New York Times*/CBS News, 2010: 30).

These expressions of 'Othering' (whereby the interests of one grouping are defined in opposition to another grouping) laid a basis for the construction of coalitional blocs while closing off and precluding others. They overlapped with other divides. Many rested, either explicitly or implicitly, around the question: 'who pays for the debt?' There was a divide between the employed and those without jobs, which was then reinforced by economic recovery: 'Where economic recovery is improving the security of those who have jobs, while leaving others unemployed, it is gradually translating economic dualism into political dualism' (Hall, 2013: 147).

The study of the Right in terms of social and demographic groupings can also be approached in another way. Many accounts, including those written more than half a century ago, consider the perceptions and understandings of particular constituencies by emphasizing the ways in which these are shaped by economic and social circumstances and, in particular, changes in those circumstances. Thus, for many years, the study of 'extremist' movements on the Right was guided, if only implicitly, by notions of modernization, structural dispossession, inter-class cleavages and the generation of 'collective grievances' (Bell, 1963: 19). These processes, it was said, laid a basis for 'extremist' perceptions and outlooks. As Seymour Martin Lipset argued in his 1960 book, *Political Man: The Social Bases of Politics*:

> Extremist movements have much in common. They appeal to the disgruntled and the psychologically homeless, to the personal failures, the socially isolated, the economically insecure, the uneducated, unsophisticated, and authoritarian persons at every level of the society.
>
> (Lipset, 1960: 175)

Similarly, in a 1964 account, Richard Hofstadter talked in similar terms and emphasized the irrationalist political psychologies of many movement participants. He spoke of 'the paranoid style, simply because no other word adequately evokes the sense of heated exaggeration, suspiciousness, and conspiratorial fantasy' (Hofstadter, 1996, orig. 1964: 3).[2]

Although now very dated, these early studies inform more recent accounts of Rightist movements in the US. Like the early studies they depict Rightist movements in terms of structural maladjustment and dispossession. They stress the radical Right's associations with particular social and cultural groupings that feel under siege, such as the white South or evangelical Protestants. During the 1990s (and again more recently), the concept of 'angry white men' provided an axis for the study of the Republican Right and Christian conservative movements as well as the militia and survivalist movements (Baker, 2012).

Seen in this way, movements of the Right, including the Tea Party movement, are a 'hold-out' or 'backlash' against 'modernization', globalization, structural economic strains and the shifts that are remoulding the US as a less overtly religious and more racially and ethnically diverse society in which women and minorities play a more visible and egalitarian role. For example, Chip Berlet ties the growth and development of the movement to the structural economic strains facing whites in middle- and lower-income groupings:

> much of what steams the tea bag contingent is legitimate. They see their jobs vanish in front of their eyes as Wall Street gets trillions. They see their wages stagnate. They worry that their children will be even less well off than they are. They sense that Washington doesn't really care about them. On top of that, many are distraught about seeing their sons and daughters coming home in wheelchairs or body bags. With no one appearing to champion their cause, they line up with the anti-Obama crowd, and they stir in some of their social worries about gay marriage and abortion, dark-skinned immigrants, and a black man in the White House.
>
> (Berlet, 2010)[3]

Ideas

Ideational or discursive explanations can also be employed. Peter Hall has noted the failure of a new or alternative policy paradigm to emerge during the crisis years that might displace market-based thinking (Hall, 2013: 146). Just as Edward Heath's Conservative government (1970–74) performed a U-turn after initially tacking towards free market objectives and quickly fell back on established Keynesian remedies and reflated the British economy because there was no alternative policy paradigm (that only came when Margaret Thatcher and her immediate circle embraced monetarism), so the absence of an alternative paradigm or economic policy framework in the 'Great Recession' allowed fiscal retrenchment to take centre-stage.

And, as Chapter 6 noted, the concept of 'austerity' around which the politics of fiscal retrenchment are structured has an intrinsic moral and cultural appeal insofar as it corresponds closely with widely held assumptions and judgements. Seen in this way, spending reductions are the inevitable payback for over-spending by the reckless and profligate. At times, in these representations, the reckless are relatively small groups indulging their own ideological passions. In the UK, Labour's record in government and the performance of Gordon Brown (as both Chancellor of the Exchequer and then prime minister) have been depicted in this way. And, often, if instances of over-spending and debt appear overseas, it is not only the politicians who are represented as reckless but instead entire nations and peoples. The Greek crises that at times raised the possibility of an exit from the eurozone, or even the possible disintegration of the shared currency, were represented in these terms. The crisis and the austerity programmes that followed were inevitable and deserved retribution for cultural traits that steered individuals away from honest endeavour and labour and turned them instead towards profligacy, corruption and structural inefficiencies: 'austerity is the penance – the virtuous pain after the immoral party' (Blyth, 2013: 13). Economic processes are, as Blyth records, represented in terms of a morality play.

The 'morality play' to which Blyth refers was ideationally reinforced and bolstered by particular strands of economic thought, intellectual frameworks and the popular application of concepts derived from them (Blyth, 2013). Politics, morality and economics become entangled with each other. Periods of 'creative destruction' are necessary. Crises, as Andrew Mellon, President Herbert Hoover's Treasury Secretary, noted, 'purge the rottenness out of the system'. Beyond a certain point, as the Reinhart–Rogoff thesis suggests, government spending stifles economic growth. Furthermore, governments do not have the capacity to spend efficiently or make rational economic decisions. In many instances, government spending is tied to the winning of votes and campaigning needs that arise from the election cycle. It may well also prove to be inflationary.

In place of government spending, 'natural' economic growth requires the removal of supply-side rigidities and a lowering of the many burdens imposed upon productive industry. And, as many on the Right and indeed some on the centre-Left frequently asserted, a debt crisis cannot be resolved by incurring yet more debt.

The institutional architecture

As the book has argued, the institutional landscape can be treated as a further level or tier. Institutional literature stresses the way in which institutions mediate interests and thereby play a pivotal role in shaping outcomes. Furthermore, 'institutions' have in recent decades been redefined by the 'new institutionalism' so that they are now understood in looser and broader terms (see below).

As has been noted, it would, however, be a mistake to disregard the perspectives offered by the 'old institutionalism' of earlier years altogether. It talked of 'institutions', as the term is understood in everyday use, and emphasized formal bodies, structures and codified rules. Their role in the US political process is easily visible. The many veto points and the structural relationships derived from the principle of checks and balances shape the behaviour of actors and the character of the relationships between them.

The effects of the formal institutional architecture upon American conservatism and its policy responses during the crisis years are also readily evident. Republican victories in the November 2010 mid-term elections that gave the party a majority in the House of Representatives and denied the Democrats hopes of cloture in the Senate brought to an abrupt halt the reform process pursued by the Obama administration that had (despite the challenges involved in securing or circumventing the requirement for sixty votes so as to break Republican filibusters) brought forth the Affordable Care Act, the Dodd–Frank Act and the fiscal stimulus.

Alongside this, there were also related issues of government capacity. The limited administrative capacity of the state at federal, state and local level as well as the formal requirements governing contracts and tendering processes had an impact on the policies that could be pursued and the ways in which they could be implemented. Stimulus policies could be limited or held back by the structural inability of sub-governments to implement large-scale spending within a relatively short period. In practice, as the American Recovery and Reinvestment Act was under consideration by the Obama transition team and Congress, and it was becoming clear that the fiscal stimulus package would be very sizeable, local governments made promises about delivery that they did not have the resources to fulfil in their eagerness to secure contracts.

Having said that, and although formalized structural arrangements are an ever-present feature of political life, the embrace of the 'new institutionalism' by scholars from the 1980s onwards broadened out understandings of institutions in ways that offered a basis for more considered accounts of policy development and processes of political change. In particular, the focus on the ways in which policy legacies and established policy frameworks limit, constrain and sometimes empower actors or at the least shape the forms of change that they will in all probability pursue and perhaps secure. As Peter Hall records, as the scale and extent of the financial crisis became only too evident in the closing months of 2008, policymakers instinctively turned to policy ideas derived from the institutional frameworks within which they operated during the preceding years: 'If recession floods the basement and financial crises set fire to the roof, the first reaction of governments will not be to tear the edifice down but to address their problems with the building materials on hand' (Hall, 2013: 143). Drawing upon the distinction that defines the Varieties of Capitalism approach, Hall notes that the liberal market economies such as the US and UK sought to maintain demand levels while the coordinated market economies, most notably Germany, where the labour market is based upon industry-specific skills rather than generalizable skills, moved to preserve existing jobs given the costs that employers would face if they had to recruit and train new employees when the economy revived.

The institutional landscape thus initially pushed some countries towards stimulus policies but at the same time constrained the extent to which those policies could be pursued. They certainly prevented the passage of a second stimulus package along the lines that some, most notably Paul Krugman, advocated. This inevitably limited the economic effectiveness of the stimulus policies that were pursued and thereby facilitated the claims of those on the Right who posed a sustained ideational alternative.

Neoliberalism and economic elites

As has been noted at different points in the book, the recent history of the Right can also be understood in terms of the logics associated with neoliberalism. The Tea Party movement has, in particular, been described as the 'top-down' creation of particular financial and commercial interests. In a celebrated comment, former House of Representatives Speaker Nancy Pelosi used the word 'astroturf' to describe the movement. She was invoking a term that had been employed during the 1980s to describe the front organizations established or backed by corporations seeking commercial gain while at the same time concealing their true purposes through talk of a broader public interest (Formisano, 2012: 7).

Similarly, in an analysis that draws upon classical representations of Marxism, William I. Robinson and Mario Barrera locate the rise of the Tea Party movement within the context of capitalist decay. From this perspective, the 'Great Recession' from 2007–8 onwards was a 'restructuring crisis'. Like the crises of the 1930s and 1970s, it had 'the potential to become a systemic crisis, depending on how social agents respond to the crisis and on the element of contingency that is unpredictable and always plays some role in historical outcomes' (Robinson and Barrera, 2012: 6). This, in turn, gives rise to efforts by the transnational capitalist class to quell protests and dissent. These efforts may bring forth 'twenty-first century fascism' (Robinson and Barrera, 2012: 8). Approached in this way, the Tea Party movement should be considered alongside 'violent hate groups' and the campaigns against immigration. Taken collectively, they pave the way for institutionalized oppression insofar as all are expressions, they argue, of 'the psychopathology of white decline, sharp militarization and pervasive policing' and have 'fascistic characteristics' (Robinson and Barrera, 2012: 4).

Other class-based analyses are much more restrained in tone but also tie demands for austerity or 'constitutional government' to the interests of capital. In accounts of the UK, the disproportionate weight of finance capital has long been emphasized. Contemporary studies echo Keynes who, in his writings, asserted that the pound's return to the gold standard at pre-parity with the dollar in 1925 served the interests of the rentier. Finance capital, it was said, saw its interests lying overseas and sought only short-term returns. In contrast, domestic capital in both the extractive industries and manufacturing, which required long-run investment, suffered the consequences. The return to gold raised export prices thereby reducing international competitiveness and setting the scene for the prolonged miners' dispute and the May 1926 General Strike (Pollard, 1970).

The spirit of Keynes's critique of Britain's economic structure and policymaking processes hangs over studies of contemporary austerity politics. Indeed, in an account that could have been written in the 1920s, the Conservative Party has been described as 'effectively the political wing of the City of London' (Milne, 2011).

From this perspective, finance capital secures leverage through both structural and instrumental power.[4] It exercises structural power through the scale of its contribution to the UK economy and the embedded fear that, if policies are pursued that the City of London perceives as a challenge to its interests, financial assets would be transferred and the markets destabilized. The financial sector also seeks and secures instrumental power, in other words leverage, over specific policy-making areas through lobbying efforts and campaign contributions. *The Guardian* reported in 2011 that more than half the donations totalling £12 million given to the Conservatives during the preceding year were given by the City and banking, in particular hedge funds, financiers and private equity firms (Milne, 2011).

Friction and abrasion

Each of these tiers or levels provides a valid and legitimate approach to the study of the Right and indeed political processes more broadly. It would, of course, be trite just to state that there is interaction between these tiers or levels. The pivotal issue is instead the form and character of such interaction between the different tiers and levels. As noted above, the concept of intercurrence is tied to the points of friction, 'chafing' and abrasion between orders. It is these 'abrasion points' that play an important part in bringing forth change and shaping the forms and extent of the changes that take place. If the experience of the US Right during the course of the crisis years and the growth of the Tea Party movement is considered, five such abrasion points can be identified.

First, although at times hidden by the accommodations that both sides made and the early willingness of the 'establishment' to employ the forms of rhetoric associated with more radical forms of Rightist activism, there were profound tensions between the Tea Party movement and the Republican Party 'establishment'. These were exposed in their most visible form during efforts by Tea Partiers to dislodge Republican incumbents, most notably the defeat of House Majority Leader Eric Cantor in June 2014. Having said that, the term 'establishment' (which was popularized by the movement and figures such as former Alaska governor, Sarah Palin) should be used with caution. There are certainly Republican elites. Some are based in particular institutional locations, most notably Congress or the different state legislatures. Others control funding or the campaigning and mobilizing resources that candidates and their supporters seek to secure.

To some degree such elites, particularly those serving as elected public officials, have independent interests. In particular, those in leadership positions are compelled by their location and circumstances to recognize that crises and confrontations can be destabilizing and that politics in Washington, DC, always depends upon a degree of cross-party compromise and negotiations between Congress and the White House so that no single interest gained all of its original bargaining position. The alternative is gridlock and stasis.

However, this having been said, it would be over-simplistic to represent Republican politics in terms of 'elite' versus 'mass' or 'establishment' versus grassroots radicals. Party elites have independent interests but they are also pulled towards activists and the broader movement. Their role is characterized by what might be dubbed embedded ambivalence. At times, elites in legislative institutions have to secure bipartisan compromises but they also require broader endorsement for their actions because such endorsement confers legitimacy upon them. So as to secure re-election they seek the mobilizing and campaigning efforts of activists, campaign contributions and primary victories. Because elites are pulled in different directions at the same time, there is no sharp dividing line in the way that attempts to apply crude elite theory to the study of contemporary Republicanism may suggest.

The political career of John Boehner, Speaker of the House of Representatives, is instructive. Boehner had backed the 2001 No Child Left Behind Act, which Tea Partiers later saw as an intrusive and expansive attempt to direct school-level education, and, with more obvious reservations, the Emergency Economic Stabilization Act of 2008. Yet, he was quickly able to embrace the Tea Partiers. As *The New Yorker* later noted:

> Boehner aggressively wooed the insurgents, spending much of the summer travelling, often by motor coach, to campaign events – he attended more than a hundred and sixty – and donating millions of dollars from his own campaign chest to the challengers. He adopted the overheated Tea Party rhetoric in vowing to dismantle the Obama health-care plan ('this monstrosity'), and, after the election, he announced a renewal

> of the Republican moratorium on budgetary earmarks and forswore domestic travel by military jet, a relished perk of his predecessors.
>
> (Boyer, 2010)

Boehner's shifting political persona was driven by shifts in elite positions as they sought to connect with the movement while at the same time pursuing their own interests. This led to efforts, by Republican elites, to harness the Tea Party movement. Boehner told a private meeting of the Republican Conference: 'I urge you to get in touch with these efforts and connect with them ... The people participating in these protests will be the soldiers for our cause a year from now' (quoted in Boyer, 2010).

The processes of interaction between Tea Party activism and the Republican 'establishment' were mediated through the formal institutional architecture that governed the political process, particularly the parties and electoral systems. That architecture energized and empowered the movement by providing structures of political opportunities at pivotal moments, but also imposed limits and constraints.

In contrast with the European parties, both the Democrats and Republicans have fragmented structures. Indeed, they should be considered as networks of different organizations and constituencies rather as structured or hierarchical bodies. Furthermore, the use of primaries, caucuses and party conventions to select candidates (the last two of these offering particular opportunities to those with organizational skills and high levels of motivation, such as the supporters of Congressman Ron Paul in the 2008 and 2012 presidential contests), the sheer frequency of elections, the staggered nature of different election cycles, the calling of special elections if a member of Congress resigns or dies (an institutional feature that is absent in some European systems of government) – all of these factors give outsider groups chances and opportunities that are largely denied in other political systems. The relatively empty character of many Republican Party organizations, particularly at precinct level, also facilitated the entry and participation of committed Tea Party-aligned activists.

At the same time, political resources are distributed between multiple loci including officeholders at federal, state and local level, advocacy organizations, particular media outlets, influential ideational and policy entrepreneurs, structured networks and funding sources. Such sources may be individuals who command large sums or organizations such as 527s established either by individuals or networks so as to campaign around issues during election periods, political action committees (PACs) or the relatively new generation of 'Super PACs' that have organized 'independent' campaigns in support of particular candidates.

The impact of all these different actors has been shaped by regulatory structures. In recent years, successive US Supreme Court rulings have reduced or eliminated many of the limits and barriers that earlier legislation had sought to impose. *McCutcheon* v. *Federal Election Commission* (2014) removed aggregate campaign contribution limits that had formerly governed federal elections and contributions to candidates, parties and PACs. Following the *McCutcheon* ruling, donors can contribute to as many candidates, party committees and PACs as they wish. Although the effects of the ruling should not be exaggerated, this may rein in some of the fragmentation processes that have taken place. If candidates and party organizations can now attract more donations, election campaigns may be less subject to the decisions and actions of 'independent' organizations such as 527s or individual policy entrepreneurs.

Nonetheless, although the institutional character of the party system and the decentralized nature of campaign funding 'invited' the growth of the Tea Party movement and enabled it to defeat incumbent Senator Bob Bennett from Utah in 2010 by denying him a place on the primary ballot process, as well as removing House Majority Leader Eric Cantor in 2014, it also placed some limits upon the movement's growth and gave opportunities to 'establishment' Republicans to regroup and mobilize. As the elites regained political confidence, and became more willing to express their own interests openly, they too sought to secure resources and funding so as to deter credible primary challenges against Republican incumbents in the 2014 mid-term contests and compel those associated with Tea Partiers to concentrate their efforts on open seats or on the dislodging of a sitting Democrat. In some cases, party rules or state law provided further opportunities for Republicans fighting off Tea Party challengers. In June 2014, Mississippi Senator Thad Cochran who was backed by the National Republican Senatorial Committee fought off a sustained Tea Party effort to dislodge him by drawing in African-Americans and Democrats to vote in the Republican run-off primary.

The second critical 'abrasion point' was between the ideas of the Right, particularly those that defined the Tea Party movement, and the policy legacies created by the political and administrative efforts of preceding generations. Whereas the movement was structured around calls for 'constitutional' government, much state provision for the American 'middle class' (which, as noted earlier, often takes an invisible or only partially visible form) and, to a much lesser degree, provision for those at the lower end of the socioeconomic scale is deeply embedded. As theories of path dependence suggest, the potential cost of path-departing change rises over time as extensive institutional complementarities take shape and then crystallize. Attempts to change one area of policy would almost certainly have spillover effects in other policy areas. The political outcomes generated from the tensions between the ideational demands of militant conservatism and the policy inheritances that surround them depend upon the creative skills and the political imagination of well-placed actors. Such actors will more often than not fail in their efforts.

Chapter 5 recorded instances of that creativity. House Budget Committee Chairman and 2012 vice-presidential running-mate Congressman Paul Ryan felt required to frame his proposals for reform (the 'Ryan Plan') in terms of maintaining and extending the legacy of Medicare (and to some extent Medicaid) and thereby building upon the aspirations of President Lyndon Johnson (see p. 107). The Ryan Plan itself thereby rested upon conversion and layering rather than the immediate displacement of Medicare provision. Medicare was to become a system based upon the provision of a 'premium-support payment', market choice, subsidy and 'top up' so that individuals could add to a basic level of cover (House Budget Committee, 2012: 45).

Social Security was approached more cautiously and the goals of reformers were as a corollary much more restrained, reflecting its more deeply embedded character. There are, after all, formidable institutional obstacles to pension reform. Put crudely, most pension schemes were initially established by requiring one generation to pay the pensions of the preceding generation. Given these continuing structural arrangements, it would be difficult, and electorally dangerous, to put forward reform plans that compelled individuals to contribute to both their own pension provision and that of current senior citizens at one and the same time. This inevitably puts a 'lock' on the reforms that are feasible. The Ryan Plan spoke in cautiously positive terms about proposals for more targeted forms of benefit, but beyond this it was imprecise. It stated that if it was established that Social Security was not sustainable as the longevity of life increased and the population aged, the president would have to submit 'a plan'. Congressional leaders would be required to put forward 'their best ideas as well' and together they would 'move the conversation to solutions that save Social Security' (House Budget Committee, 2012: 56).

All this ties together with a third (albeit related) 'abrasion point'. Although it has not as yet taken a developed form, there has also been chafing and abrasion between the free market commitments of the Tea Party movement and the self-defined interests of the constituencies upon which it draws. As has been noted, senior citizens are disproportionately represented in the movement's ranks. Thus, when polls were conducted, respondents gave mixed answers when asked about those forms of government provision of which seniors were direct beneficiaries. According to the *New York Times*/CBS News poll (April 2010), 92 per cent of Tea Party supporters predictably favoured a smaller government providing fewer services rather than a larger government offering more (*The New York Times*/CBS News, 2010: 14). Some 73 per cent said that they would accept cuts to Social Security and Medicare, but nonetheless the programmes were regarded in broadly positive terms, while 62 per cent of Tea Party respondents said, for example, that their benefits were 'worth the costs of those programs for taxpayers' (*The New York Times*/CBS News, 2010: 26). Although there was intense opposition to the individual mandate, included within the Affordable Care Act, that required nearly all individuals to purchase health insurance coverage or face a tax penalty, there was substantial backing (56 per cent) for the provision in the Act that required health insurance companies to accept all those with pre-existing health conditions (such as chronic illnesses or disabilities), although such conditions would inevitably impose significant costs upon them (*The New York Times*/CBS News, 2010: 26).

Fourth, there was periodic chafing and abrasion between the Tea Party movement (and at times the Republican elites) and business interests. There were differences when the fiscal stimulus (the American Recovery and Reinvestment Act) was under consideration in early 2009. Although they had some reservations, the peak business organizations and individual companies welcomed the Act, seeing it as a boost to consumer demand and in some instances hoping for tendering opportunities. The US Chamber of Commerce's Executive Vice President of Government Affairs said in a press statement:

> While we're concerned with individual items in this package, the whole is more important than the individual parts. The global economy is in uncharted and dangerous waters and inaction from Washington is not an option ... Spending on 'shovel-ready' construction projects, expanding broadband access, and modernizing our health care information are major steps toward boosting our nation's infrastructure and creating American jobs.
>
> (US Chamber of Commerce, 2009)

In contrast to business attitudes, however (and as noted in Chapter 5), there was almost unanimity among Congressional Republicans that the American Recovery and Reinvestment Act (ARRA) should be rejected. Although later tensions between Tea Party groupings and business interests were for the most part kept in check by a sense of shared opposition to the Obama administration, the perceived effects of its regulatory policies and the costs imposed by healthcare reform, there were periodic clashes.

There were significant strains when it seemed that the federal government debt ceiling would not be increased during the government shutdown in October 2013. As the shutdown approached, a broad coalition of 251 business and trade organizations led by the US Chamber of Commerce wrote an open letter to members of Congress opposing the move, saying: 'It is not in the best interest of the employers, employees or the American people to risk a government shutdown that will be economically disruptive and create even more uncertainties for the U.S. economy' (quoted in Wilkie, 2013). Speaking in January 2014, Thomas Donohue, President and CEO of the US Chamber of Commerce, drew a distinction between the ranks of the early Tea Party movement, who were, he said, 'good people', and the movement's later adherents:

> It's the group of people that have hitched their trailer to the tea party name and want to come to Washington and shut down the government and not pay our debts and do that sort of thing ... That we're not going to be supporting.
>
> (quoted in Morganteen, 2014)

Then, in mid-2014, Tea Party protests against the Export–Import Bank, a government agency that provided assistance for foreign purchasers of US planes, lorries and other products (which the movement represented as a form of 'crony capitalism' and 'corporate welfare'), pitted the movement against the US Chamber of Commerce (Goldfarb and Yeager, 2014).

Fifth, there were processes of ideational tensions and stresses *within* the Right, in other words between its constituent groupings, stands and factions. The abrading between the Tea Party movement's free market commitments and the interests of the groupings upon which it drew have already been noted. However, there were also tensions and strains between the movement's emphasis upon economic issues and the influence of religious or cultural conservatism that had defined important sections of the Republican Right from the late 1970s onwards. Indeed, some figures associated with the religious Right feared that the Tea Party movement was a repudiation or at the least an abandonment of moral issues. There were periodic clashes and the differences between the factions affected the 2012 Republican presidential primaries by dividing votes between Senator Rick Santorum, seen as a champion of moral conservatism, and Congressman Ron Paul, who stressed economic issues and market freedoms.

Consequences

All in all, the shape and character of the American Right during the crisis years owe much to the chafing and abrasion between the different tiers that define it. The 'abrasion points' between Tea Party activism and Republican elites produced unstable and destabilizing political outcomes that inevitably enfeebled campaigning efforts by the party's candidates. The 2012 presidential primaries dragged on (a process exacerbated by the Republican Party's rules governing the pre-nomination period) and Governor Mitt Romney, who had been compelled to tack heavily Rightwards during the primary campaign, had relatively few assets as a candidate. Indeed, he could be regarded as the 'lowest common denominator' in a frequently bitter contest. He secured the nomination not so much because of his own strengths (although his business record and experience as governor in Massachusetts, customarily regarded as the most Democratic and bluest of states, could potentially have served as such), but because the other contenders seeking the Republican presidential nomination, particularly former House Speaker Newt Gingrich and former Senator Rick Santorum, had significant political and personal 'negatives'.

In Congress, the tensions between activists and party elites led Republican legislators to steer an erratic and uneven course. While Republican leaders at times adopted fearsome rhetoric in their denunciations of the Obama White House, it could not be matched by their deeds leading to eleventh-hour compromises and the abandonment of the 2013 government shutdown.

At the same time, the tensions and abrasions between tiers caused profound difficulties when it came to generating new policy ideas that would pose a sustained and electorally credible alternative to the reforms pursued by the Obama White House and Congressional Democrats. Put another way, processes that are comparable with intercurrence stifled significant parts of the US knowledge regime.

The concept of 'knowledge regimes' requires some unpacking. Knowledge regimes are the 'sets of actors, organizations, and institutions that produce and disseminate policy ideas that affect how policy-making and production regimes are organized and operate in the first place' (Campbell and Pedersen, 2011: 167). Think tanks, such as the Heritage Foundation, the Cato Institute and the American Enterprise Institute for Public Policy Research (AEI), as well as some advocacy and scholarly research organizations play a pivotal role in such regimes insofar as their activities are structured around the generation, development and transmission of policy ideas.

It has been argued that liberal market economies such as the US and UK are characterized by competitive, market-oriented knowledge regimes, structured by their relationship with the production and policy regimes, within which there are winners and losers.

> Of course, competition and conflict over ideas exist within all types of knowledge regimes. Our point is that the manner in which this is handled and whether it produces winners and losers or compromise and consensus depend on the institutional configuration of the political economy in question.
>
> (Campbell and Pedersen, 2011: 168)

From this perspective, there are, however, important differences between the liberal market economies. Decentralized and open states such as the US are likely to have 'market-oriented knowledge regimes that are highly competitive and are often partisan and adversarial'. In contrast, more centralized and closed states, most notably the UK, 'also tend to have competitive knowledge regimes, but the level of partisan competition is tempered politically by public funding for knowledge producers in civil society and by the state's own analytic capacities' (Campbell and Pedersen, 2011: 168).

By stressing the competitiveness of the US knowledge regime, there appears to be a high level of symmetry or a 'fit' between the character of the knowledge regime and that of the production and policymaking regimes. However, there are reasons to question the extent to which the contemporary US knowledge regime is competitive (either in terms of think tanks' and other research organizations' relationships to each other, or in the nature of the bidding process whereby they secure access to policymakers). Indeed, it is more credible to argue that the US knowledge regime has a largely cartelized character. Its relationship with other regimes is thereby much less of a 'fit' than it might initially appear.

Regime cartelization goes a long way beyond a simple dividing line between Left and Right. Within both the Left and Right, the major think tanks have established their own distinct, separate and discrete 'market' segments or spheres. Within the conservative Right, the AEI considers policy in relatively broad terms and focuses, in particular, on foreign policy issues. It has been closely associated with a 'neoconservative' vision of the US's global role. For its part, the Heritage Foundation often undertakes more meso-level research work and has specialized in ensuring that its conclusions and findings can be conveyed to legislators in an accessible form that could be utilized on Capitol Hill and, at times when the White House is held by the Republicans, within the administration. More significantly, although Heritage Action (which was founded in 2010 as an advocacy arm) has at times challenged the Republicans' Congressional leadership, with which it has strained relations, the Heritage Foundation itself has long been closely aligned with conservative and Republican 'orthodoxy' and has sought to reconcile those within the conservative movement who emphasize the primacy of economic issues and those who emphasize the pivotal character of social and cultural concerns. The Cato Institute has much more of an overtly libertarian character. Cato stresses free market principles, and largely concentrates on economic issues such as tax reform and deregulation, but at the same time shies away from social conservatism. Indeed, it has associated itself with calls to constrain the role of the state in regulating social questions, opposes many US military actions overseas and has criticized the extension of state powers through measures such as the USA Patriot Act of 2001.

When new think tanks have been created (and the process of expansion has in part been driven by processes of partisan and ideational polarization, the growth of founding sources, the opening up of further areas of contestation within the US polity and, at least arguably, the search for employment and influence by former members of Congress or successive administrations), they have not operated as competitors seeking to secure a market segment already held by another research unit. Instead, they have staked out, occupied and effectively dominated a sector of the knowledge market that had hitherto been undeveloped or at least under-developed.

The think tanks created in recent decades within the conservative orbit have thus for the most part been directed towards small and narrow niches (defined in terms of either area or ideology) that had hitherto attracted relatively little attention. The Project for the New American Century (1997–2006), which considered foreign and defence policy issues from a neoconservative perspective, and the Ethics and Public Policy Center, which was formed in 1976 and is 'dedicated to applying the Judeo-Christian moral tradition to critical issues of public policy', are broadly representative examples (Ethics and Public Policy Center, 2012).

The effects of cartelization fuse together with the effects of partisan and ideational polarization. Over recent decades, the parties have moved further from each other and a large proportion of Congressional votes have closely followed party lines, whereas in the mid-century years, coalitional blocs were generally built *across* party lines on a bill-by-bill basis. This has had important consequences for the Right. As Jacob Hacker and Paul Pierson argue, the process of ideological and partisan polarization has been *asymmetric* in character. By this they mean that the Republicans have moved far further ideologically in terms of political positioning than the Democrats. Indeed, they argue, by the early 2000s, the median Senate Republican was 'essentially twice as conservative' as in the early 1970s (Hacker and Pierson, 2005: 29).

There has been a further parallel development. Over recent decades, as processes of ideational and partisan polarization have become more pronounced, new gatekeepers and gatekeeping processes have emerged. They define what is, or is not, legitimate within the relatively narrow ideational parameters that define the contemporary Right. Accounts suggest, for example, that figures such as Grover Norquist, president of Americans for Tax Reform, have been pivotal. A report in *Mother Jones* has described the regular Wednesday morning meetings convened by Norquist:

> The invitation-only meetings Norquist hosts have become a hot ticket for Washington's conservative in crowd, the place for GOP players to brainstorm, swap intelligence, and see and be seen. The 100-plus people who come each week are the powers who run the federal government – congressmen, lobbyists, senior White House and Senate staffers, industry-group leaders, and Right-wing policy wonks.
>
> (Scherer, 2004)

Such meetings, within which Norquist himself is *primus inter pares*, have been said to play a pivotal role in determining which policy ideas go forward and which are sidelined or cast aside.

Norquist has added to the scope of his influence through the use of the 'Taxpayer Protection Pledge' that was to be signed by election candidates. In 2011, the *New York Times* estimated that 95 per cent of Congressional Republicans had taken the pledge never to raise taxes for any reason. If a tax deduction is removed, the subsequent increase in revenue will be matched with further tax reductions (*The New York Times*, 2011).

Taken together, cartelization, polarization, gatekeeping and the processes of chafing and abrasion between the Right's different factions structure the character of the policy development process. Cartelization stifles any prospect of ideational competition and thus suppresses policy innovation. Polarization and gatekeeping limit the range of policy ideas that are regarded as acceptable or credible insofar as the principal political parties, which were once broad and heterogeneous coalitional blocs, are now defined by firm and relatively narrow sets of ideological principles.[5] Thus, policy proposals that, for example, endorse the notion of global warming or even give credence to it now lie beyond the bounds of legitimate conservative discourse.

Given all of this, the US conservative think tanks have largely steered away from policy initiation. Instead, they build upon, extend and develop ideas that have already been embraced and accepted within the Right. Such ideas will not only have survived gatekeeping processes but will also be acceptable to most of the different factions within the Right. In practice, few policy ideas can surmount these obstacles.

Thus, as has been widely noted, the American Right has played a major role in blocking or seeking to block the policy reforms promoted by the Obama White House and the Congressional Democrats, but it has been largely unable to develop its own policy alternatives.

Intercurrence and the British Right

The contrasting fate of the British Right during the recession years can similarly be assessed in terms of tiers and processes that are akin to intercurrence. Again, those tiers can be identified by considering the principal forms of literature that have defined the study of the Right.

If the British Right is studied at the level of party, there have self-evidently been tensions, at times subdued and at other moments visceral, between the Conservatives and their coalition partners, the Liberal Democrats. Some, particularly those in the Home Office, Department for Education and the Department for Energy and Climate Change, have been widely reported.[6] The tensions were, however, held in check by the political investment that the Conservatives had made in the coalition government, the commitment to maintain the arrangement over a five-year period and the seeming unpopularity of the Liberal Democrats, who feared an electoral disaster.

There were, however, other processes of chafing and abrasion. There were profound ideational tensions between the Cameron project and traditionalist Conservative constituencies as those constituencies resented what they perceived and understood as a modernization project imposed by unrepresentative elites. In particular, the stresses came to a head around issues such as same-sex marriage, HS2, immigration and Britain's relationship with the European Union. These stresses led to tensions within the party but also fuelled the further and continued growth of the United Kingdom Independence Party.

In many ways, the chafing between these different sentiments and policies were navigated fairly effectively by the Conservative leadership, although there were forecasts that the EU could still cause a split within the party that would be on a scale comparable with the ruptures that took place in 1846 when the Corn Laws were repealed. The latent tensions within the party were evident in 2013–14. Whereas some (including David Cameron himself) asserted that they backed membership of a reformed EU, others leaned towards withdrawal or argued that they could only support continued membership if there were fundamental reforms that changed the structural character of the EU. The pledge to hold a referendum on Britain's continued membership of the EU after renegotiations had taken place held the party together, although there were efforts by those whose faith in the leadership was limited to bring the referendum forward and to place the commitment on a statutory basis.

There were also tensions around the 'Big Society'. There had been stresses during the 2010 general election campaign as efforts to promote the Big Society jarred with more established Conservative ideas and the motivations of party activists. These tensions, and the weakness of the constituencies that supported the project, led to it being relegated to a lowly place on the political agenda. Localism caused rather more friction as tensions inevitably arose between the commitment to localism and the principle of subsidiarity and the government's efforts to brand itself and pursue national policy goals. This arose, for example, in the efforts of Eric Pickles, the Local Government Secretary, to restrict the ability of local councils to regulate car parking. In June 2014, it was announced that councils would be prohibited from using CCTV cameras and drivers would be encouraged to appeal against the issue of parking tickets (Hope, 2014). Similarly, the commitment to the devolution of authority over school administration to schools themselves, through the expansion of academies and 'free schools', created strains when it was alleged that the governance of some schools had been 'infiltrated' by Muslim activists.

There were further strains if economic policy is considered. The reliance on the Bank of England's commitment to quantitative easing as a way of maintaining demand levels, which was pursued in the absence of an activist fiscal policy, created a threat of new asset bubbles as wealth-holders sought a higher rate of return than the very low or negative real interest rates offered to savers by banks. There were also tensions, or at least potential tensions, between the Help-to-Buy programme, which offered financial guarantees to first-time home buyers, a grouping pivotal in the representations of social mobility to which Conservative ideational frames were tied and important to Conservative-leaning constituencies, and the broad economic strategy that the government pursued.[7] While (in the six months leading up to March 2014) Help-to-Buy loans only constituted 1.3 per cent of the total number of mortgages taken out (and many of these were in the more disadvantaged parts of the country), they had indirect effects insofar as they fuelled expectations that house prices would continue rising, thus putting further upward pressure on prices. Indeed, between March 2013 and March 2014, average London house prices rose by 17 per cent (Douglas, 2014). Inevitably, the property bubble exacerbated the regional disparities that the government was committed to reducing, thereby further slowing labour mobility across the country still further.

Conclusion

The chapter has focused on the processes of abrasion between different institutional structures and ideational orders as well as the strains within particular policy regimes or between competing sets of policy ideas. It has been argued that outcomes are in large part shaped by the form and character of the abrasion processes that take place as they interact with each other, as well as the efforts of actors to manage or coexist with those processes. Thus, the US Right was driven by the tensions between the Tea Party movement, Republican elites, ideas, constituencies and, at times, business interests. In the UK, the abrasion was often less visible and actors seemed to navigate between orders and ideas with greater success and aplomb, although the tensions often seemed to have the capacity to break out into open forms of political warfare.

Notes

1 FreedomWorks was led until 2012 by former Republican House of Representatives Majority Leader Dick Armey.

2 As an illustration, Hofstadter cited the celebrated claim by Robert Welch, founder of the John Birch Society, that President Dwight Eisenhower was 'a dedicated, conscious agent of the Communist conspiracy' (quoted in Hofstadter, 1996: 28).

3 This account, which stands in contrast to those that represent the Tea Party movement as a reaction against those most severely hit by economic shifts, has to be squared with empirical surveys of the movement indicating that participants were drawn from more affluent groupings and older age cohorts (*The New York Times*/CBS News, 2010: 41).

4 The distinction between the structural and instrumental power of business is drawn from Jacob Hacker and Paul Pierson (Hacker and Pierson, 2002).

5 Both the Republicans and Democrats were for long periods relatively diverse coalitions. Both parties represented within their ranks very different interests and ideational groupings. The passage of legislation required and secured the construction of cross-party coalitions.

6 There were also intra-Conservative clashes, most notably the battles between the Home Office and the Department for Education in mid-2014.

7 The Help-to-Buy scheme might also be regarded as a quasi-Keynesian mechanism aimed at boosting consumer demand.

8

A permanently leaner state?

The concluding chapter considers the durability of the processes of restructuring and the efforts to create a permanently leaner state that are now taking place, particularly in the UK. It argues that despite the radicalism of the changes being ushered in, they are nonetheless vulnerable to later roll-back

In surveying the state and its institutional 'stickiness', Chapter 2 suggested that gradual change processes may have a rather more limited character than it sometimes appears. While the scholarly pendulum has now swung decisively towards accounts that stress the capacity of gradual reform processes, based upon, for example, layering, drift or conversion, to bring forth long-run transformations, such processes can also by their very nature provide openings and opportunities that enable some of those opposed to a reform to instigate counter-mobilizations that may then rein in and in some circumstances roll back that reform. Or, actors can run up against many more institutional obstacles than they had originally anticipated. In short, the capacity of gradualism to bring forth significant change cannot be assured but is instead contingent upon particular settings and circumstances. It cannot, in other words, be taken for granted.

Limits of gradualism

There is certainly evidence in both the UK and the US to support such a picture. Despite the Cameron government's commitment to fiscal 'consolidation', the early targets for deficit reduction and the repayment of debt within the lifetime of the 2010–15 parliament had to be substantially revised because of persistently lower-than-expected growth, reduced revenues and increased demands upon government. According to the Office for Budget Responsibility (OBR), the cyclically adjusted current budget would be in surplus (at 1.5 per cent of GDP) only by 2018–19 (Office for Budget Responsibility, 2014: 16). Furthermore, by 2013–14, the Chancellor of the Exchequer had to revise his earlier forecasts that the debt to GDP ratio would fall between 2014/15 and 2015/16.[1] According to commentators: 'We are still as far away from the (budget deficit) target as we were in 2010 ... Indeed, it would not be surprising if not just 2015 but also 2020 was an "austerity" election' (quoted in *BBC News*, 2013b).

Thus, given all of this, further and continuing expenditure cuts were required. Nonetheless, political exigencies intervened. For the most part the budget cuts were postponed until after the 2015 general election and for some on the Right this put a question mark against their likelihood. Writing in a *Spectator* blog, Fraser Nelson noted the scale of the cuts implied by the government's figures but also pointed to the ways in which intensely painful decisions were being pushed into an unforeseeable future: 'the years 2015–20 are being used as dumping ground, for problems deemed too difficult to solve in 2010–15. A crisis deferred, rather than a crisis addressed' (Nelson, 2014).

The government has proved ready to pull back and reach an accommodation on other issues, particularly when it seemed that it might have to pay a political price for a particular measure. Some 2012 budget provisions, for example, were reversed. And the transfer of Michael Gove from his post as Education Secretary in July 2014 seemed to have a significance for the government's reforming zeal. Gove had been identified with the more radical edges of the government, but some of his changes had, in contrast with the principles associated with the 'Big Society' and localism, rested upon compulsion rather than inducements. His strident opposition to parents removing their children from school for family holidays during term-time had provoked some ire. There were also indications that the scope for further cuts might be limited. In particular, there were indications that there would be substantial opposition to any further cuts in defence expenditure.

Furthermore, the introduction of Universal Credit, which merges six benefits for those of working age into one and was the flagship policy of the Department of Work and Pensions under Iain Duncan Smith, turned out to be a prolonged and administratively painful affair. The project appears to have hit a reef of institutional rocks. By November 2013, just 3,610 people had signed up to receive it. Its failure to be implemented has been blamed on 'years of wasted money, political turmoil, Whitehall infighting, failed IT and departmental chaos' (Jee, 2014). Despite all the coalition government's pledges, there were claims that welfare expenditure was continuing to rise. In August 2014, Rachel Reeves, Duncan Smith's 'shadow', asserted that the number of working people on housing benefit was set to double between 2010 and 2018 (Savage, 2014). She stated: 'The government's flagship welfare reforms are in chaos. Millions of taxpayers' money has been wasted on the £12.8bn Universal Credit which less than 7,000 people are claiming' (quoted in Johnstone, 2014).[2]

Other barriers to reform may lie ahead. Although growth rates have picked up, the impact of the crisis on real living standards, income inequality and a sense of generalized 'unfairness' (all of which are themes emphasized by the Labour Party in its different campaigns) may take a toll on the Conservatives' electoral fortunes, although a study of British opinion suggests that the relationship between economic perceptions (and the extent to which they are optimistic or pessimistic about the future) and support for the political parties has broken down. The coalition government did not gain credit from the rise in optimism from early 2013 and may therefore as a corollary not lose if perceptions change (Whiteley *et al.*, 2014).

In the US, efforts to create a leaner state also faced difficulties. The federal government budget sequester, which came into effect from March 2013 onwards, imposed expenditure cuts. However, although the impact upon service provision should not be underestimated (see below), and despite the seemingly 'automatic' character of the sequestration process, departments and agencies engaged in processes of adaptation. Despite the severity of the cuts, the government found ways, at least in the early months of the sequester, of alleviating the impact. In some instances, as *The Washington Post* reported, 'agencies dug into their budgets and found millions they could spare ... Congress passed a law that allocated new funds or shifted money around ... lawmakers signed off on an agency's proposal to "reprogram" its money' (Fahrenthold and Rein, 2013). As the *Post* report indicates, when faced by the prospect of a backlash from significant constituencies and interests, policymakers stepped in to modify the process. Less than two months after the sequester came into effect, Congress voted to give the Federal Aviation Administration (FAA) the authority to limit the furloughs imposed on air traffic controllers by the process. *The Washington Post* commented:

> All it took was a few days of flight delays to undo part of the sequester. And it exemplifies the way Congress has responded to the $1.2 trillion across-the-board-spending cuts: randomly, and almost entirely for reasons of publicity rather than policy.
>
> (Weiner, 2013)

Then, at the end of 2013, the sequestration caps for Fiscal Year (FY) 2014 and FY2015 were revised upwards.

Shrinking the state

Nonetheless, although gradual change processes may provide greater opportunities for counter-mobilizations than some accounts suggest, thereby allowing them to be reined in, change however defined is self-evidently taking place in the UK. In other words, the shift in the character of the frame through which fiscal retrenchment and austerity is represented (and the embrace of the permanently 'leaner' state) has been backed up by what military strategists call 'events on the ground'. The contours of the British state are changing. Certainly there was good news for government strategists in mid-2014. The International Monetary Fund, which had a year earlier seemed very anxious about the Chancellor of the Exchequer's strategy, forecast 3.2 per cent growth for 2014 and 2.7 per cent for 2015. In other words, the UK was 'growing faster than those of every other major developed country' (Holehouse, 2014).

Furthermore, although the budget deficit and overall debt remained higher than projected (because of continuing unemployment and disappointing growth figures during the coalition government's early years), overall government expenditure has been shrinking as a share of GDP.[3] The privatization of government functions and services has been not only implemented but routinized. In sum, the British government has used expenditure reductions as well as gradual change mechanisms such as conversion (through the restructuring of relationships within the National Health Service), drift (by allowing the real value of benefits to fall) and layering (by, for example, introducing free schools 'on top' of the state sector) to bring about far-reaching shifts. Thus, as the book has argued, the radicalism of the Cameron government should not be underestimated. The post-war state is finally, it seems, being overturned.

Although taking place within a very different political and institutional context, and while there has been a less marked shift in the way that retrenchment is framed, the story in the US is not entirely dissimilar. The debt ceiling limit and (despite the efforts by departments and agencies to adapt to its effects, as discussed above) the budget sequester took their toll on overall government spending and the delivery of provision. At the same time, there were signs of modest economic growth and (in part because of withdrawal from the labour market) the percentages that were unemployed fell to 6.3 per cent in April 2014. Stephen Moore of *The Wall Street Journal* and Heritage Foundation claimed a victory for the Right and retrenchment when it came to economic policy outcomes:

> Mr. Obama has inadvertently chained himself to fiscal restraints that could flatten federal spending for the rest of his presidency ... the deficit is on a path to drop steadily at least through 2015. Already the deficit has fallen from its Mount Everest peak of 10.2% of gross domestic product in 2009, to about 4% this year. That's a bullish six percentage points less of the GDP of new federal debt each year.
>
> (Moore, 2013)

And, Moore emphasized, the areas that were being subject to the most severe cuts were (because they were disproportionately represented in discretionary non-defence-spending categories) those policy areas that had long been associated with the Left:

> The sequester is squeezing the very programs liberals care most about – including the National Endowment for the Arts, green-energy subsidies, the Environmental Protection Agency and National Public Radio. Outside Washington, the sequester is forcing a fiscal retrenchment for such liberal special-interest groups as Planned Parenthood and the National Council of La Raza, which have grown dependent on government largess.
>
> (Moore, 2013)

Revolutionary and reformational change

There is, then, a seeming contradiction. The book has suggested that the capacity of gradual change mechanisms can be much more limited than it sometimes appears, but has also argued that the Cameron government has enacted reforms and US policymakers have imposed 'automatic' processes of expenditure reduction that appear to go far in terms of restructuring the British and American states and might well be described as cumulatively transformational.

How then should this contradiction be resolved? There are two answers. First, although gradual change can face greater difficulties than accounts suggest, it can still in some circumstances bring forth transformational change, although, as noted below, that change may be more weakly embedded than the change brought about using more radical and ruptural strategies.

Some forms of gradual change are more likely to succeed than others. Much depends upon the nature of the change and the extent to which it is permissive (insofar as it opens up new possibilities rather than prohibiting established practices), how far it is taking place within policy areas where government agencies have substantial implementation and enforcement capacities, the architecture of incentives and disincentives that might encourage compliance, the number of institutional gaps or openings that could be exploited by those who oppose a measure and the spread of constituencies between self-perceived 'winners' and 'losers' and their capacity to form coalitional blocs. Assessed in these terms, there was every likelihood that fiscal retrenchment and state restructuring processes could, despite the proliferation of obstacles, be implemented.

A second answer lies in the character of transformations. 'Transformation' refers to a complete or total change but is, beyond that, a relatively loose and imprecise term. The other synonyms that are sometimes employed such as 'dramatic' do not assist. Instead of using the term 'transformational' it is more useful to distinguish between *revolutionary* and *reformational* change. Both are far-reaching, fundamental and can be dramatic, but there are important differences.

The concept of *revolutionary* change can best be understood by turning to the revolutionary tradition itself. Leon Trotsky, the Russian revolutionary theorist and founder of the Red Army who, after his duel with Stalin and other Soviet leaders, was exiled and eventually murdered, considered just this question as he reflected upon the political character of the Soviet Union after it had cast him out. The USSR was, Trotsky asserted during the 1930s, a degenerated workers' state. Capitalism had been overthrown in the second of the 1917 revolutions and (despite zigzags such as the New Economic Policy) property collectivized. Planning had enabled the USSR to make economic leaps from 1929 onwards that would not be conceivable within a capitalist order. And yet despite this, as Trotsky noted in *The Revolution Betrayed* (1937), which was written on the eve of the first Moscow show trial, the country was presided over by a tyrannical and parasitic bureaucratic elite that increasingly resorted to totalitarian terror to enforce its rule.

Nonetheless, despite the terror and the totalitarian character of political rule, Trotsky firmly insisted to some wayward followers who argued otherwise that capitalism had not been restored in the USSR. However politically degenerated, it remained a workers' state. The nationalization of the means of production, and the supersession of the economic laws that governed market economies such as the falling rate of profit, ensured this. Capitalism and bourgeois rule could only again come to Russia if there was a counter-revolution that had both political and economic consequences. Such a counter-revolution would not be confined to the political realm but would instead destroy collective ownership, restore private property to the bourgeoisie, displace the ruling Stalinist caste (whose rule rested upon a nationalized economy) and eliminate the resistance of the proletariat who would be instinctively loyal to collectivized property relations. In other words, 'on the road to capitalism the counterrevolution would have to break the resistance of the workers' (Trotsky, 2006, orig. 1937: 239–240).[4] Put in the language of contemporary institutionalism, revolutions create deeply embedded structures and arrangements.

The class character of the Soviet Union is today a profoundly arcane subject. Nonetheless, Trotsky's analysis identifies four defining features of revolutionary change. It overturns heavily embedded logics and structures and imposes other heavily embedded logics and structures in their place. Change is not limited to one sphere or realm but there are instead extensive spillover effects and interconnections. It is likely to have sustained positive feedback effects, being thereby bolstered and reinforced over time. The institutional bases used by those who opposed revolutionary forms of change will have been largely or wholly removed. Put in stark and simple terms, revolutionary change requires a revolution. And the rolling back of a revolution requires a counter-revolution.

In contrast, what might be termed *reformational* change may be far-reaching and indeed have momentous consequences, but because it has been brought forth by gradual change processes it is likely (because of the settings in which gradual change generally takes place and the cautious, piecemeal strategies adopted by reformers) to be much more shallowly embedded. It is therefore more vulnerable to modification or roll-back, and change in one realm may not be tied to change in another realm. Positive feedback effects will be limited even over substantial periods of time. Some institutional bases associated with the *ancien régime* are likely to remain. Reformational change will also, because it is more weakly embedded, be open and susceptible to the use of gradual change mechanisms that are much more likely to be more efficacious than in regimes created through revolutionary change.

Leaner states

Should the restructuring processes, which are certainly dramatic in scale, pursued by the Cameron government and through budgetary restraint processes in the US be regarded as revolutionary or reformational? The evidence presented in the book suggests the latter.

Restructuring has been based upon gradual change mechanisms and sometimes, as has been seen, subject to roll-back. Although the British and American states will be squeezed and shorn, the long-run effects may be limited. There is every reason therefore to think that, as in earlier years, the state will re-establish itself relatively speedily. There are seven principal reasons for this.

First, there is no convincing evidence that the concept of a permanently 'leaner' state has been embraced by public opinion in either the UK or the US. Indeed, although large numbers loosely endorse 'limited government' as an abstract proposition, many entitlement programmes are ideationally embedded and remain a political 'third rail'. Policymakers are likely to back away, as President Bush's efforts to reform Social Security after his 2004 re-election victory illustrate.[5] As the shock waves created by Hurricane Katrina's devastation of New Orleans in 2005 illustrate, the federal government is still widely believed to have extensive social obligations particularly in times of crisis and for those seen as guiltless victims.

Second, the relative costs of increasing government expenditure again at some point in the future are comparatively low. It is an incremental process that only constitutes, to use Peter Hall's typology, first-order change, whereby the settings of existing policy instruments are changed.[6] As such, expenditure increases have relatively low levels of political visibility. And, the political costs of not meeting demands, particularly if they come from a well-placed constituency, may be fairly high.

Third, neoliberal reformers have for the most part been unable to engage in what has been termed 'deck-stacking' (which rational choice theorists emphasize), by which mechanisms are constructed by those enacting a reform that would deter, prevent or raise the costs of later efforts to repeal or modify the reform (Patashnik and Zelizer, 2013: 1074). Despite, for example, earlier conservative efforts in the US to pass a balanced budget amendment to the US Constitution or, more fancifully, proposals for a restored gold standard or freely competing currencies to displace the dollar, there are relatively few institutional constraints upon later fiscal expansion.

Fourth, the demands upon government will almost certainly grow in the years to come as demography shifts towards an older population, more people live independently rather than in established family units and, in particular, if there are persistently low levels of economic growth over a prolonged period.

Fifth, the demands for infrastructural projects such as broadband expansion or further high-speed connections, many of which may not be sustainable in pure market terms and will therefore require taxpayer funds, will continue and are likely to intensify.

Sixth, although there has, as been noted, been extensive privatization in the UK, many services have not readily lent themselves to private ownership. Indeed, Network Rail (which owns the railway infrastructure) went into administration and its borrowing is now guaranteed by the government. The National Health Service has proved resistant to the introduction of quasi-market mechanisms.

Last, the failure of the Right to pursue or sustain the projects that are associated with compassionate conservatism or the 'Big Society' has added to what might be termed a civic vacuum. Few voluntary organizations have taken over, or are likely to take over, responsibility for the provision of services or the delivery of care. Civic cohesion remains at relatively low levels.

All of this is further testimony to the widely cited concept of the 'double movement' introduced by Karl Polanyi in *The Great Transformation* (1944). From a Polanyian perspective, as Fred Block has noted, efforts to disembed markets by allowing them to become more self-regulating will fail. Markets require and indeed necessitate state intervention insofar as the state adjusts credit availability and the money supply and is drawn into labour market policymaking through, for example, educational provision and the regulation of migration. More broadly, the uncertainties and insecurities created by periodic movements towards freer markets inevitably give rise to a countermovement providing a measure of social protection (the 'double movement'). Thus the gold standard, which seemingly functioned 'automatically', profoundly limited the options open to policymakers insofar as countries had through their exchange rate to maintain a fixed parity with a given weight of gold and at the same time limit their money supply to their gold holdings, gave rise to sustained efforts by nations to protect themselves from the system's effects or at least mitigate its impact. As the British experience of the gold standard between 1925 (when it returned at pre-war parity) and 1931 made clear (and membership of the eurozone has emphasized more recently), adherence to the gold standard particularly at high rates of exchange can require very difficult and painful processes of adjustment and deflation as efforts are made to bring down the domestic price level so as to increase a country's international competitiveness. This in turn causes hardship and at times social turmoil. In some cases, although Polanyi often seems to have social-democratic or New Deal forms of social protectionism in mind, the protective impulse that arose in response to the gold standard took the form of nationalism or imperialism: 'disembedding the market is similar to stretching a giant elastic band ... With further stretching, either the band will snap – representing social disintegration – or the economy will revert to a more embedded position' (Block, 2001: xxv).

Although there is always a possibility that countries will take further refuge in nationalism if the populist upsurge against the EU continues or intensifies, it seems more probable that, as in the past, state social provision will again expand at some point so as to meet the perceived needs and demands of a citizenry facing more than a decade of minimal growth and living standards that have slipped back dramatically. David Cameron may indeed secure his 'leaner' state, but it will quickly reacquire considerable fat.

Notes

1 The Office for Budget Responsibility (OBR) forecast in March 2014 that the Public Sector Net Debt would peak at 78.7 per cent of GDP in 2015–16 and only fall by a 'small margin' the following year (Office for Budget Responsibility, 2014: 7).

2 Iain Duncan Smith, however, pointed to changes in the labour market. In an August 2014 speech, he stressed that the proportion of workless households was the lowest ever recorded. He attributed this in part to the cap on the total benefits payable and housing benefit reforms (Goodman, 2014).

3 There are, however, some difficulties monitoring government accounts and tracking spending levels, particularly where funds are transferred to self-governing institutions. If, for example, an academy school or foundation trust hospital underspends funds that have money that has been transferred, this is recorded as an underspend in the overall government accounts. These funds can, however, be spent at a later date (Harris and McCrae, 2013: 6).

4 These issues, of course, caused considerable theoretical difficulties for Trotsky's latter-day adherents when in 1989–91 the Soviet bloc collapsed and capitalism was indeed restored.

5 See p. 44.

6 See p. 83 for an outline of Hall's typology.

Bibliography

Adonis, Andrew (2013) *5 Days in May: The Coalition and Beyond*, London: Biteback Publishing.

Alesina, Alberto and Veronique de Rugy (2014) 'A review of the scholarship on austerity', in Alberto Alesina, Romina Boccia, Ryan Bourne, Salim Furth, David Howden, Filip Jolevski, Miguel Marin, Matthew Melchiorre, Derrick Morgan, Dalibor Rohac and Veronique de Rugy (eds), *Europe's Fiscal Crisis Revealed: An In-Depth Analysis of Spending, Austerity, and Growth*, Washington, DC: Heritage Foundation. Online: www.heritage.org/research/reports/2014/06/europes-fiscal-crisis-revealed-an-in-depth-analysis-of-spending-austerity-and-growth.

Armitstead, Louise (2014) 'IMF accepts it was wrong on George Osborne's austerity', *The Daily Telegraph*, 6 June. Online: www.telegraph.co.uk/finance/economics/10881540/IMF-accepts-it-was-wrong-on-George-Osbornes-austerity.html.

Ashbee, Edward (2003) 'The US Republicans: Lessons for the Conservatives?', in Mark Garnett and Philip Lynch (eds), *The Conservatives in Crisis*, Manchester: Manchester University Press, 29–48.

Ashford, Nigel (1990) *Reaganomics and Thatcherism: From Ideas to Policy*, Lecture #248 on Political Thought, Washington, DC: Heritage Foundation. Online: www.heritage.org/research/lecture/reagonomics-and-thatchehsm-from-ideas-to-policy.

Baker, Kevin (2012) 'Angry white men: Can the G.O.P. genuinely change its attitude toward minorities and women?', *Harper's Magazine*, 8 November. Online: http://harpers.org/blog/2012/11/angry-white-men.

Bale, Tim (2010) *The Conservative Party from Thatcher to Cameron*, Cambridge: Polity.

Bale, Tim (2012) 'Whither the Tory Left? The demise of progressive Conservatism', *Public Policy Research*, 19:2, 84–91.

Ball, Molly (2014) 'Eric Cantor's loss: A stunning upset', *The Atlantic*, 10 June. Online: www.theatlantic.com/politics/archive/2014/06/eric-cantor-loses-in-stunning-upset/372550.

Banks, James, Richard Blundell and James Smith (2004) 'Wealth portfolios in the United Kingdom and the United States', in David A. Wise (ed.), *Perspectives on the Economics of Aging*, National Bureau of Economic Research. Online: www.nber.org/books/wise04-1.

Barry, Frank and Michael B. Devereux (1995) 'The "Expansionary Fiscal Contraction" hypothesis: A neo-Keynesian analysis', *Oxford Economic Papers*, 47:2, April, 249–264.

Bartels, Larry M. (2006) 'What's the matter with *What's the Matter with Kansas?*', *Quarterly Journal of Political Science*, 1, 201–206.

Bartlett, Bruce (2010) 'Tax cuts and "starving the beast"', *Forbes*, 7 May. Online: www.forbes.com/2010/05/06/tax-cuts-republicans-starve-the-beast-columnists-bruce-bartlett.html.

BBC News (2008) 'Darling unveils borrowing gamble', *BBC News*, 24 November. Online: http://news.bbc.co.uk/2/hi/7745340.stm.

BBC News (2010) 'Spending Review 2010: George Osborne wields the axe', *BBC News*, 20 October. Online: www.bbc.co.uk/news/uk-politics-11579979.

BBC News (2012) 'Private cash needed to boost roads network, says David Cameron', *BBC News*, 19 March. Online: www.bbc.com/news/uk-politics-17423693.

BBC News (2013a) 'UK economy is turning corner, George Osborne says', *BBC News*, 9 September. Online: www.bbc.co.uk/news/business-24011795.

BBC News (2013b) 'Austerity "may last until 2020"', *BBC News*, 7 June. Online: www.bbc.com/news/business-22819843.

BBC News (2014) 'Economy tracker: GDP', *BBC News*, 28 January. Online: www.bbc.com/news/10613201.

Béland, Daniel (2009) 'Ideas, institutions, and policy change', *Journal of European Public Policy*, 16:5, 701–718.

Béland, Daniel and Alex Waddan (2008) 'Taking "Big Government Conservatism" seriously? The Bush presidency reconsidered', *The Political Quarterly*, 79:1, January–March, 109–118.

Bell, Daniel (1963) *The Radical Right: The New American Right Expanded and Updated*, New York: Doubleday and Company.

Benford, Robert D. and David A. Snow (2000) 'Framing processes and social movements: An overview and assessment', *Annual Review of Sociology*, 26, 611–639.

Berezin, Mabel (2013) 'The normalization of the Right in post-security Europe', in Armin Schäfer and Wolfgang Streeck (eds), *Politics in the Age of Austerity*, Cambridge: Polity, 239–261.

Berk, Gerald, Dennis C. Galvan and Victoria Hattam (eds) (2013) *Political Creativity: Reconfiguring Institutional Order and Change*, Philadelphia: University of Pennsylvania Press.

Berlet, Chip (2010) 'Taking tea partiers seriously', *The Progressive*, February. Online: www.progressive.org/berlet0210c.html.

Berlet, Chip (2012) 'Collectivists, communists, labor bosses, and treason: The Tea Parties as right-wing populist counter-subversion panic', *Critical Sociology*, 38:4, 565–587.

Bevir, Mark and R.A.W. Rhodes (1998) 'Narratives of "Thatcherism"', *West European Politics*, 21:1, 97–119.

Block, Fred (2001) 'Introduction', in Karl Polanyi (2001, orig. 1944) *The Great Transformation: The Political and Economic Origins of Our Time*, Boston: Beacon Press, xviii–xxxviii.

Blond, Philip (2009) 'Rise of the red Tories', *Prospect*, 28 February. Online: www.prospectmagazine.co.uk/magazine/riseoftheredtories/#.U5s4pxZ_iyM.

Blyth, Mark (2013) *Austerity: The History of a Dangerous Idea*, Oxford: Oxford University Press.

Boesler, Matthew (2013) 'Now it's time to start talking about the economic impact of a full sequester', *Business Insider*, 10 January. Online: www.businessinsider.com/us-gdp-impact-of-cuts-in-full-sequester2013-1.

Bonnett, Kevin, Simon Bromley, Bob Jessop and Tom Ling (1985) 'Thatcherism and the politics of hegemony: A reply to Stuart Hall', *New Left Review*, September/October, 153, 87–101.

Booth, Philip (2011) *VAT Rise Is Bad Economics, Further Spending Cuts Are Needed to Get Deficit Down*, London: Institute of Economic Affairs, 4 January. Online: www.iea.org.uk/in-the-media/press-release/vat-rise-is-bad-economics-further-spending-cuts-are-needed-to-get-deficit.

Booth, Philip (2014) *Spending Cuts Must Be More Comprehensive*, London: Institute of Economic Affairs, 6 January. Online: www.iea.org.uk/in-the-media/press-release/spending-cuts-must-be-more-comprehensive.

Boyer, Peter J. (2010) 'House rule: Will John Boehner control the Tea Party Congress?', *The New Yorker*, 13 December. Online: www.newyorker.com/reporting/2010/12/13/101213fa_fact_boyer?currentPage=all.

Brant-Zawadzki, A. and D. Teo (2009) 'Anatomy of the Tea Party movement: Tea Party patriots', *The Huffington Post – The Blog*, 11 December. Online: www.huffingtonpost.com/alex-brantzawadzki/anatomy-of-the-tea-party_b_380567.html.

Brogan, Benedict (2010) '*Red Tory: How Left and Right Have Broken Britain and How We Can Fix It* by Phillip Blond: Review', *The Daily Telegraph*, 25 March. Online: www.telegraph.co.uk/culture/books/bookreviews/7523149/Red-Tory-How-Left-and-Right-Have-Broken-Britain-and-How-We-Can-Fix-it-by-Phillip-Blond-review.html.

Bulpitt, Jim (1986) 'The discipline of the new democracy: Mrs Thatcher's domestic statecraft', *Political Studies*, 34, 19–39.

Bureau of Economic Analysis (2014) *National Economic Accounts: Percent Change from Preceding Period*, Washington, DC: Bureau of Economic Analysis. Online: www.bea.gov/national/index.htm#gdp.

Bureau of Labor Statistics (2014) *Unemployment Rate*, Washington, DC: Bureau of Labor Statistics. Online: http://data.bls.gov/timeseries/LNS14000000.

Cameron, David (2011) 'How we will release the grip of state control', *The Daily Telegraph*, 20 February. Online: www.telegraph.co.uk/comment/8337239/How-we-will-release-the-grip-of-state-control.html.

Campbell, John L. (1998) 'Institutional analysis and the role of ideas in political economy', *Theory and Society*, 27:3, 377–409.

Campbell, John L. (2004) *Institutional Change and Globalization*, Princeton, NJ: Princeton University Press

Campbell, John L. and Ove Kaj Pedersen (2011) 'Knowledge regimes and comparative political economy', in D. Béland and R.H. Cox (eds), *Ideas and Politics in Social Science Research*, Oxford: Oxford University Press, 167–190.

Carlin, Brendan (2007) 'Tories vow to match Labour spending', *The Daily Telegraph*, 3 September. Online: www.telegraph.co.uk/news/uknews/1562023/Tories-vow-to-match-Labour-spending.html.

Cato Institute (2009) *With All Due Respect Mr. President, That Is Not True*, London: Cato Institute. Online: www.cato.org/sites/cato.org/files/documents/cato_stimulus.pdf.

Centre for Social Justice (2008) *Breakthrough Britain – Briefing Paper 2: Economic Dependency and Worklessness*, London: Centre for Social Justice. Online: www.centreforsocialjustice.org.uk/UserStorage/pdf/Pdf%20Exec%20summaries/BBExecEcDependency.pdf.

Cerny, Philip G. (1997) 'Paradoxes of the competition state: The dynamics of political globalization', *Government and Opposition*, 32:2, April, 251–274.

Channel 4 News (2012) 'Osborne unveils £10bn benefits cut package', *Channel 4 News*, 8 October. Online: www.channel4.com/news/osborne-unveils-10bn-benefits-cut-package.

Chote, Robert, Rowena Crawford, Carl Emmerson and Gemma Tetlow (2010) *Filling the Hole: How Do the Three Main UK Parties Plan to Repair the Public Finances?*, 2010 Election Briefing Note No. 12 (IFS BN99), London: Institute for Fiscal Studies.

Church Urban Fund (2013) *Guide to Welfare Reforms 2010–2017*, London: Church Urban Fund.

CNN (2009) 'Obama, George H.W. Bush unite to support volunteerism', *CNN*, 16 October. Online: http://edition.cnn.com/2009/POLITICS/10/16/obama.bush.volunteerism/index.html?eref=ib_us.

ComRes (2014) *Paul Sykes – EP2014 Post-Election Analysis Poll*, London: ComRes. Online: http://comres.co.uk/polls/EP2014_Analysis_Poll_31_May_2014_FINAL_3468.pdf.

Condon, Stephanie (2011) 'Poll: One in four Americans think Obama was not born in US', CBS News, 21 April. Online: www.cbsnews.com/8301-503544_162-20056061-503544.html.

Confederation of British Industry (2013) *Our Global Future: The Business Vision for a Reformed EU*, London: Confederation of British Industry. Online: www.cbi.org.uk/media/2451423/our_global_future.pdf.

Congressional Budget Office (2012) *Economic Effects of Policies Contributing to Fiscal Tightening in 2013*, Washington, DC: Congressional Budget Office, November. Online: http://cbo.gov/publication/43694.

Conservative Party (1979) *Conservative General Election Manifesto*, London: The Conservative Party. Online: www.margaretthatcher.org/document/110858.

Conservative Party (2010) *Invitation to Join the Government of Britain: The Conservative Manifesto 2010*, London: The Conservative Party.

Crafts, Nicholas (2013) *The Economic Legacy of Mrs Thatcher*, The CAGE Background Briefing Series, 20, July.

Crawford, Rowena and Paul Johnson (2011) *The Changing Composition of Public Spending*, IFS Briefing Note 119, London: Institute for Fiscal Studies.

Crossley, Thomas F., Hamish Low and Matthew Wakefield (2009) 'The economics of a temporary VAT cut', *Fiscal Studies* (IFS Working Papers), London: Institute for Fiscal Studies, 30:1, March.

Crouch, Colin (2011) *The Strange Non-Death of Neoliberalism*, Cambridge: Polity.

The Daily Telegraph (2010) Budget 2010: Full text of George Osborne's statement, *The Daily Telegraph*, 22 June. Online: www.telegraph.co.uk/finance/budget/7846849/Budget-2010-Full-text-of-George-Osbornes-statement.html.

d'Ancona, Matthew (2013) 'Last chance saloon: The history and future of Tory modernization', in Ryan Shorthouse and Guy Stagg (eds), *Tory Modernisation 2.0: The Future of the Conservative Party*, London: Bright Blue Campaign, 12–24.

Dewan, Shaila (2014) 'In jobless youth, U.S. is said to pay high price', *The New York Times*, 6 January. Online: www.nytimes.com/2014/01/07/business/economy/in-jobless-youth-nation-is-said-to-pay-high-price.html?_r=0.

Dilworth, Richardson (2009) 'Adventures in intercurrence', *Historical Methods*, Fall, 42:4, 143–147.

Disch, Lisa (2011) 'Tea Party movement: The American "Precariat"', *Representation*, 47:2, 123–135.

Dorey, Peter (2007) 'A new direction or another false dawn? David Cameron and the crisis of British Conservatism', *British Politics*, 2, 137–166.

Douglas, Jason (2014) 'Is UK's house buying support having a London effect?', *The Wall Street Journal* (Real Time Economics), 29 May. Online: http://blogs.wsj.com/economics/2014/05/29/is-uks-house-buying-support-having-a-london-effect.

Draper, Robert (2013) *When the Tea Party Came to Town: Inside the U.S. House of Representatives' Most Combative, Dysfunctional, and Infuriating Term in Modern History*, New York: Simon & Schuster.

Driver, Stephen and Luke Martell (1997) 'New Labour's communitarianisms', *Critical Social Policy*, 17:3, 27–46.

Dugan, Emily (2013) 'Number of long-term jobless hits 20-year high – and most haven't worked for two years', *The Independent*, 17 July. Online: www.independent.co.uk/news/business/news/number-of-longterm-jobless-hits-20year-high-and-most-havent-worked-for-two-years-8713535.html.

The Economist (2012) 'I never promised you a rose garden', *The Economist*, 12 May. Online: www.economist.com/node/21554567.

Edmonds, Timothy, Dominic Webb and Rob Long (2011) *The Economic Crisis: Policy Responses*, London: House of Commons Library. Online: www.parliament.uk/business/publications/research/briefing-papers/SN04968/the-economic-crisis-policy-responses.

Edwards, Rosalind (2004) 'Present and absent in troubling ways: Families and social capital debates', *The Sociological Review*, 52:1, February, 1–21.

Edwards, Tim (2011) 'NHS reforms: A guide to the controversial bill', *The Week*, 19 January. Online: www.theweek.co.uk/politics/nhs-reform/8501/nhs-reforms-guide-controversial-bill#ixzz33Q7mcFym.

Emmerson, Carl and Christine Frayne (2005) *Election Briefing 2005*, London: Institute for Fiscal Studies.

Ethics and Public Policy Center (2012) *About*, Washington, DC: Ethics and Public Policy Center. Online: www.eppc.org/about.

Fahrenthold, David A. and Lisa Rein (2013) 'They said the sequester would be scary. Mostly, they were wrong', *The Washington Post*, 30 June. Online: www.washintonpost.com/politics/they-said-the-sequester-would-be-scary-mostly-they-were-wrong/2013/06/30/73bdbbfc-da7a-11e2-8ed8-7adf8eba6e9a_story.html.

Foley, Michael W. and Bob Edwards (1997) 'Social capital debate – Editors' introduction: Escape from politics? Social theory and the social capital debate', *American Behavioral Scientist*, 40, 550–561.

Ford, Robert and Matthew Goodwin (2014) *Revolt on the Right: Explaining Support for the Radical Right in Britain*, Abingdon: Routledge.

Formisano, R.P. (2012) *The Tea Party*, Baltimore, MD: Johns Hopkins University Press.

Frymer, Paul (2008) *Black and Blue: African Americans, the Labor Movement and the Decline of the Democratic Party*, Princeton, NJ: Princeton University Press.

Gamble, Andrew (1988) *The Free Economy and the Strong State: The Politics of Thatcherism*, Basingstoke: Palgrave Macmillan.

Gamble, Andrew (2014) 'Austerity as statecraft', *Parliamentary Affairs* (Advance Access), 11 July.

Gamson, William A. (1992) *Talking Politics*, Cambridge: Cambridge University Press.

Garnett, Mark (2003) 'A question of definition? Ideology and the Conservative Party', in Philip Lynch and Mark Garnett (eds), *The Conservatives in Crisis: The Tories after 1997*, Manchester: Manchester University Press, 107–124.

Gerring, John (2003) 'APD from a methodological point of view', *Studies in American Political Development*, 17, Spring, 82–102.

Gleeson, Denis (1986) 'Life skills training and the politics of personal effectiveness', *The Sociological Review*, 34:2, May, 381–395.

Glenn, Brian J. and Steven M. Teles (2009) *Conservatism and American Political Development*, Oxford: Oxford University Press.

Goldfarb, Zachary A. and Holly Yeager (2014) 'Long-building conservative anger at Export-Import Bank reaches boiling point', *The Washington Post*, 28 June. Online: www.washingtonpost.com/business/economy/long-building-conservative-anger-at-export-import-bank-reaches-boiling-point/2014/06/27/cce4a87a-fe01-11e3-b1f4-8e77c632c07b_story.html.

Good, Chris (2012) 'Norquist's tax pledge: What it is and how it started', *ABC News*, 26 November. Online: http://abcnews.go.com/blogs/politics/2012/11/norquists-tax-pledge-what-it-is-and-how-it-started.

Goodman, Paul (2014) 'The work ethic of Iain Duncan Smith', *Conservative Home*, 12 August. Online: www.conservativehome.com/thetorydiary/2014/08/the-reforming-work-of-iain-duncan-smith.html.

Gov.uk (2013) *Lord Mayor's Banquet 2013: Prime Minister's speech*, 11 November. Online: www.gov.uk/government/speeches/lord-mayors-banquet-2013-prime-ministers-speech.

The Guardian (2006) 'Full text of Cameron's speech on young offenders', *The Guardian*, 2 November. Online: www.theguardian.com/politics/2006/nov/02/conservatives.ukcrime1.

The Guardian (2013) 'UK public spending since 1963', *The Guardian*. Online: www.guardian.co.uk/news/datablog/2010/apr/25/uk-public-spending-1963.

Hacker, Jacob S. (2004) 'Privatizing risk without privatizing the welfare state: The hidden politics of social policy retrenchment in the United States', *American Political Science Review*, 98:2, 243–260.

Hacker, Jacob and Paul Pierson (2002) 'Business power and social policy: Employers and the formation of the American welfare state', *Politics & Society*, 30:2, 277–325.

Hacker, Jacob and Paul Pierson (2005) *Off Center: The Republican Revolution and the Erosion of American Democracy*, New Haven, CT: Yale University Press.

Hall, Ben, Alex Barker and Chris Bryant (2009) 'Sarkozy claims credit on tighter regulation', *Financial Times*, 2 April. Online: www.ft.com/intl/cms/s/0/10b0bbee-1fb3-11de-a1df-00144feabdc0.html#axzz391qvwPXj.

Hall, Peter A. (1993) 'Policy paradigms, social learning, and the state: The case of economic policymaking in Britain' *Comparative Politics*, 23 (April), 275–296.

Hall, Peter A. (2002) 'Great Britain: The role of government and the distribution of social capital', in Robert D. Putnam (ed.), *Democracies in Flux: The Evolution of Social Capital in Contemporary Society*, Oxford: Oxford University Press.

Hall, Peter A. (2013) 'The political origins of our economic discontents', in Miles Kahler and David A. Lake (eds), *Politics in the New Hard Times*, Ithaca, NY: Cornell Paperbacks, 129–149.

Hall, Peter A. and David Soskice (2001) *Varieties of Capitalism: The Institutional Foundations of Comparative Advantage*, Oxford: Oxford University Press.

Hall, Stuart (1988) *The Hard Road to Renewal: Thatcherism and the Crisis of the Left*, London: Verso.

Harris, Joshua and Julian McCrae (2013) *The 2015–16 Spending Round: A Briefing Note to Accompany the IfG/IFS Press Briefing on 7 June 2013*, London: Institute for Government. Online: www.instituteforgovernment.org.uk/sites/default/files/publications/Spending%20Round%20briefing%20note%20final.pdf.

Hay, Colin (1996) 'Narrating crisis: The discursive construction of the "Winter of Discontent"', *Sociology*, 30:2, 253–277.

Hay, Colin and Stephen Farrall (2014) 'Interrogating and conceptualizing the legacy of Thatcherism', in Stephen Farrall and Colin Hay (eds), *The Legacy of Thatcherism: Assessing and Exploring Thatcherite Social and Economic Policies*, London and Oxford: The British Academy/Oxford University Press, 3–30.

Hayton, Richard (2012) *Reconstructing Conservatism? The Conservative Party in Opposition, 1997–2010*, Manchester: Manchester University Press.

Heffernan, Richard (2000) *New Labour and Thatcherism: Political Change in Britain*, Basingstoke: Palgrave Macmillan.

Heilemann, John and Mark Halperin (2010) *Game Change: Obama and the Clintons, McCain and Palin, and the Race of a Lifetime*, New York: Harper.

Herbert, Jon (2011) 'The struggles of an "orthodox innovator": George W Bush, the conservative movement, and domestic policy', in Joel D. Aberbach and Gillian Peele (eds), *Crisis of Conservatism? The Republican Party, the Conservative Movement, and American Politics*, Oxford: Oxford University Press.

Herszenhorn, David (2009) 'A smaller, faster stimulus plan, but still with a lot of money', *The New York Times*, 13 February. Online: www.nytimes.com.

Herszenhorn, David M., Carl Hulse and Sheryl Gay Stolberg (2008) 'Talks implode during a day of chaos; Fate of bailout plan remains unresolved', *The New York Times*, 25 September. Online: www.nytimes.com/2008/09/26/business/26bailout.html?pagewanted=all&_r=0.

Hills, John (1998) *Thatcherism, New Labour and the Welfare State*, London: Centre for Analysis of Social Exclusion, London School of Economics. Online: http://eprints.lse.ac.uk/5553/1/Thatcherism_New_Labour_and_the_Welfare_State.pdf?origin=publication_detail.

HM Government (2010) *The Coalition: Our Programme for Government*, London: HM Government.

HM Treasury (2010) *The Spending Review Framework*, London: HM Treasury, Cm 7872.

Hofstadter, Richard (1996, orig. 1964) *The Paranoid Style in American Politics and Other Essays*, Cambridge, MA: Harvard University Press.

Holehouse, Matthew (2014) 'UK has fastest-growing economy, International Monetary Fund says', *The Daily Telegraph*, 24 July. Online: www.telegraph.co.uk/finance/economics/10988849/UK-has-fastest-growing-economy-International-Monetary-Fund-says.html.

Hope, Christopher (2014) 'Ban on CCTV parking fines for unwitting motorists', *The Daily Telegraph*, 21 June. Online: www.telegraph.co.uk/news/politics/10915510/Ban-on-CCTV-parking-fines-for-unwitting-motorists.html.

Horowitz, David (2009) 'How conservatives should celebrate the inauguration', *Townhall.com*, 20 January. Online: http://townhall.com/columnists/davidhorowitz/2009/01/20/how_conservatives_should_celebrate_the_inauguration/page/full.

House Budget Committee (2012) *The Path to Prosperity: A Blueprint for American Renewal* (Fiscal Year 2013 Budget Resolution), Washington, DC: House Budget Committee.

Howard, Christopher (1997) *The Hidden Welfare State: Tax Expenditures and Social Policy in the United States*, Princeton, NJ: Princeton Paperbacks.

Howard, Christopher (2007) *The Welfare State Nobody Knows: Debunking Myths about Us Social Policy*, Princeton, NJ: Princeton University Press.

The Huffington Post UK (2013) 'Coalition's planning reforms watered down to give neighbours a say after backbench revolt', *The Huffington Post UK*, 20 April. Online: www.huffingtonpost.co.uk/2013/04/20/planning-permission-reforms_n_3121940.html.

Hutton, Will (2013) 'Osborne wants to take us back to 1948. Time to look forward instead', *The Guardian*, 8 December.

Hyman, Richard (1999) 'Strikes in the UK: Withering away?', *Eiro Online*, 28 July. Online: www.eurofound.europa.eu/eiro/1999/07/feature/uk9907215f.htm.

International Monetary Fund (2012) *World Economic Outlook Database*. Online: www.imf.org/external/pubs/ft/weo/2012/02/weodata/index.aspx.

Isidore, Chris (2008) 'Bailout plan rejected – supporters scramble', *CNN Money*, 29 September. Online: http://money.cnn.com/2008/09/29/news/economy/bailout.

Jacobs, Lawrence R. and Desmond King (2009) 'The political crisis of the American state: The unsustainable state in a time of unraveling', in Lawrence Jacobs and Desmond King (eds), *The Unsustainable American State*, Oxford: Oxford University Press, 3–33.

Jee, Charlotte (2014) 'Universal Credit: The anatomy of a government failure', *The New Statesman*, 11 April. Online: www.newstatesman.com/politics/2014/04/universal-credit-anatomy-government-failure.

Jessop, Bob, Kevin Bonnett, Simon Bromley and Tom Ling (1988) *Thatcherism: A Tale of Two Nations*, Cambridge: Polity Press.

Johnstone, Richard (2014) 'IDS: Welfare reform delivering "social recovery"', Public Finance, 11 August. Online: www.publicfinance.co.uk/news/2014/08/ids-welfare-reform-delivering-social-recovery.

Jones, Robert P. and Daniel Cox (2010) *Religion and the Tea Party in the 2010 Election: An Analysis of the Third Biennial American Values Survey*, Washington, DC: Public Religion Research Institute. Online: http://publicreligion.org/site/wp-content/uploads/2010/05/Religion-and-the-Tea-Party-in-the-2010-Election-American-Values-Survey.pdf.

Kampfner, John (2008) 'Margaret Thatcher, inspiration to New Labour', *The Daily Telegraph*, 17 April. Online: www.telegraph.co.uk/news/newstopics/themargaretthatcheryears/1895878/Margaret-Thatcher-inspiration-to-New-Labour.html.

Kellner, Peter (2013) 'Why Northerners don't vote Tory', *YouGov*, 21 October. Online: http://yougov.co.uk/news/2013/10/21/why-northerners-dont-vote-tory.

King, Desmond S. (1987) *The New Right: Politics, Markets and Citizenship*, London: Macmillan; Chicago: Dorsey Press.

King, Desmond S. and Rogers M. Smith (2005) 'Racial orders in American Political Development', *The American Political Science Review*, 99:1, February, 75–92.

Klein, Ezra (2011) 'The Tea Party and the debt ceiling', *The Washington Post*, 14 July. Online: www.washingtonpost.com/blogs/wonkblog/post/the-tea-party-and-the-debt-ceiling/2011/07/11/gIQAHaldEI_blog.html.

Kristol, Irving (1978) *Two Cheers for Capitalism*, New York: Basic Books.

Krugman, Paul (2008) 'Amity Shlaes strikes again', *The New York Times – Conscience of a Liberal*, 19 November. Online: http://krugman.blogs.nytimes.com/2008/11/19/amity-shlaes-strikes-again.

Krugman, Paul (2012) 'What's in the Ryan Plan?', *The New York Times – Conscience of a Liberal*, 16 August. Online: http://krugman.blogs.nytimes.com/2012/08/16/whats-in-the-ryan-plan.

Krugman, Paul (2013) 'How the case for austerity has crumbled', *The New York Review of Books*, 6 June. Online: www.nybooks.com/articles/archives/2013/jun/06/how-case-austerity-has-crumbled.

Kuo, David (2006) *Tempting Faith: An Inside Story of Political Seduction*, New York: Free Press.

Labour Party (2010) *The Labour Party Manifesto 2010*, London: The Labour Party.

Laws, David (2010) *22 Days in May: The Birth of the Lib Dem–Conservative Coalition*, London: Biteback Publishing.

Leach, Adam (2013) 'UK public sector is world's second-largest outsourcing market', *Supply Management*, 22 March. Online: www.supplymanagement.com/news/2013/uk-public-sector-is-worlds-second-largest-outsourcing-market.

Lee, Simon (2011) 'No Plan B: The Coalition agenda for the economy', in Simon Lee and Matt Beech (eds), *The Cameron–Clegg Government: Coalition Politics in an Age of Austerity*, Basingstoke: Palgrave Macmillan, 59–74.

Le Grand, Julian (2011) ' Cameron's NHS reform is no health revolution', *Financial Times*, 19 January. Online: www.ft.com/intl/cms/s/0/43c4e79e-241b-11e0-a89a-00144feab49a.html#axzz33Q4jRT4V.

Le Grand, Julian, Nicholas Mays and Jennifer Dixon (1998) 'The reforms: Success or failure or neither?' in Julian Le Grand, Nicholas Mays and Jo-Ann Mulligan (eds), *Learning from the NHS Internal Market*, London: King's Fund.

Leppard, David (2013) 'Asians and Africans must pay £3,000 to enter Britain', *The Sunday Times*, 23 June. Online: www.thesundaytimes.co.uk/sto/news/uk_news/National/article1277753.ece.

Leys, Colin (1990) 'Still a question of hegemony', *New Left Review*, May–June, 181, 119–128.

Lieberman, Robert C. (2002) 'Ideas, institutions, and political order: Explaining political change', *The American Political Science Review*, 96:4, December, 697–712.

Lilico, Andrew, Neil O'Brien and Adam Atashzai (2009) *Controlling Public Spending: The Scale of the Challenge*, Policy Exchange – Research Note. Online: www.policyexchange.org.uk/images/publications/controlling%20public%20spending%20-%20jun%2009.pdf.

Lipset, Seymour Martin (1960) *Political Man: The Social Bases of Politics*, New York: Doubleday and Company.

Lo, Clarence Y.H. (2012) 'AstroTurf versus grass roots: Scenes from early Tea Party mobilization', in Larry Rosenthal and Christine Trost (eds), *Steep: The Precipitous Rise of the Tea Party*, Oakland, CA: University of California Press, 98–130.

Lynch, Philip and Richard Whitaker (2013) 'Where there is discord, can they bring harmony? Managing intra-party dissent on European integration in the Conservative Party', *British Journal of Politics and International Relations*, 15:3, August, 317–339.

Lynch, Philip, Richard Whitaker and Gemma Loomes (2011) *The UK Independence Party: Analysing Its Candidates and Supporters*, Working Paper – Department of Politics and International Relations, University of Leicester.

Mahoney, James (2000) 'Path dependence in historical sociology', *Theory and Society*, 29:4, August, 507–548.

Mahoney, James and Kathleen Thelen (2010) 'A theory of gradual institutional change', in James Mahoney and Kathleen Thelen (eds), *Explaining Institutional Change: Ambiguity, Agency, and Power*, Cambridge: Cambridge University Press, 1–37.

Marsh, David (1995) 'Explaining "Thatcherite" policies: Beyond uni-dimensional explanation', *Political Studies*, 43, 595–613.

Maude, Francis (2013) 'Foreword', in Ryan Shorthouse and Guy Stagg (eds), *Tory Modernisation 2.0: The Future of the Conservative Party*, London: Bright Blue Campaign, 2–4.

Mays, Nicholas, Anna Dixon and Lorelei Jones (2011) 'Return to the market: Objectives and evolution of New Labour's market reforms', in *Understanding New Labour's Market Reforms of the English NHS*, London: The King's Fund. Online: www.kingsfund.org.uk/sites/files/kf/chapter-1-Return-to-the-market-objectives-evolution-new-labours-market-reforms-sept11.pdf.

McCain, Robert Stacy (2009) 'Tea Party Nation', *The American Spectator*, 13 November. Online: http://spectator.org/archives/2009/11/13/tea-party-nation/print.

McSmith, Andy (2000) 'Join Nafta and ignore threats of EU, says Redwood', *The Daily Telegraph*, 26 July. Online: www.telegraph.co.uk/news/uknews/1350571/Join-Nafta-and-ignore-threats-of-EU-says-Redwood.html.

Meagher, Kevin (2013) 'Uncut poll reveals public blame last Labour government, not Tories, for today's benefits bill', *Labour Uncut*, 12 September. Online: http://labour-uncut.co.uk/2013/09/12/uncut-poll-reveals-public-blame-last-labour-government-not-tories-for-today's-benefits-bill/#more-17150.

Meagher, Richard (2012) 'The "vast right-wing conspiracy": Media and conservative networks', *New Political Science*, 34:4, 469–484.

Mechanic, David (1995) 'The Americanization of the British National Health Service', *Health Affairs*, 14:2, 51–67.

Metro (2012) 'David Cameron: Conservatives are for strivers not skivers', *Metro*, 16 April. Online: http://metro.co.uk/2012/04/16/david-cameron-conservatives-are-for-strivers-not-skivers-390621.

Mettler, Suzanne (2011) *The Submerged State: How Invisible Government Policies Undermine American Democracy (Chicago Studies in American Politics)*, Chicago: University of Chicago Press.

Miller, William J., Jeremy D. Walling and Brian P. Smentkowski (2012) 'Adding pieces to the chess set: New players for an old game', in William J. Miller and Jeremy D. Walling (eds), *Tea Party Effects on 2010 US Senate Elections*, Lanham, MD: Lexington Books, 361–374.

Milne, Seamus (2011) 'The class interests at the heart of David Cameron's plan', *The Guardian*, 5 October. Online: www.theguardian.com/commentisfree/2011/oct/05/david-cameron-conservative-party-city-of-london.

Minford, Patrick (2001) 'Economic view: The Tories' golden chance', *The Daily Telegraph*, 8 January.

Mirza-Davies, James (2014) *NEET: Young People Not in Education, Employment or Training*, London: The House of Commons Library, Standard Note, SN/EP/06705.

Mitchell, Daniel J. (2012) 'A Lesson for Krugman, et al, about Canada's Real Fiscal Restraint vs. the United Kingdom's Faux Austerity', *International Liberty*, 18 February. Online: http://danieljmitchell.wordpress.com/2012/02/18/a-lesson-for-krugman-et-al-about-canadas-real-fiscal-restraint-vs-the-united-kingdoms-faux-austerity.

Montgomerie, Tim (2011) 'The Class of 2010 is reshaping the Tory party for the better', *The Daily Telegraph*, 25 June. Online: www.telegraph.co.uk/news/politics/david-cameron/8598650/The-Class-of-2010-is-reshaping-the-Tory-party-for-the-better.html.

Moore, Stephen (2013) 'The budget sequester is a success', *The Wall Street Journal*, 11 August. Online: http://online.wsj.com/news/articles/SB10001424127887323477604579000933006361834.

Morgan, Kimberly J. and Andrea Louise Campbell (2011) *The Delegated Welfare State: Medicare, Markets, and the Governance of Social Policy*, Oxford: Oxford University Press.

Morganteen, Jeff (2014) 'U.S. Chamber of Commerce vows to oppose GOP's far-right wing', *CNBC*, 8 January. Online: www.cnbc.com/id/101320541.

Murray, Charles (1984) *Losing Ground: American Social Policy, 1950–1980*, New York: Basic Books.

Nelson, Fraser (2014) 'Budget 2014: What Osborne didn't tell us about the crunch to come', *The Spectator*, 23 March. Online: http://blogs.spectator.co.uk/coffeehouse/2014/03/budget-2014-three-more-scary-graphs-about-the-crunch-to-come.

The New York Times (1996) 'Politics; Gingrich on Medicare', *The New York Times*, 20 July. Online: www.nytimes.com/1996/07/20/us/politics-gingrich-on-medicare.html.

The New York Times (2011) 'Signing away the Right to govern', *The New York Times*, 18 July. Online: www.nytimes.com/2011/07/19/opinion/19tue1.html?_r=0.

The New York Times/CBS News (2010) *National Survey of Tea Party Supporters*, 5–12 April. Online: http://s3.amazonaws.com/nytdocs/docs/312/312.pdf.

Norman, Jesse and Janan Ganesh (2006) *Compassionate Conservatism: What It Is; Why We Need It*, London: Policy Exchange

Office for Budget Responsibility (2014) *Office for Budget Responsibility: Economic and Fiscal Outlook*, Presented to Parliament by the Economic Secretary to the Treasury by Command of Her Majesty, Cm 8820.

Organisation for Economic Cooperation and Development (2009) *The Effectiveness and Scope of Fiscal Stimulus, OECD Economic Outlook, Interim Report March 2009*. Online: www.oecd.org/economy/outlook/42421337.pdf.

Organisation for Economic Cooperation and Development (2010) *United Kingdom Policies for a Sustainable Recovery*, Paris: Organisation for Economic Cooperation and Development. Online: www.oecd.org/unitedkingdom/45642018.pdf.

Ormerod, Paul (2011) 'Expansionary fiscal contraction', *Institute of Economic Affairs*, 9 November. Online: www.iea.org.uk/blog/expansionary-fiscal-contraction.

Orren, Karen (1995) 'Ideas and institutions', *Polity*, XXVIII: 1, Fall, 97–101.

Orren, Karen and Stephen Skowronek (1994) 'Beyond the iconography of order: Notes for a "New Institutionalism"', in L. Dodd and C. Jillson (eds), *The Dynamics of American Politics*, Boulder, CO: Westview Press, 311–330.

Orren, Karen and Stephen Skowronek (2002) 'The study of American Political Development', in Ira Katznelson and Helen V. Milner (eds), *Political Science: The State of the Discipline*, New York and London: W.W. Norton & Co., 722–754.

Orren, Karen and Stephen Skowronek (2004) *The Search for American Political Development*, Cambridge: Cambridge University Press.

Park, Alison, Caroline Bryson, Elizabeth Clery, John Curtice and Miranda Phillips (eds) (2013) *British Social Attitudes: The 30th Report*, London: NatCen Social Research.

Patashnik, Eric M. (2008) *Reforms at Risk: What Happens after Major Policy Changes Are Enacted*, Princeton, NJ: Princeton University Press.

Patashnik, Eric M. and Julian E. Zelizer (2013) 'The struggle to remake politics: Liberal reform and the limits of policy feedback in the contemporary American state', *Perspectives on Politics*, 11:4, December, 1071–1087.

Paul, Ron (2004) *Mises and Austrian Economics: A Personal View*, Auburn, AL: Ludwig von Mises Institute.

Perry, Mark (2010) *The Great Mancession of 2008–2009: Statement before the House Ways and Means Committee Subcommittee on Income Security and Family Support on 'Responsible Fatherhood' Programs*, Washington, DC: American Enterprise Institute.

Peston, Robert (2013) 'Chancellor's return to 1948', *BBC News*, 5 December. Online: www.bbc.com/news/business-2524020.

Peters, Jeremy W. (2012) 'For tax pledge and its author, a test of time', *The New York Times*, 19 November. Online: www.nytimes.com/2012/11/20/us/politics/grover-norquist-author-of-antitax-pledge-faces-big-test.html?_r=0.

Pew Research Center for the People and the Press (2013) *If No Deal Is Struck, Four-in-Ten Say Let the Sequester Happen*, 21 February. Online: www.people-press.org/2013/02/21/if-no-deal-is-struck-four-in-ten-say-let-the-sequester-happen.

Pierson, Paul (1994) *Dismantling the Welfare State? Reagan, Thatcher, and the Politics of Retrenchment*, Cambridge: Cambridge University Press.

Pierson, Paul (1996) 'The new politics of the welfare state', *World Politics*, 48:2, 143–179.

Pierson, Paul (2000) 'Increasing returns, path dependence, and the study of politics', *The American Political Science Review*, 94:2, 251–267.

Pierson, Paul (2001) 'Coping with permanent austerity: Welfare state restructuring in affluent democracies', in Paul Pierson (ed.), *The New Politics of the Welfare State*, Oxford: Oxford University Press, 410–456.

Plimmer, Gill (2014) 'Outsourcers win high-value deals', *Financial Times*, 18 May.

Plotke, David (1996) *Building a Democratic Political Order: Reshaping American Liberalism in the 1930s*, Cambridge: Cambridge University Press.

Pollard, Sidney (1970) 'Editor's introduction', in Sidney Pollard (ed.), *The Gold Standard and Employment Policies between the Wars*, London: University Paperbacks, 1–26.

PollingReport.com (2013a) *Health Policy*. Online: www.pollingreport.com/health5.htm (p. 5).

PollingReport.com (2013b) *Major Institutions – Government: Federal*. Online: www.pollingreport.com/institut.htm#Federal.

PollingReport.com (2013c) *Budget, Taxes, Economic Policy*. Online: www.pollingreport.com/budget.htm.

Porter, Andrew (2010) 'Britain to emulate Canada's radical solution to tackle debt', *The Daily Telegraph*, 6 June. Online: www.telegraph.co.uk/news/politics/7807347/Britain-to-emulate-Canadas-radical-solution-to-tackle-debt.html.

Postel, Charles (2012) 'The Tea Party in historical perspective', in Larry Rosenthal and Christine Trost (eds), *Steep: The Precipitous Rise of the Tea Party*, Berkeley and Los Angeles, CA: University of California Press, 25–46.

Powell, Frederick (2007) *The Politics of Civil Society*, Bristol: The Policy Press.

Purtill, Corinne (2013) 'Thatcher in Cameron's clothing', *Real Clear World*, 19 November. Online: www.realclearworld.com/articles/2013/11/19/thatcher_in_camerons_clothing.html.

Putnam, Robert (1995) 'Bowling alone: America's declining social capital', *Journal of Democracy*, 6:1, January, 65–78.

Quinn, Thomas, Judith Bara and John Bartle (2011) 'The UK Coalition Agreement of 2010: Who won?', *The Journal of Elections, Public Opinion & Parties*, 21:2, May, 295–312.

Rauchway, Eric (2010) 'New Deal denialism', *Dissent*, Winter, 68–72.

Reiland, Ralph R. (2013) 'Thatcher's revolution', *The New American*, 24 April. Online: www.thenewamerican.com/reviews/opinion/item/15202-thatcher-s-revolution.

Reinhart, Carmen M. and Kenneth S. Rogoff (2010) *Growth in a Time of Debt*, NBER Working Paper 15639, Cambridge: National Bureau of Economic Research. Online: www.nber.org/papers/w15639.

Republican National Convention (1980) *Republican Party Platform of 1980*. Online: www.presidency.ucsb.edu/ws/?pid=25844.

ResPublica (2009) *David Cameron: The Big Society*. Online: www.respublica.org.uk/item/ResPublica-mentioned-in-Camerons-speech-ggtc.

Reynolds, Alan (2010) *The 'Stimulus' Actually Raised Unemployment*, Washington, DC: Cato Institute, 10 February. Online: www.cato.org/publications/commentary/stimulus-actually-raised-unemployment.

Rhodes, R.A.W. (1994) 'The hollowing out of the state: The changing nature of public service in Britain', *The Political Quarterly*, 65:2, April, 138–151.

Richman, Sheldon L. (1988) 'The sad legacy of Ronald Reagan', *The Free Market*, 6:10, October. Online: http://mises.org/freemarket_detail.aspx?control=488.

Riedl, Brian M. (2010) *White House Report Claims Stimulus Success – Despite 3.5 Million Job Losses*, Washington, DC: The Heritage Foundation, 14 January. Online: www.heritage.org/research/reports/2010/01/white-house-report-claims-stimulus-success-despite-3-million-job-losses.

Roberts, Russell (2008) 'Does Bear Stearns bailout set a bad precedent?', *All Things Considered (National Public Radio)*, 25 March. Online: www.npr.org/templates/story/story.php?storyId=89064840.

Robinson, William I. and Mario Barrera (2012) 'Global capitalism and twenty-first century fascism: A US case study', *Race and Class*, 53:3, 4, 4–29.

Rodgers, Daniel T. (2005) 'The search for American Political Development (review)', *Journal of Interdisciplinary History*, 36:2, 275–276.

Ross, Fiona (2007) 'Policy histories and partisan leadership in presidential studies: The case of social security,' in George C. Edwards III and Desmond King (eds), *The Polarized Presidency of George W. Bush*, Oxford: Oxford University Press, 419–446.

Roulstone, Alan and Simon Prideaux (2008) 'More policies, greater inclusion? Exploring the contradictions of New Labour inclusive education policy', *International Studies in Sociology of Education*, 18:1, 15–29.

Rove, Karl (2013) 'Karl Rove: The GOP's self-defeating "defunding" strategy', *The Wall Street Journal*, 18 September. Online: http://online.wsj.com.

Rudalevige, Andrew (2011) *Government in a Box': Challenges of Policy Implementation in the American System*, Washington, DC: American Enterprise Institute. Online: www.aei.org/files/2011/05/23/Rudalevige-Final%20Conference%20Draft.pdf.

Saad, Lydia (2010) 'Verdict on Healthcare Reform Bill still divided', *Gallup Politics*, 22 June. Online: www.gallup.com/poll/140981/verdict-healthcare-reform-bill-divided.aspx.

Sahadi, Jeanne (2009) 'Senate passes $787 billion stimulus bill', *CNN Money*, 15 February. Online: http://money.cnn.com.

Savage, Michael (2014) 'Broken welfare system "drove up migration"', *The Times*, 11 August.

Schäfer, Armin and Wolfgang Streeck (2013) 'Introduction: Politics in the Age of Austerity', in Armin Schäfer and Wolfgang Streeck (eds), *Politics in the Age of Austerity*, Cambridge: Polity, 1–25.

Scheiber, Noam (2011) *The Escape Artists: How Obama's Team Fumbled the Recovery*, New York: Simon & Schuster.

Scherer, Michael (2004) 'Grover Norquist: The soul of the new machine', *Mother Jones*, January–February. Online: http://motherjones.com/politics/2004/01/grover-norquist-soul-new-machine.

Schreiber, E.M. (1971) '"Where the Ducks Are": Southern strategy versus fourth party', *The Public Opinion Quarterly*, 35:2, Summer, 157–167.

Schreiber, Ronnee (2012) 'Mama Grizzlies compete for office', *New Political Science*, 34:4, 549–563.

Seager, Ashley (2006) 'CBI tells Brown to plug gap in public coffers', *The Guardian*, 7 November. Online: www.theguardian.com/business/2005/nov/07/politics.economicpolicy.

Shah, Neil (2013) 'More young adults live with parents', *The Wall Street Journal*, 28 August, A2.

Sheingate, Adam (2014) 'Institutional dynamics and American Political Development', *Annual Review of Political Science*, 17, 461–477.

Shlaes, Amity (2008a) 'Don't repeat errors of New Deal', *New York Post*, 10 November. Online: http://nypost.com/2008/11/10/dont-repeat-errors-of-new-deal.

Shlaes, Amity (2008b) 'Obama will take us backward by channeling Keynes', *Bloomberg*, 19 November. Online: www.bloomberg.com/apps/news?pid=newsarchive&refer=columnist_shlaes&sid=a1CNR7igi8KU.

Shlaes, Amity (2008c) 'The Krugman recipe for Depression', *The Wall Street Journal*, 29 November. Online: http://online.wsj.com/news/articles/SB122792327402265913?mg=reno64-wsj&url=http%3A%2F%2Fonline.wsj.com%2Farticle%2FSB122792327402265913.html.

Simons, Ned (2013) 'Tory MPs more rebellious than any backbenchers since 1945, who are the top 5?', *The Huffington Post*, 14 May. Online: www.huffingtonpost.co.uk/2013/05/14/tory-rebels-david-cameron_n_3271051.html?utm_hp_ref=uk.

Skidelsky, Robert (2009) *Keynes: The Return of the Master*, London: Allen Lane.

Skocpol, Theda (1992) *Protecting Soldiers and Mothers: The Political Origins of Social Policy in the United States*, Cambridge, MA: The Belknap Press of Harvard University Press.

Skocpol, Theda and Vanessa Williamson (2012) *The Tea Party and the Remaking of Republican Conservatism*, Oxford: Oxford University Press.

Skowronek, Stephen (1995) 'Order and change', *Polity*, 28:1, Fall, 91–96.

Skowronek, Stephen (2009) 'An attenuated reconstruction: The conservative turn in American political development', in Brian J. Glenn and Steven M. Teles (eds), *Conservatism and American Political Development*, Oxford: Oxford University Press, 348–63.

Smith, Rogers M. (2006) 'Which comes first, the ideas or the institutions?', in Ian Shapiro, Stephen Skowronek and Daniel Galvin (eds), *Rethinking Political Institutions: The Art of the State*, New York: New York University Press.

Stanley, Liam (2014) 'We're reaping what we sowed': Everyday crisis narratives and acquiescence to the age of austerity', *New Political Economy* (published online), DOI: 10.1080/13563467.2013.861412.

Streeck, Wolfgang (2009) *Institutions in History: Bringing Capitalism Back in*, MPIfG Discussion Paper 09/8, Cologne: Max Planck Institute for the Study of Societies.

Streeck, Wolfgang and Kathleen Thelen (2005) 'Institutional change in advanced political economies', in Wolfgang Streeck and Kathleen Thelen (eds), *Beyond Continuity*, Oxford: Oxford University Press.

Summers, Lawrence (2013) 'The end of the line', *Financial Times*, 12 April. Online: www.ft.com/intl/cms/s/2/5097537a-a034-11e2-a6e1-00144feabdc0.html#axzz34vqHPZNT.

Suskind, Ron (2011) *Confidence Men: Wall Street, Washington, and the Education of a President*, New York: Harper.

Taibbi, Matt (2010) 'The truth about the Tea Party', *Rolling Stone*, 28 September. Online: www.rollingstone.com/politics/news/matt-taibbi-on-the-tea-party-20100928.

Tanner, Michael and Charles Hughes (2013) *The Work versus Welfare Trade-Off: An Analysis of the Total Level of Welfare Benefits by State*, Washington, DC: Cato Institute.

Taylor, Ciaren, Andrew Jowett and Michael Hardie (2014) *An Examination of Falling Real Wages, 2010–2013*, Newport: Office for National Statistics.

Taylor, Matthew (2014) 'Two-third of voters in Tory marginals want NHS exempt from US trade pact', *The Guardian*, 7 August. Online: www.theguardian.com/society/2014/aug/07/voters-want-nhs-exempt-us-trade-pact-ttip-eu-privatisation.

Taylor-Gooby, Peter (2012) 'Root and branch restructuring to achieve major cuts: The social policy programme of the 2010 UK coalition government', *Social Policy & Administration*, 46:1, February, 61–82.

Taylor-Gooby, Peter and Gerry Stoker (2011) 'The coalition programme: A new vision for Britain or politics as usual?' *The Political Quarterly*, January–March, 82:1, 4–15.

Teles, Steven (2011) 'Compassionate conservatism: Domestic policy, and the politics of ideational change', in Joel D. Aberbach and Gillian Peele (eds), *Crisis of Conservatism? The Republican Party, the Conservative Movement, and American Politics after Bush*, Oxford: Oxford University Press, 178–211.

Thatcher, Margaret (2008, orig. 1988) 'Full text of Margaret Thatcher's speech to the College of Europe: "The Bruges Speech"', *The Daily Telegraph*, 19 September. Online: www.telegraph.co.uk/comment/personal-view/3562258/Full-text-of-Margaret-Thatchers-speech-to-the-College-of-Europe-The-Bruges-Speech.html.

Thompson, Derek (2014) 'The shame of America's long-term unemployment crisis', *The Atlantic*, 6 February. Online: www.theatlantic.com/business/archive/2014/02/the-shame-of-americas-long-term-unemployment-crisis/283655.

Tonkiss, Katherine and Katharine Dommett (2012) *The Bonfires of Quangos Has Thus Far Only Smouldered*. Online: http://blogs.lse.ac.uk/politicsandpolicy/archives/29739.

Trotsky, Leon (2006, orig. 1937) *The Revolution Betrayed: What Is the Soviet Union and Where Is It Going?* Delhi: Aakar Books.

UK Polling Report (2014) *YouGov Voting Intention since 2010*. Online: http://ukpollingreport.co.uk/yougov-voting-intention.

US Chamber of Commerce (2009) *U.S. Chamber Outlines Support for Legislation that Creates Jobs, Helps Small Businesses*, 11 February. Online: www.uschamber.com/press-release/us-chamber-outlines-support-legislation-creates-jobs-helps-small-businesses.

US Government Spending (2014) *Government Spending Chart*. Online: www.usgovernmentspending.com/spending_chart_1980_2007USp_15c2li011mcn_F0f.

van Apeldoorn, Bastiaan (2009) 'The contradictions of "embedded neoliberalism" and Europe's multi-level legitimacy crisis: The European project and its limits', in Bastiaan Van Apeldoorn, Laura Horn and Jan Drahokoupil) (eds), *Contradictions and Limits of Neoliberal European Governance: From Lisbon to Lisbon*, Basingstoke: Palgrave, 21–43.

Wade, Richard (2013) *Conservative Party Economic Policy: From Heath in Opposition to Cameron in Coalition*, Basingstoke: Palgrave Macmillan.

The Wall Street Journal (2008) 'In crisis, opportunity for Obama', *The Wall Street Journal*, 21 November. Online: http://online.wsj.com/news/articles/SB122721278056345271.

Wallison, Peter J. (2011) 'Three narratives about the financial crisis', *Cato Journal*, 31:3, Fall, 535–549.

Watt, Nicholas (2014) 'Local government cuts hitting poorest areas hardest, figures show', *The Guardian*, 30 January. Online: www.theguardian.com/society/2014/jan/30/local-government-cuts-poorest-areas.

Weigel, David (2011) 'The Don't-Tread-on-Meter: Defeat from the jaws of victory!', *Slate*, 15 March. Online: www.slate.com/articles/news_and_politics/politics/2011/03/the_donttreadonmeter.html.

Weiner, Rachel (2013) 'How is Congress dealing with the sequester? Randomly', *The Washington Post* (The Fix), 26 April. Online: www.washingtonpost.com/blogs/the-fix/wp/2013/04/26/how-congress-is-dealing-with-the-sequester-randomly.

Weisenthal, Joe (2013) 'Warren Buffett: During the financial crisis, George W. Bush made the greatest economic statement of all time', *Business Insider*, 9 December. Online: www.businessinsider.com/warren-buffett-on-george-w-bush-2013-12#ixzz2zK7FfWqE.

Weiss, Robert P. (2001) 'Charitable choice as neoliberal social welfare strategy', *Social Justice*, 28:1, 35–53.

Weyland, Kurt (2008) 'Toward a new theory of institutional change', *World Politics*, 60, January, 281–314.

White, Michael (2012) 'David and the Nordic goliaths', *The Guardian*, 9 February. Online: www.guardian.co.uk/politics/2012/feb/09/david-cameron-nordic-goliaths-sweden.

The White House (2011) *Remarks by the President on Fiscal Policy*, 13 April. Online: www.whitehouse.gov/the-press-office/2011/04/13/remarks-president-fiscal-policy.

Whiteley, Paul, Harold D. Clarke, David Sanders and Marianne C. Stewart (2014) 'The economic and electoral consequences of austerity policies in Britain', *Parliamentary Affairs*, First View, 11 July.

Wilkie, Christina (2013) 'Huge business coalition led by U.S. Chamber of Commerce urges Congress to fund the government', *The Huffington Post*, 30 September. Online: www.huffingtonpost.com/2013/09/30/chamber-of-commerce-government-shutdown_n_4018959.html.

Williams, Daniel K. (2010) *God's Own Party: The Making of the Christian Right*, Oxford: Oxford University Press.

Williamson, Vanessa, Theda Skocpol and John Coggin (2011) 'The Tea Party and the remaking of Republican conservatism', *Perspectives on Politics*, March, 9:1, 25–43.

Willetts, David (1994) *Civic Conservatism*, London: Social Market Foundation.

Willetts, David (2013) Beyond bare-earth Conservatism: The future of the British economy', in Ryan Shorthouse and Guy Stagg (eds), *Tory Modernisation 2.0: The Future of the Conservative Party*, London: Bright Blue Campaign, 25–35.

Wintour, Patrick (2010a) 'Coalition is more radical than Thatcher government, says senior Tory minister', *The Guardian*, 30 July. Online: www.theguardian.com/politics/2010/jul/30/coalition-government-reforms-francis-maude.

Wintour, Patrick (2010b) 'Labour MPs suspicious of Mervyn King's role in coalition talks', *The Guardian*, 2 December. Online: www.theguardian.com/politics/2010/dec/02/labour-suspicious-mervyn-king-coalition.

Wintour, Patrick (2012) 'Heseltine's No 10 report blasts coalition over growth strategy', *The Guardian*, 31 October. Online: www.theguardian.com/politics/2012/oct/31/heseltine-report-blasts-coalition-growth.

Woods, Thomas (2009) *Meltdown: A Free-Market Look at Why the Stock Market Collapsed, the Economy Tanked, and Government Bailouts Will Make Things Worse*, Washington, DC: Regnery Publishing.

The World Bank (2011) *Overview: Social Capital*, Washington, DC: The World Bank. Online: http://go.worldbank.org/C0QTRW4QF0.

Wrong, Dennis (1983) 'Two cheers for Irving Kristol', *The New Republic*, 30 October. Online: www.newrepublic.com/article/two-cheers-irving-kristol.

Zernike, Kate and Megan Thee-Brenan (2010) 'Poll finds Tea Party backers wealthier and more educated', *The New York Times*, 14 April. Online: www.nytimes.com/2010/04/15/us/politics/15poll.html.

Zeskind, Leonard (2011) 'A nation dispossessed: The Tea Party movement and race', *Critical Sociology*, 38:4, 495–509.

Index

AARP 22
Aberbach, Joel D. 185, 193
abortion 13, 58, 101, 105, 153
abrasion 6, 14–16, 22, 28, 145, 148–51, 153, 155, 157, 159–63, 165–9
actors 4–6, 8–11, 14–16, 18–19, 22–3, 25–8, 30, 34, 37, 42–3, 45–8, 75, 84–5, 98, 105, 107, 114, 148, 150–1, 155, 159–60, 164, 168–70
Adam Smith Institute 130
Adonis, Andrew 124, 179
agency 5, 11, 13, 24, 26–7, 30, 41–2, 60, 98–9, 148, 150–2, 162, 172
American International Group 80
American Political Development 6, 14–15, 19, 21–4, 26–9, 53, 102, 149–50, 184, 186, 189–92
American Recovery and Reinvestment Act 17, 86, 89–93, 95, 97, 104, 109, 155, 162
AmeriCorps 59
Anglosphere 4
APD *see* American Political Development
Apeldoorn, Bastiaan van 10, 194
Armey, Dick 58, 169
ARRA *see* American Recovery and Reinvestment Act
Ashford, Nigel 36, 179
astroturf 117, 152, 156
austerity 2–3, 5, 17, 81, 84, 93–6, 115, 120, 123, 125, 128, 133, 138, 141–3, 146, 154, 157, 170, 172, 179, 187, 189–90, 193–4

Bachmann, Michele 101–2, 109, 114
backbenchers 8, 192
bailout 3, 17, 52, 79–80, 85, 120, 185–6, 191
Bale, Tim 8, 63, 179
Balls, Ed 146
Barnes, Fred 41
Bartels, Larry 105, 179
BBC 85, 126, 135, 138, 170, 180
Bear Stearns 79, 191
Beech, Matt 187
Beltway 57, 106
Berk, Gerald 29–30, 180
Berlet, Chip 100, 118, 153, 180
Bevan, Aneurin 15
Bevir, Mark 11, 180
Birtherism 100
Bismarck, Otto von 9, 22
Blair, Tony 35, 45, 55, 65, 69, 71, 128, 147
Blairism 71–2, 139
Blond, Phillip 69, 72, 77, 180–1
Blunkett, David 77
Blyth, Mark 146, 154, 180
BNP *see* British National Party
Boehner, John 92, 113, 158–9, 181
Bricolage 98
British National Party, 144, 147
Broadband 127, 162, 176
Brokerage 107–8
Brown, Gordon 45, 72–3, 76, 84–5, 118, 121, 124, 154, 192
Brown, Scott 99, 106
Bruges 33, 193
Budgets 41, 43, 83, 90, 111, 126, 137, 172
Buffett, Warren 80–1, 194
Bush, George H. W. 52, 57, 59, 182

Bush, George W. 2–3, 7, 39, 41, 44, 53, 59–62, 66, 73, 76, 79, 81, 85, 87, 111–13, 115–16, 118, 176, 180, 185, 191, 193–4
business 16, 34, 43–4, 69, 75, 79, 84, 87–8, 90, 112, 114, 120, 123, 131–2, 145, 162–3, 169, 180, 182–5, 190, 192–4

cabinet 9, 129
Cameron, David 2, 6–7, 16, 66, 70–3, 77, 126–31, 133–7, 139–42, 145–6, 150, 167, 170, 173, 175, 177, 179–81, 183–4, 187–8, 191, 194
Canada 2, 64, 133, 189–90
Cantor, Eric 116–17, 158, 160, 179
capitalism 3, 10–11, 28, 35, 56, 69, 73, 92, 162, 174–5, 178, 191
Carter, Jimmy 35–6, 41
Cato Institute 2, 52, 86, 164–5, 181, 193–4
Causality 96, 148
CBI *see* Confederation of British Industry
Cerny, Philip G. 34, 181
Chancellor of the Exchequer 32, 42, 72, 78, 84–5, 120, 123, 125–6, 129–30, 139, 154, 170, 172, 190
Chicago 5, 98, 186, 188
Chote, Robert 45, 121, 124, 182
citizenship 62, 68, 127
class 10, 12–13, 15, 35, 57, 99–100, 116, 142–5, 149, 152, 156–7, 160, 175, 188
Clegg, Nick 124, 187
clientelism 95, 125
Clinton, Bill 36, 39, 55, 58–9, 110, 113
cloture 155
CNN 59, 80, 182, 186, 192
communitarianism 65, 69
compassionate conservatism 59–62, 66–7, 70, 73, 76, 176
competitiveness 31–2, 34, 75, 157, 164, 177
complementarities 11, 14, 20–3, 26, 28, 43–4, 149, 160
Confederation of British Industry 75, 84, 131–2, 182, 192
Congress iv, 39, 41–2, 44, 55, 58, 73, 79–80, 85, 89–92, 95, 97–8, 103–4, 106–7, 109–12, 114–16, 151, 155, 158–9, 162–3, 165, 172, 181, 194
conservatism 5–6, 9–10, 17, 19, 41, 53, 56–62, 65–73, 76, 101, 131, 148, 150, 155, 160, 163, 165, 176, 193–4
Conservatives 11, 13, 17, 31, 34, 64–6, 69, 71, 73–4, 76, 85, 105, 121–4, 128–9, 133, 139–46, 148, 150, 157, 167, 171, 179, 184, 188
see also Tories
contestation 14, 34, 48, 53, 165
contingency 106, 150, 156
continuity 6, 29, 137
contraction 93–6, 115, 126, 132–3, 141, 189
councils 33, 50, 126, 141, 168
Crewe, Ivor 34
Crouch, Colin 43, 182

Dansk Folkeparti 71, 143, 145
Darling, Alistair 78, 84, 120, 180
debt 2, 17, 52, 78, 83, 92–3, 96, 110–15, 121, 125–6, 131, 133, 137, 150, 152, 154, 162, 170, 172–3, 187, 190
deficit 44, 141
Democrats 9, 13, 28, 41–2, 55, 60, 71, 80, 90–1, 96, 99, 105–6, 111–15, 121, 123–6, 128–9, 140–1, 150, 155, 159–60, 164, 166–7, 169
demography 15, 176
deregulation 33, 36, 131, 165
devolution 146, 168
DiIulio, John 61
Dodd–Frank Wall Street Reform and Consumer Protection Act 108–9, 155
Dole, Bob 56

earmarks 159
Eisenhower, Dwight 82, 169
elections 4, 16, 51, 58–9, 62, 64, 71, 90, 97, 102, 111, 113, 144–5, 155, 159–60
elites 13, 57, 97, 100, 107, 116–18, 149, 151, 156, 158–60, 162–3, 167, 169
empowerment 22, 59
entitlements 62
equilibrium 6–7, 44
EU *see* European Union
Eurocommunism 12

Europe, 3–4, 16, 31–3, 64, 94, 102, 125, 127, 137, 144–5, 147, 180, 193–4
European Union 10, 15–16, 52, 64, 73, 125, 128, 130–1, 144–5, 146–7, 167, 177, 182, 188
Euroscepticism 63–4, 128, 131, 145
eurozone 17, 94, 133, 154, 177

Fannie Mae 3, 78, 102
fascism 156, 191
federalism 64
feedback 21, 175, 190
fractures 63, 85, 116, 129
fragmentation 106, 160
frames 98, 107, 117, 168
framing 17, 47, 53, 126, 141–2
France 34, 143
Freddie Mac 3, 78, 102
FreedomWorks 169
friction 14, 16, 22–3, 25–6, 28, 145, 150, 157, 168
Friedman, Milton 89
Frymer, Paul 24, 183

Gadsden flag 97–9, 101, 103, 105, 107, 109, 111, 113, 115, 117, 119
Gallup 116, 192
Gamble, Andrew 52, 146, 183
gatekeeping 46, 166
GDP *see* Gross Domestic Product
Geithner, Timothy 97
gender 21, 59, 101, 142
Germany 34, 131, 156
Gingrich, Newt 7, 55, 58, 97, 151, 163, 189
globalization 153, 181
Goldwater, Barry 9, 89
GOP 166, 189, 191
see also Republicans
governance 23, 102, 168
gradualism 7, 45–8, 51–2, 170
Gramsci, Antonio 12
Greece 94, 125, 146
Greenspan, Alan 56, 87
gridlock 16, 158
Gross Domestic Product 1–2, 16, 34, 38–42, 44–5, 52, 55, 83–4, 90–1, 93, 108, 112, 121, 136, 170, 172–3, 177, 180

Hacker, Jacob 7, 13, 37, 45–6, 75, 165–6, 169, 184
Hague, William 64, 66, 129
Hastert, Dennis 118
Hay, Colin 11, 32, 143, 149, 185
Hayton, Richard 11, 185
Heath, Edward 32, 154, 194
Hegemony 12, 14, 34–5, 84, 149, 180, 187
Herbert, Jon 53, 154, 185
Heseltine, Michael 146, 148, 195
historical institutionalism 6, 11, 21, 24–9, 43, 142, 149
Hofstadter, Richard 99, 153, 169, 185
Howard, Christopher 103, 186
Howard, Michael 64
Howe, Geoffrey 32, 148

identity 89, 99, 101, 112–13, 142–4
IEA *see* Institute of Economic Affairs
IMF *see* International Monetary Fund
immigration 15, 56, 64, 71, 100, 130, 143–4, 146–7, 156, 167
impeachment 58
imperialism 177
incongruities 28
incrementalism 47
incumbents 59, 158, 160
indebtedness 78, 125, 136
individualism 12, 59, 69, 142
industries 28, 32, 105, 157
inequalities 3, 69
infrastructure 122, 127, 134, 162, 176
Institute of Economic Affairs 63, 130
institutionalism 6, 11, 18, 21–22, 26–7, 43, 105–6, 142, 149, 155, 175
intercurrence 6, 14–16, 18, 20–9, 148–50, 157, 164, 167, 182
International Monetary Fund 2, 125–6, 146, 172, 179, 185–6
investment 3, 10, 32, 36, 44, 79, 81–2, 86–8, 116–17, 123–4, 126–7, 132, 135, 157, 167

Jessop, Bob 180, 186
joblessness 1, 81
jobs 53, 68, 91–2, 121, 133, 152–3, 156, 162, 194
Johnson, Boris 66, 145
Johnson, Lyndon 28, 89, 96, 107, 161
JPMorgan Chase 79
judiciary 134

Kennedy, Edward (Ted) 99, 106
Keynes, John Maynard 3, 82, 157, 192
Keynesianism 7, 10, 43, 83–4, 86, 91, 96, 143
Keynesians 82, 87
King, Desmond 24, 102, 186, 191
King, Mervyn 132
Kristol, Irving 69, 187, 195
Krugman, Paul 91, 93–4, 96, 108, 156, 187, 189, 192
Kuo, David 61, 187

Labour Party 13, 17, 21, 25, 31, 33, 35–6, 39, 41, 44, 53, 55, 63–5, 69, 71–5, 77, 84–5, 89, 120–2, 124, 126, 128–9, 134, 141–3, 145–6, 154, 171, 181, 183, 185–8, 191, 195
lacunae 48
Lawson, Nigel 32
layering 7, 26, 108, 141, 161, 170, 173
legacies 6, 21, 106, 149, 155, 160
legislation 20, 37, 46, 58, 80, 99, 112, 114–15, 129, 159, 169, 194
Lehman Brothers 79–80
leverage 9, 13, 41, 157
liberal market economies 4, 28, 131–2, 156, 164
liberalism 9, 12, 18, 68–70, 105, 125, 128, 131
libertarians 57, 86–7, 107, 118
Lilley, Peter 63, 128
Limbaugh, Rush 151
Lipset, Seymour Martin 153, 187
LMEs, *see* liberal market economies
lobbying 22, 58–9, 74, 157
lobbyists 118, 166
localism 66, 69, 138–9, 145, 168, 171
losers 48–9, 65, 95, 104, 107, 143, 164, 174

Mahoney, James 7, 11, 37, 48, 133, 188
Major, John 34, 39, 64, 66, 130, 134, 136, 147
malinvestment 86–7
manufacturing 157
Marxism 7, 12, 156
Maude, Francis 71, 141, 143, 188
McCain, John 62, 89, 96, 98, 185, 188
McConnell, Mitch 92
Medicaid 103–4, 108, 111, 114–15, 160
Medicare 7, 21, 41, 43, 103–4, 107–9, 111, 114–15, 160–1, 189
Mellon, Andrew 154
Mexico 64
Michigan 98
migrants 56
migration 177, 192
Miliband, Ed 142
Minford, Patrick 64–5, 188
minorities 24, 100, 104, 109, 144, 153, 179
Mises, Ludwig von 86, 190
modernization 25, 63, 70–1, 139, 152–3, 167, 182
modernizers 71
monetarism 32, 83, 129, 143, 154
Montgomerie, Tim 128, 189
mortgages 3, 43, 78–9, 95, 168
multiplier 82, 112
Murray, Charles 68, 189
mutualization 138

NAFTA *see* North American Free Trade Agreement
narratives 11, 35, 78–9, 81, 83, 85, 87, 89, 91, 93, 95, 101, 142, 193–4
National Bureau of Economic Research 92, 179, 191
National Health Service 11, 14–15, 51, 65, 128–30, 134, 136, 138, 141, 173, 176, 183, 187–8, 193
nationalization 69, 71, 174
NBER *see* National Bureau of Economic Research

neoconservatives 20, 61, 69
neoliberalism 6, 10, 20, 54–5, 57, 59, 61–3, 65, 67, 69, 71, 73, 75, 77, 82–3, 107, 130, 149, 156, 194
NHS *see* National Health Service
Nixon, Richard M. 13
Norquist, Grover 55–6, 166, 184, 192
North American Free Trade Agreement 64, 99

Obamacare 29, 104, 109, 112–14
OECD *see* Organisation for Economic Cooperation and Development
Olasky, Marvin 60
ordering 22, 28
orders 6, 14–16, 22–9, 110, 149–50, 157, 168–9, 186
Organisation for Economic Cooperation and Development 42, 67, 84, 90, 120, 125–6, 189
Ormerod, Paul 93–4
Orren, Karen 21–3, 25–30, 118, 189–90
Orszag, Peter 90–1
Osborne, George 72, 85, 123, 125–6, 129, 139, 146, 179–82, 186, 189
Othering 152
outsourcing 124, 134–5, 137, 187
overheating 82
ownership 33, 92, 147, 175–6

PACs *see* political action committees
Palin, Sarah 89, 96, 101–2, 158, 185
paradigm 3, 83–4, 96, 122, 143, 153–4
partisanship 57, 117–18
Patashnik, Eric 46–7, 176, 190
paths 6, 11, 14, 23, 43, 52, 133, 140, 147
Paul, Rand 99, 114
Paulson, Hank 81
Pelosi, Nancy 152, 156
pensioners 43, 50, 65
Perot, Ross 110
Peston, Robert 133, 190
Pew Research Center for the People and the Press 115
philanthropy 62
Pickles, Eric 138, 168
Pierson, Paul 23, 33, 38, 43–4, 47, 75, 136–7, 140, 165–6, 169, 184, 190
Planned Parenthood 109, 173
Polanyi, Karl 177, 180
political action committees 159–60
populism 3, 12–13, 57, 71, 117, 143–4, 149
pork 41, 89, 92
porousness 76, 90
Portillo, Michael 71
poverty 28, 36, 59–60, 68, 70, 127
presidency 28, 52, 54, 62, 89, 110, 116, 173, 180, 191
primaries 58, 74, 99, 101, 159, 163
privatization 19–20, 32, 37, 44–5, 49, 52, 134, 147, 172, 176
producerism 57, 118
productivity 34, 44, 126
Professional Air Traffic Controllers' Organization 36
progressivism 57, 118
protectionism 28, 177
punctuated equilibrium 7, 44
Putnam, Robert 18, 67–8, 184, 191

quangos 124, 135–6

Reagan, Ronald 5, 10, 13, 29, 35–9, 41–2, 50, 52–5, 57, 59, 89, 136, 190–1
Reaganomics 10–11, 31, 35, 37–8, 45, 74, 179
realignment 9, 148
rebalancing 123, 129, 146
recovery 1–2, 17, 34, 42, 51, 70, 81–3, 85–6, 88, 92, 96, 99, 115, 123–5, 131–3, 152, 186
Redwood, John 64, 128, 130, 188
referendum 16, 128, 145, 167
regime 10, 13–16, 18, 20, 25, 29, 33, 44, 50, 52, 84, 129, 164
regulation 33–4, 53, 64, 92, 102, 131, 177, 184
Reid, Harry 119
Reinhart, Carmen 92–3, 96, 115, 119, 154, 191
rentier 157
repertoire 12

Republicans 7, 9, 54–9, 61–2, 69, 73, 80, 85, 89, 91–2, 99, 101–2, 105–7, 109–19, 151, 159–60, 162, 165–6, 169, 179
ResPublica 73, 191
restructuring 5, 7, 41, 128–31, 133–4, 136, 156, 170, 173–5, 190, 193
retirement 37, 107–8
retrenchment 2–3, 5, 7, 17, 38–9, 43–5, 49, 72, 95, 111, 115, 117, 120–1, 123, 125–7, 129–31, 133, 135–7, 139–43, 145–7, 154, 172–4, 184
revenue 36, 56, 108, 115, 135, 166
revolution 5, 29, 31, 35, 37, 39, 58, 63, 84, 175, 187, 191
Rhineland capitalism 35
Rogoff, Kenneth 92–3, 96, 115, 119, 154, 191
Romney, Mitt 62, 106–7, 109, 116, 119, 163
Roosevelt, Franklin D. 69, 81, 88
Rothbard, Murray 86
Rove, Karl 113, 191
Rubio, Marco 114
Rudalevige, Andrew 106, 192
Russia 175
Ryan, Paul 93, 107–8, 160–1, 179, 182, 187–8, 195

Santelli, Rick 97–8
Santorum, Rick 163
Sarkozy, Nicolas 4, 184
Scheiber, Noam 90–1, 192
securitization 3, 79, 102
Senate 42, 56, 58, 90–2, 97, 99, 102, 106, 109, 113–14, 116, 119, 155, 166, 188, 192
seniors 104, 107–8, 116, 161
sequestration 111–12, 172
Sheingate, Adam 22, 28, 192
Shlaes, Amity 88–9, 96, 187, 192
shrinkage 17, 31, 54, 128, 145
shutdown 107, 113–14, 162–3, 194
Skidelsky, Robert 3, 82, 192
Skocpol, Theda 28, 99–101, 105, 151, 192, 194
Skowronek, Stephen 21–3, 25–30, 35, 118, 189–90, 192–3
Smith, Iain Duncan 63, 68, 76, 128, 171, 178
Smith, Rogers 24–6
sovereignty 15, 99
Specter, Arlen 91
stability 17, 23, 32, 44, 90, 122
stabilizers 84, 132
stasis 16, 158
statecraft 11, 181, 183
stateness 103
stickiness 17, 76, 140, 170
stimulus 3, 17, 79, 83, 85–6, 88–92, 95, 120, 155–6, 162, 181, 185, 191–2
Streeck, Wolfgang 7, 47, 137, 143, 180, 192–3
subsidiarity 168
Summers, Lawrence 44, 90–1, 193
sunbelt 10

taxation 35–6, 50, 72, 85, 111
Tea Party movement 3, 5, 17–18, 59, 94, 97–111, 113–14, 116–19, 142, 151–3, 156–63, 169, 180–3, 186–90, 192–5
Teles, Steven M. 53, 59–60, 76, 184, 192–3
tendering 60, 62, 102, 135, 155, 162
tensions 6, 15–16, 18, 22–3, 27–9, 57, 73, 97, 105, 107, 112, 116, 145, 158, 160, 162–3, 167–9
Thatcherism 185
The Spectator 66, 188–9
Tocqueville, Alexis de 67
Tories 63, 65, 69, 71, 133, 148, 180–1, 184, 188
  see also Conservatives
trade 20, 31–4, 36, 52, 64, 140, 144, 147, 162, 193
Treasury 42, 44, 79–80, 82, 84, 90, 97, 120, 123, 126, 146, 154, 185, 189
triangulation 59
Trotsky, Leon 174–5, 178, 193

UKIP *see* United Kingdom Independence Party
underclass 57, 67–8, 100
unemployment 1, 31–2, 70, 75, 81–2, 84, 89, 112, 136–7, 172, 191, 193
United Kingdom Independence Party 13, 18, 120, 139, 142–6, 167

value added tax 35, 50, 83, 120, 130, 141, 182
Varieties of Capitalism 4, 28, 131, 156, 185
VAT *see* value added tax
vectors 24
veto 41, 47, 108, 155
Virginia 116
Volcker, Paul 35
volunteering 62, 67
volunteerism 182

Waddan, Alex 41, 180
Washington DC 2, 10, 55, 93, 117, 153, 158, 162, 166, 172–3, 179, 181–4, 186–7, 190–5
wealth 86, 104, 118, 123, 127, 135, 168
welfare 4, 11–12, 34, 36–8, 45, 52–3, 56, 58–60, 62, 67–9, 91, 100, 103, 107, 121, 126–7, 136–7, 139, 142, 163, 171, 184, 186, 190, 192, 194
Westminster 4, 8, 73, 144
Weyland, Kurt 48–9, 194
Whitehall 8, 73, 171
Willetts, David 65–6, 70, 73, 195
Wilson, Woodrow 29
women 60, 62, 67, 101–2, 104–5, 118, 122, 151, 153, 179
workfare 36, 52, 68

Youth Training Scheme 49–50
YTS *see* Youth Training Scheme